The Republic of Ireland –
Economic and Social Ecology in a Layered Perspective

Andrea Jende

The Republic of Ireland – Economic and Social Ecology in a Layered Perspective

PETER LANG

Bibliographic Information published by the Deutsche Nationalbibliothek
The Deutsche Nationalbibliothek lists this publication in the Deutsche Nationalbibliografie; detailed bibliographic data is available online at http://dnb.d-nb.de.

Library of Congress Cataloging-in-Publication Data
A CIP catalog record for this book has been applied for at the Library of Congress.

Zugl.: Freiberg (Sachsen), Techn. Univ., Diss., 2020

Coverimage: © Andrea Jende

105
ISBN 978-3-631-84148-8 (Print)
E-ISBN 978-3-631-84801-2 (E-PDF)
E-ISBN 978-3-631-84802-9 (EPUB)
E-ISBN 978-3-631-84803-6 (MOBI)
DOI 10.3726/b18070

Peter Lang – Berlin · Bern · Bruxelles · New York · Oxford · Warszawa · Wien

This publication has been peer reviewed.

www.peterlang.com

Preface

"When it comes to analyzing financial crises, Andrea Jende points out that more than mere economic data is needed to fully explain their causes. That is why she makes a case to also consider various human factors which go beyond mere economic data because these factors often provide a richer and fuller understanding of how and why a financial crisis emerges and unfolds. Typically, analyses of a financial crisis focus on the monetary policy or lending practices while ignoring other factors that could possibly influence the behavior and decision-making processes prior to and during such a crisis. The author notes that other factors need to be included as well in such an analysis. That is why she examined the 2007/ 2008 financial crisis in the Republic of Ireland from this broader perspective so as to determine how the human factor contributed to that crisis. In doing so, she took a closer look at Irish history, society, and culture to ascertain if any of those factors might influence the behavior and decision-making process observed during the 2007/ 2008 financial crisis in Ireland. By applying a broader, more comprehensive analysis, the author sought to isolate and understand how these factors influence people's behaviors during a crisis. This is actually similar to what behavioral economics seeks to do as well. In order to conduct this comprehensive analysis, the author developed and applied a social and economic ecological approach in a layered perspective which is based on Bronfenbrenner's Social Ecological Model so as to systematically examine the influences and interactions of the cultural, social, and economic environments at various levels over a longer period of time. The author is able to demonstrate that this approach works and provides a richer insight into the analysis of the 2007/ 2008 financial crisis in the Republic of Ireland. The author concludes that the same method can also be used to analyze other economic crises. She has, thus, created a tool for a better and fuller understanding of economic crises."

Michael B. Hinner, Ph.D., M.A.,
Professor, TU Bergakademie Freiberg

"Efforts to understand human activities, which are by nature inherently multifaceted and interwoven, presents a significant challenge to the many fields of social research. As a result, research studies commonly focus on only one or two causal factors, which tends to impede a more comprehensive understanding of the social phenomenon being examined. The question then is how to identify and evaluate the many different influences that contribute to human behaviors and decisions across varying contexts? Andrea Jende's research provides an avenue for gaining greater insight into unraveling that challenge.

Using the 2008–2007 economic crisis in the Republic of Ireland as the model, Ms. Jende examines selected variables not commonly considered part of an economic study. Moving away from the traditional single level problem analysis approach to research, she endeavors to determine how certain economic activities are influenced by multiple human factors, such as culturally influenced behaviors and decision-making processes, across multiple contexts (e.g., household, political, financial, and media). In addition to demonstrating the applicability of employing a multilevel analytical framework, the results also add to the growing body of contemporary behavioral economics research.

The study also illustrates the applicability of Urie Bronfenbrenner's layered systems model in determining the role of cultural and social change in decision making within an economic transition context. The results demonstrate that individuals exist in multiple, interconnected physical and social contexts, which are dynamic to varying degrees and both collectively and individually exert an influence on personal preferences.

Ms. Jende's research will be of interest to a broad interdisciplinary group of academic researchers and students as it offers a means of interconnecting multiple disciplines, such as anthropology, economics, social psychology, sociology, etc. Moreover, the study demonstrates an avenue for discerning the dynamics of cultural values rather than relying on the widely accepted statistic models presented by Hofstede, Trompenaars, Lewis, the Globe Study, etc.

In short, Jende's work illustrates the multiple, interconnected physical and social contexts that characterize human activities and demonstration the utility of employing a multilayered model in determining the interaction between social, economic and cultural factors. Her study clearly brings out the benefits of applying an interdisciplinary approach in order to gain a fuller understanding of human behaviors."

Edwin R. McDaniel, Ph.D., M.A.,
Harbin Institute of Technology

To:
Michael B. Hinner and Ed McDaniel, who inspired me
my friends, who supported me
and to
my family, who believed in me

Table of Contents

List of Figures

List of Tables

Introduction

Motivation

In 2007, the dominant topic in the media was the emerging global economic crisis. In the following months, leading politicians and financial experts stated that they were shocked when they were confronted with the true extent of the crisis (Kloepfer, 2008; Reinhart and Rogoff, 2009). The *New York Times* even titled the crisis as a 'near-death experience' for the European economic and monetary union (Castle, 2013). Many banks all over Europe and also in the USA had to be saved from bankruptcy so that governments were forced to lend hitherto unprecedented aid to the global financial system (Kloepfer, 2008; Dill, 2009). Even today, over ten years after the crisis, many private households but also entire nations, such as Greece and Italy, are still suffering from its effects (Ettel and Zschäpitz, 2015). In the years that followed the crisis, there were many discussions and publications concerning the causes and course of the crisis. According to Reinhart and Rogoff (2009) many decision-makers in politics and business argued that this crisis was not comparable to any past situation. However, after analyzing different crises of the past 800 years, Reinhart and Rogoff conclude that the same mistakes were made over and over again. This time, some contexts had also been ignored completely which led to the massive recession (Eichengreen, 2015). Yet, despite the findings of past analyses and a better informed policy regarding macro-economic aspects, the recent economic crisis could not be prevented. Although it is known how crises develop and in spite of the knowledge about economic and political instruments for the prevention of crisis, both the government and the economy seem to be powerless against the recurrence of crises (Reinhart and Rogoff, 2009). This led to the motivation to find out whether other factors exist that could promote the emergence of financial crises – factors that were neglected in previous economic analyses.

Scope

In order to identify further possible factors that contribute to the emergence of a financial crisis, it was necessary to select a national economy as research subject which was significantly affected by the financial crisis of 2007. Thus, the Republic of Ireland appeared to be a suitable subject of investigation due to its extraordinary economic development in the last few decades. The country experienced an unprecedented economic upturn – unique in Europe and often compared to the fast rise of the Asian Tiger economies and is therefore also labeled the Celtic Tiger. However, a decade later, the financial crisis hit the Irish economy and Ireland experienced an exceptional economic breakdown. As a result, it ended up as one of the euro zone nations besides Greece, Portugal, Spain, and Cyprus that was hit so hard by the economic crisis that it had to enter the international bailout program (Castle, 2013). When Ireland is generally mentioned in the course of this dissertation this always refers specifically to the Republic of Ireland.

The holistic analysis carried out here is intended to identify factors – besides an analysis focusing only on economic factors – that may have influenced the economic development of Ireland. Therefore, the analysis includes economic aspects but also the human factor in line with the basic assumption of the dissertation that economic decisions are made by human beings.

This dissertation argues that economic developments, such as crises, can be better understood if not only the instruments of an economic system, such as monetary policy or lending practices, are analyzed but also the human factor is taken into account. It assumes that merely examining the economic processes leads to misleading results when non-economic factors, such as influences on behavior and decision-making processes, are neglected in the analysis (Lee, 1989). Therefore, various factors that influenced behavior and decision-making processes in many different areas, such as private households, politics, financial institutions, and the media, are examined with regard to their contribution to the crisis. This approach can be assigned to the research field of behavioral economics which deals with human behavior in economic situations. Behavioral economists investigate the way people make economic choices and judgments (Cialdini, 2018). Lin (2011) stresses the importance of the interdisciplinary field of behavioral economics because its application offers new insights. The core assumption is that economic actors are not as reasonable as the idealized *homo economicus* (the economic actor who acts absolutely rational to maximize his or her own utility) of neoclassical economic theory but instead make their decisions depending on many other influences (Thaler, 2016; Lin, 2011; Rolle, 2005).

Consequently, an analysis of the influences and interactions of the cultural, social and economic environments results in a holistic picture of Irish social and economic development. Thus, the dissertation deals with *Social and Economic Ecology in a Layered Perspective.*

Theoretical and Practical Relevance of the Research

Many researchers, such as Slater, Snyder, and Hayes (2006), Zhang and Ting-Toomey (2014), and Lejano and Stokols (2013), emphasize the benefits of the application of a layered perspective or multi-level theoretical framework. Slater, Snyder, and Hayes (2006) argue that there are multiple benefits, for instance, for the field of communication research because the analysis of communication must also take into account biological, psychological, sociological, and cultural phenomena. They state that this research field has suffered because the researchers were, for example psychologists, sociologists, or anthropologists and, therefore, only considered their respective research issues and thus, neglected seeing the whole picture (Slater, Snyder, and Hayes, 2006).

Consequently, other research areas which include multiple phenomena can also benefit from a multi-level theoretical framework because this approach allows the inclusion of various issues and, therefore, provides a comprehensive analysis. Slater, Snyder, and Hayes (2006) further argue that an appreciation and understanding of a multi-level theoretical framework can move many research fields forward significantly in terms of formulating and addressing important questions by simultaneously considering multiple levels of analysis. The multi-level theoretical framework is helpful in many interrelated ways, i.e. for the simultaneous analysis of data collected at several levels and when having to cope with changes in data occurring over time (Slater, Snyder, and Hayes, 2006).

The layered perspective or multi-level framework that is used for the analyzing part in this dissertation incorporates, as the name suggests, various layers into the analysis. Culture is also such a layer. It is assumed that culture is an all-encompassing influencing ecological factor. Thus, a multi-level perspective is also able to reveal the interrelations between culture, human behavior and decision-making processes with regard to social and economic developments.

This dissertation also has practical relevance for, among others, the field of economics. The recent global economic crisis of 2007 showed that security mechanisms of both the government and the economy failed to prevent the crisis (Reinhart and Rogoff, 2009). Since then, various instruments, have been examined. For instance, Dewatripont, Rochet and Tirole (2010) discuss instruments for crisis prevention in the banking sector in their book *Balancing the Banks: Global Lessons from the Financial Crisis*. They provide, among others, regulatory reforms, such as sound guidelines for ways to deal with distressed banks in the future. In contrast to examining the instruments, this dissertation focuses especially on examining the human factor. Humans, as economic actors, build and form the instruments through their actions and decisions. Therefore, the human factor, specifically the behavior and decision-making processes of the economic actors, is the decisive factor determining the nature of the instruments. This dissertation argues for the importance of including non-economic factors in economic analysis. According to Lee (1989) the results can be misleading when non-economic factors are neglected because humans never act entirely rationally in their economic decisions (Shiller, 2000). As a result, economic development cannot be understood by simply looking at economic indicators. The question of how far and to what extent culture and other influences affect human behavior and decision-making processes which, in turn, guide social and economic destiny is examined. After all, in the end, all decisions are made by humans. Therefore, this dissertation shows how strongly culture influences human behavior and decision-making processes and in this way, shows the impact of culture on social and economic development.

With regard to the application of a multi-level theoretical framework, this dissertation shows the possible benefits of such an approach for research. First, this approach allows a holistic analysis because lower and higher influencing levels are taken into account (Slater, Snyder, and Hayes, 2006; Oetzel, 2009; Lejano and Stokols, 2013; Zhang and Ting-Toomey, 2014). Second, it shows that this model can be used in many different areas, such as for examining societal but also economic development. Third, it shows that the basic idea of multi-level theorization can be applied in different ways, such as with a layered perspective based on a bottom-up, top-down and interactive effects approach (Oetzel, 2009) but also as subsystems that can be illustrated as a series of layers (Zhang and Ting-Toomey, 2014). Fourth, the application of multi-level theoretical framework is well-suited for developmental phenomena because it is possible to examine and explain change in a particular characteristic over time, and the approach reveals the impact of other variables on change (Slater, Snyder, and Hayes, 2006). The fifth benefit is that the model can be applied to reveal a general development, such as the social development of a country by placing society at the center of consideration. At the same time, this model is suitable for the examination of specific research issues, such as the influences that contributed to an economic crisis. Finally, the model is able to reveal how different areas (in this case social and economic) are related to each other.

A main point of criticism of the multi-level theoretical framework is that it is too extensive, due to its ability to include many issues. However, this dissertation aims to show how to select and stress the relevant factors with regard to a certain issue (Oetzel, 2009).

Current State of Research of the Multi-Level Framework

A multi-level framework model, called social ecology model, first emerged in the early 1900s and evolved over subsequent decades (Lejano and Stokols, 2013). The social ecological framework with its layered perspective was adopted by many researchers and transferred to their respective fields of research, such as child development in Bronfenbrenner's (1977) case, intercultural communication by Oetzel (2009) and Zhang and Ting-Toomey (2014) or health behavior change by Stokols (1992; 1996) as well as by Schneider and Stokols (2009). The model offers a holistic view because "[t]he field of social ecology gives greater attention to the social, institutional, and cultural contexts of people – environment relations…" (Stokols, 1992, p. 7).

In 2009, Oetzel published his book *Intercultural Communication: A Layered Approach* in which he used an approach with an ecological perspective on intercultural communication. The model he applied included a bottom-up, top-down, and interactive effects approach, as is also used in this dissertation in the first and second part of the analysis.

The third part of the analysis is based on the scientific publications of Urie Bronfenbrenner, a developmental psychologist. He formulated the ecological system approach for human development, beginning in childhood, assuming that in order to understand human development, the entire ecological system in which a child grows up must be taken into account. His framework focuses on the subsystems of the human ecological surroundings, as well as on the ways in which these subsystems interact with and influence each other. This framework is conceptualized in four ecological systems (micro-, meso-, exo- and macrosystem) that an individual interacts with. Each system is located within the next larger one with the microsystem being closest to the individual person and the macrosystem being furthest away. Bronfenbrenner's early model has occasionally been criticized for not taking into account the active role of the individual in his or her own development, such as the individual's biological characteristics (e.g. age, gender) (Bronfenbrenner, 1979). Later, the PPCT (Process, Person, Context, and Time) model was developed. This model includes the chronosystem based on the four establishing principles – process, person, context, and time – and their interactions which constituted Bronfenbrenner's original basis for the bioecological theory. The chronosystem focuses on the interaction between the different systems and how they affect one another over time (Bronfenbrenner and Morris, 1998).

Zhang and Ting-Toomey (2014) also conduct research in the field of intercultural communication like Oetzel (2009). Their analysis of an intercultural conflict situation applies a social ecological perspective based on the subsystems of the human ecological surroundings. Cultural differences that lead to misinterpretation in communication are at the center of their analysis. They state that past intercultural studies tend to use a single level approach. However, intercultural conflict is always a multi-layered and multi-contextual phenomenon which is why a methodology should be applied that helps to explain this complexity.

Other important scientific publications in this area include the works by Stokols (1992, 1996). He uses a social ecological approach to examine health issues, such as the establishment and maintenance of healthy environments. He (1996) argues that most public health challenges, such as encouraging people to exercise regularly, are too complex to be understood adequately from single levels of analysis. In contrast, a social ecological approach is able to integrate different levels, such as psychological, organizational, and cultural levels to provide a comprehensive picture.

Later, Stokols and his colleague Lejano (2013) published the article "Social ecology, sustainability, and economics", in which they demonstrate the wide applicability of the social ecological framework and advocate the application of the social ecological framework for the investigation of economic issues, too.

In conclusion, the various publications show that a multi-level framework can be applied in very different ways and research areas to explain interrelations for a variety of issues. Further, it offers a holistic picture that other models cannot provide.

Objective and Problem Statement

The main focus of this dissertation, is testing the application of a multi-level framework to reveal the ecological influences on behavior and decision-making processes which affect social and economic development. Further, the dissertation aims at identifying possible links between economic development and social change.

Influences on behavior and decision-making processes are always multilayered and multi-contextual (Oetzel, 2009). Thus, in terms of inner influences, this dissertation does not consider the single individual but, in accordance with a cultural-anthropological approach, a society. These inner influences explain the attitudes and values of a society. External influences come from the systems in which a society is embedded, such as the political and economic system. It is presupposed that these systems have not emerged free from cultural influences – culture is pervasive. Thus, behavior and decision-making processes which determine the direction of social and economic developments are also influenced by culture (Keller, 1982; Kutschker and Schmid, 2011). Consequently, social and economic developments are significantly influenced and shaped by culture (DiMaggio, 1994). Therefore, this dissertation argues for the necessity of taking into account the frequently neglected factor culture when examining economic issues. Cultures are dynamic as they do not exist in a vacuum and thus are constantly subject to new influences from outside – still, cultures tend to persist. Minkov (2011) argues that culture is both stable and changeable. Thus, another objective is to clarify the impact of economic development on the cultural and social transformation using the example of Ireland.

This leads to the emergence of three research questions:

- First, which influences on behavior and decision-making processes have which effects on societal development?
- Second, which influences on behavior and decision-making processes have an impact on economic development, and in particular, which of these influences on behavior and decision-making contributed to Ireland's economic crisis?
- Third, to what extent do economic developments have an impact on society and cultural values?

The first challenge is finding a model that is able to display influencing factors, such as culture. Second, such a model should also be able to illustrate change over time. The search for a suitable framework leads to the conclusion that the application of a multi-level theoretical framework is most appropriate. On the one hand, a multi-level framework is quite complex because it requires the consideration of a number of concepts and issues. On the other hand, the complexity represents the reality of interrelated systems that have an impact on one another and provides rich theoretical and practical insights. Therefore, a third challenge of this dissertation is finding a way to structure this complexity. A fourth challenge is identifying a suitable research subject. Ireland emerged as the most suitable country for the investigation of social and economic development because, as mentioned above, the country experienced extraordinary economic developments in both directions in a relatively short period of time. In addition to this, the country also changed its Constitution during the time of these economic turbulences. Therefore, a possible connection between economic development and cultural change can be examined. Finally, another challenge is, although there are specific factors that are unique to the investigated country, such as Ireland's demographic evolution, to show that the basic idea of the analysis can be applied to every other society and economic system.

Consequently, this dissertation should eventually enable other researchers to conduct a valid, reliable and repeatable study and also allow them to apply this model to their own research topics.

Brief Description of the Research Design

The research design describes the types of inquiry within different methods approaches that provide specific direction for procedures in a research study. Thus, it has to be considered which approach should be used to study a topic. "Informing this decision should be the philosophical assumptions the researcher brings to the study; procedures of inquiry (called research designs)..." (Creswell, 2013, p.3).

First, the question of the research method has to be considered and a qualitative research method is best-fitting and therefore selected for the analysis of influencing factors. However, some findings are supported by quantitative data.

Second, the data collection for the analysis relies mainly on literature, official reports, such as the report of the inquiry commission, and financial reports. Some data of large-scale and longitudinal survey research programs are also taken into account. Thus, the data collection is based on a comprehensive review of literature and examination of open-source documents.

Third, the special feature of the chosen analysis model is that the number of issues that can be taken into account is basically limitless. However, this does not mean that everything matters (Oetzel, 2009). With regard to the research issue, namely identifying the environmental influences on behavior and decision-making processes, some factors matter more than others. The challenge of applying a layered perspective framework lies in the determination of its theoretical limits because expanding these limits further enhances the explanatory nature of this heuristic theoretical framework (Zhang and Ting-Toomey, 2014; Oetzel, 2009). Therefore, those factors are selected that led to significant changes, such as legislation change. In addition, influences on the behavior and decisions of some key decision-makers are examined because their decisions had a significant impact on further developments.

Finally, in order to gain a better understanding of the ways in which the environment influences human behavior and decision-making processes, this dissertation concludes that the multi-level framework fits best to examine the respective issues. Therefore, the analysis is divided into three sections based on a multi-level framework. The Irish society is placed at the center of the first part of the analysis (Chapter Five) with the central issue being how and why the Irish society developed in a certain direction. This section analyzes which factors affected the behavior and decisions of key influencers and also analyzes the consequences of these decisions for society. It therefore helps to gain a better understanding of the influencing factors that led to trend-setting decisions which in turn swayed the development of the Irish society.

In Chapter Six, the Irish economy is at the center of consideration. In particular, this section focuses on Ireland's dramatic economic slump, also known as the fall of the Celtic Tiger. The analysis reveals the behavior and decisions of key figures and shows the interaction of some important influencing factors that finally led to the fall of the Celtic Tiger.

Both chapters use a bottom-up, top-down, and interactive effects approach in contrast to Chapter Seven. Chapter Seven takes into account time as an important factor to reveal change. Thus, Chapter Seven reveals cultural change in light of economic developments using the knowledge of the previous chapters by taking into account a framework that focuses on the subsystems of the human ecological surroundings, as well as on the ways in which these subsystems interact with and influence each other. The subsystems are illustrated as a series of layers.

Dissertation Outline

This dissertation is organized in eight chapters. Chapter One deals with the role of history, culture, and identity because these factors influence all areas of human behavior and decision-making. In Chapter Two, some theoretical frameworks for the description of culture are presented and examined. The review and conclusion reveal that the social ecological theory is the most suitable of the presented analyzing methodology. In Chapter Three, the theoretical approach of Chapter One is applied to Ireland. Chapter Three gives an overview of Irish history, Irish culture, and the self-conception of Irish people, i.e. their identity, which contributes to the explanation of the social and economic development of Ireland. Therefore, this chapter provides the basis for the analysis in Chapters Five, Six, and Seven. Chapter Four focuses on the period of the beginning of the rise and abrupt decline of the Irish economy, which started in 2007 with the advent of the global financial crisis. This chapter provides the basis for the analysis in Chapters Six and Seven.

Chapter Five, Six and Seven are the chapters containing the analysis based on a multi-level framework and aim at answering the research questions. Each chapter deals with one of the research questions showing that a multi-level framework is able to provide answers to each of the respective research questions: Chapter Five then examines the various influencing factors on human behavior and decision-making processes that contributed to the social development of Ireland. Chapter Six analyzes the influences on individual behavior and decision-making with regard to their effects on Irish economy. Finally, based on the findings of the previous chapters, Chapter Seven investigates whether there are interrelations between economic development, social development, and cultural change. Chapter Eight deals with the answers of the research questions. It further provides a discussion about the theoretical and practical implications of the application of the layered perspective and offers recommendations for further research.

Chapter 1: The Role of History, Culture and Identity

DiMaggio (1994) states that "[m]ost of us are accustomed to the view, assimilated by social research and theory, that economic relations influence ideas, worldviews, and symbols. That the reverse is true, that aspects of culture shape economic institutions and affairs, is less well understood..." (DiMaggio, 1994, p. 27). Therefore, it is important to take into account a country's culture when looking at its economy which is also part of this dissertation. Sen (2007a) claims that sociologists, anthropologists, and historians have often criticized the tendency of economists to pay too little attention to culture when studying the functioning and development of societies and economies. He states that economists can benefit from paying more attention to the influence of culture on economic and social issues. For instance, authorities such as the World Bank are dominated by the way of thinking of economists and financial experts. The fact that economists often neglect the importance of culture is reflected in their predictions and approaches. Therefore, Sen (2007a) argues that cultural dimensions require a closer examination as part of an analysis of social and economic developments. Culture should be taken into account in order to develop sound economic strategies. The question is not whether culture matters, the question is in which way is culture important and further in which different ways can culture influence developments? How can these influences be better understood and how can they affect developments? Therefore, the nature of these relationships and their implications that affect the behavior and decisions of economic actors and politicians are of interest (Sen, 2007a).

A people's culture is largely imperceptible to the people belonging to it. People only become aware of the differences existing between different cultures when they are confronted with these directly. All human beings are surrounded by culture. There is no culture-free zone (Keller, 1982; Kutschker and Schmid, 2011). Further, culture provides people with an identity while culture itself is shaped by history to a large extent. Therefore, history plays an important role in the formation of identity. History ascribes sense to the lives of a group of people giving them a collective meaning regarding who they are, where they come from, and which direction to take in the future. Identifying with their heritage and developing a strong cultural identity is very important for many people. "A shared history invests ethnic identity with social value... The ways in which a people understand their collective, cultural history can have profound effects on an individual's sense of identity" (Wexler, 2009, p. 270). "[S]ocial memory functions as a historical interpretation that imbues individuals and communities with meaning and presents strategies for future collective action" (Wexler, 2009, p. 270).

In Chapter Three, the theoretical concept of history, culture and identity, explained below, is applied to Ireland. The analyses of the Chapters Five, Six and Seven put this concept in context and shows the impact of history, culture and identity on behavior and decision-making processes with reference to the social and economic developments in Ireland.

1 History

The term 'history' is often used synonymously with the term 'past'. However there is a difference. The past is the entire collection of everything (e.g. events, personal happenings, opinions, and so on) that has ever happened anywhere prior to this moment. In contrast, history is the study, interpretation, and recording of past events and their recollections in a way that gives meaning to people (Cheprasov, 2003).

Historical memory is also called 'collective memory' or 'social memory'. It refers to the way by which groups of people create and then identify with specific narratives about historical periods or events. Historical memory is fluid because 'history' has not the same meaning as 'past'. History is the interpretation of the past. An interpretation allows different versions based on present moment and personal biases in time. These interpretations can change over time and thus, history can be re-written and recalled in a different way once again (Cheprasov, 2003).

As a consequence, written history is a personal description of past events. It illustrates what was an important happening or an important era but may also reflect the opinion, attitude, or values of the writer. The distinction between what people remember and document about the past and what happened in the past needs to be considered in a differentiated approach. Historians should attempt to reconstruct the past as it 'actually' was (Darnton, 2003). While the past is the actual event, history is the story. An author highlights what he or she, respectively his or her group, considers important about the past. This is also a matter of who gets to be remembered and who is ignored (Loewen, 2000). These descriptions identify how the author, respectively his or her group, sees the past, which values are highlighted, what he or she wanted to be remembered for, and how he or she sees others (Oetzel, 2009). Consequently, written history is, for instance, influenced by inner elements like the author's personal view of the world. However, it can also be influenced by outer elements. Some aspects of history, for instance, may be highlighted or extenuated for political reasons in order to strengthen one party and to weaken another party. In this way, written history can also be influenced by particular goals the author, or someone else having power over the author, wanted to reach.

Remains and artefacts can function as silent witnesses of what happened in the past and are therefore part of history, but they need to be interpreted. Due to new technology, such as DNA or isotopic analysis, better analyses of these remains and artefacts are possible. The improvement of technology opens up new fields of research, offers new explanations, and allows researchers to pose new questions (Wiederschein, 2012). As a consequence, history can be seen in a new light. Researchers are able to reinterpret the past, search for new sources and find new meanings in old documents or deposited artefacts. In this light, new perspectives and new knowledge lead to a better understanding of the past (McNeill, 1985). A collective memory as a set of ideas, images, and feelings about the past is anchored in the resources which the individuals share (Irwin-Zarecka, 1994). Thus, collective memory "refers to the shared pool of information held in the memories of two or more members of a group" (Weinberg, 2014, p. 143). Consequently, when resources are updated due to new knowledge and conclusions about historical events, collective memory may change, in the same way as personal memories can change.

1.1 History and Collective Memory

Major historical events have particular relevance for a group of people, most of them are able to remember them and therefore, these events become part of the collective memory and contribute to forming cultural identity (Lerner, 1997).

People who share collective memories usually share cultural identities. However, identity groups cannot be distinctly defined. In addition, there is often a high degree of internal diversity among individuals within large collectivities. Collective memories of a specific event may vary in parts. There can be widespread consensus and high agreement on some parts while others are remembered differently regarding content or emphasis or may even evoke complete disagreement. For instance, while it is undeniable that the Great Famine (please see Chapter Three, Section 1.4) is deeply engraved in the memories of the Irish people, opinions about the behavior of the British Government are divergent. On the one hand, some sources state that it is questionable whether the British Government played a significant role regarding the starvation of the

Irish population and that the Irish people would not have fared better, even if they had been independent. O Grádá states that "…genocide includes murderous intent, and it must be said that not even the most bigoted and racist commentators of the day sought the extermination of the Irish" (O Grádá, 2000, p. 10). On the other hand, other sources, state that "[t]he treatment of the Irish people by the British Government during the Famine has been described as genocide – race murder" (Woodham Smith, 1991, p. 407). These parties refer to the refusal of the British Government to provide help after 1847, to the political oppression and the resulting dependence on the potato as only food source and also to the compulsory food exports from Ireland to Britain during the Famine (Woodham Smith, 1991; Murphy, 2013; Coogan, 2012).

Although an individual is part of a culture, he or she must not necessarily agree on all details. There is consensus in a specific collective, for instance, about the meaning of symbols, but individuals may vary greatly regarding thoughts, feelings, and behavior about them (Shweder and LeVine, 1984).

The collective memory of major historical events does not always consist of bare facts about the past. Instead, an essential characteristic is the moral, political, and social lessons they transmit. Memory is experienced through the eyes and minds of the participants in the events and their descendants by transmitting the experience from generation to generation. Collective memory is, among others, built on the basis of information found in scripts written at that time, from the view of the writer of history books, commemorative events, and also in stories and legends. However, differences can arise regarding 'what' is remembered which are linked to 'who' is remembering (Ross, 2013).

Collective memories are maintained, communicated, developed, reinforced, and transformed, for instance, through narratives, rituals, and symbols. The intensity of collective memories may vary, so that not all collective memories are equally apparent for all members of an ethnic group. Collective memories serve the interests and goals of different people. Consequently, this highlights how interests motivate actions and define meanings. For instance, the Irish saint St. Patrick (please see Chapter Three, Section 3.2.2) became 'more and more sacred' in the stories over the centuries because interest groups wanted to strengthen their supremacy and it was easier to do this with the grace of a more powerful saint (Kinealy, 2004; McCaffrey and Eaton, 2002). Further, when identities are endangered, people protect them through rituals and symbols that reinforce collective memories. For instance, although the Irish adopted the Christian faith, they also held on to their Celtic rituals and symbols (Ross, 2013).

1.2 History and Identity

History, among other things, is an important factor contributing to the formation of identity which is explained in this chapter, Section 3. Historical data provide details about how groups, institutions, and nations were formed. Further, the data shed light on how they developed, whether they coalesced or fell apart. In this way, history tells the national story, highlighting distinctive events of the national experience and consequently creating an understanding of national values (Stearns, 1998). Also, history is the story of an individual's life and generation. It is the story of a person's family and of the group he or she belongs to. Thus, it is also a source of personal identity (please see this chapter, Section 3.2.1) (Lerner, 1997). A person loses his or her identity without individual memory. Consequently, this person would not know how to act in encounters with others, for instance, another nationality or some special group within national borders.

1.3 Historical Trauma

Trauma is ancient Greek and is translated as 'wound'. A wound can be a physical injury due to external force or a psychological injury through shock (Kluge and Seebold, 2002). Various cultures have experienced events threatening their life during their personal history or the history of earlier generations that left severe negative impressions. For instance, a situation in which the majority of people were suffering because of confrontation with a natural catastrophe, such as crop failure which in turn results in famine or war. However, people can also be affected by events they did not experience directly but which were transmitted from generation to generation. "Evidence supports that traumatic events from as long as 400 years ago have mental and physical health impacts on people today" (Oetzel, 2009, p. 344). When people today are affected in a negative way by these negative events from a long time ago, it is called a historical trauma (Oetzel, 2009).

Carrillo and Tello (2008) connect historical trauma to health related problems, such as depression and anxiety. Historical trauma is unresolved trauma and grief that continues to adversely affect the lives of survivors of such trauma and manifests itself in all types of unhealthy behavioral patterns. They highlight that historical trauma is passed on from one generation to the next. Consequently, if an individual or his or her ancestors experienced or witnessed these extremely negative events, this could have a direct impact on the respective individual. It could result in mental imbalance and in self-destructive behavior in an attempt to cope with these imbalances (Carrillo and Tello, 2008).

1.4 Conclusion – The Importance of History for the Present

A nation is not freestanding and self-contained. It is connected with and partially shaped by its surroundings (Bender, 2006). Hofstede (2003) states that much of the cultural variety in the present world can be explained only by history. Having knowledge of an individual's own historical heritage and that of others helps to understand current values and institutions (Samovar et al., 2013). Oetzel (2009) argues that history matters because it is part of collective memory and cultural identity. There are historical events which are traumatic and historical relations have consequences for today. From the collective memory aspect, history matters because it is part of how individuals see themselves, how they define themselves, and the meaning individuals derive from their lives. Historical trauma focuses on how victims and their descendants have been influenced through intergenerational trauma (Oetzel, 2009). The historian Peter N. Stearns (1998) even goes further by saying that the word 'culture' can be exchanged for the word 'history' because history offers the only extensive evidential basis for the examination, analysis, and explanation of understanding how people act and societies function. Further, history also provides explanations to understand how societies and cultures emerged and developed over time. The past influences the present and the future. Consequently, a retrospect is able to shed light on the causes of change. In addition, history provides adequate explanations to understand which elements of an institution or a society persist despite change. History is therefore a valuable resource to understand culture, society, and change (Stearns, 1998; Korostelina, 2008). Although this dissertation focuses on history, other factors, such as geography or climate for example, also exert an influence in shaping culture and cultural values.

2 Culture

The word 'culture' with its modern technical or anthropological meaning was established in English by the anthropologist Sir Edward B. Tylor, who states in 1871 that "CULTURE or Civilization, taken in its wide ethnographic sense, is that complex whole which includes knowledge, belief, art, morals, law, custom, and any other capabilities and habits acquired by man as a member of society" (Tylor, 1920, p. 1). Harrison and Huntington (2002) state that "[t]he term 'culture,' of course, has had multiple meanings in different disciplines and different contexts" (Harrison and Huntington, 2000, p. xv). As a result, researchers from different disciplines using the term 'culture' imply various meanings. The anthropologists Kroeber and Kluckhohn listed 164 definitions of culture

(Kutschker and Schmid, 2011). They also state that history is a central element of culture and conclude that:

> Culture consists of patterns, explicit and implicit, of and for behavior acquired and transmitted by symbols, constituting the distinctive achievement of human groups, including their embodiments in artefacts; the essential core of culture consists of traditional (i.e., historically derived and selected) ideas and especially their attached values; culture systems may, on the one hand, be considered as products of action, on the other as conditioning elements of further action (Kroeber and Kluckhohn, 1952, p. 181).

Other researchers also emphasize the importance of history by stating that culture consists of "shared motives, values, beliefs, identities, and interpretations or meanings of significant events that result from common experiences of members of collectives that are transmitted across generations" (House et al., 2004, p. 15). The way individuals perceive the world and derive meaning from it is influenced significantly by the beliefs, norms, and practices of the people and institutions surrounding them (Kassin, Fein and Markus, 2014). Consequently, human beings are influenced by their social environment which in turn is influenced by history.

In conclusion, researchers from different disciplines, such as anthropology, psychology, theology, philosophy, and sociology, have attempted to find a definition of culture which fits their respective opinions best. However, all of them seem to be in agreement that history is a decisive factor in shaping culture. Cultural identification includes individuals acknowledging their cultural attributes, such as beliefs, values, practices, norms, and history, along with understanding how these are reflected in themselves (Wexler, 2009). Cultural values have to be related to a system of meaning. Studying values involves the comparison of individuals and studying cultures means that different societies have to be compared in order to create a reference. When studying the cultural implications of values, cultural context is needed. For instance, a number of popular cultural models rely on quantitative analysis, and provide scores, for example a scale from 0–100 points to rate a certain dimension, such as power distance. However, a detached average score does not make any sense. The scores can only be understood within a context (Søndergaard, 2002). History provides that context.

2.1 Characteristics of Culture

As the term 'culture' seems to be a vague, abstract notion and because of its ambiguous concept, some authors, such as Keller (1982), Fujishin (2009), Samovar, Porter, McDaniel and Roy (2013), Haviland, Prins, McBride, and Walrath (2013), or Minkov and Hofstede (2013) list characteristics in order to define culture. The basic assumption is that "there is a limited number of common human problems for which all peoples at all times must find some solution" (Kluckhohn and Strodtbeck, 1961, p. 10). Despite the fact that "there is variability in solutions of all the problems, it is neither limitless nor random but is definitely variable within a range of possible solutions" (Kluckhohn and Strodtbeck, 1961, p. 10). There are characteristics that all cultures are likely to share when meeting common human challenges (Samovar, Porter, McDaniel and Roy, 2013). When searching for a common basis of all definitions of culture, Keller looked at specific characteristics of culture (Keller, 1982). Some of the most important ones are briefly explained below.

2.1.1 Visible and Invisible Elements of Culture

Every culture consists of visible and invisible elements. Visible elements of a culture are observable and noticeable, for instance, human behavior or material, i.e. human-made artefacts, such as literature or art. Invisible elements of a culture are beliefs, norms, values, and attitudes (Keller, 1982; Kutschker and Schmid, 2011). "The heart of a culture, [however], involves language, religion, values, traditions, and customs" (Huntington, 1996, p. 28). Language, for instance, is a noticeable element. However, the transmitted meaning may be undetectable, i.e. an invisible element, for non-members of a specific society (please see Chapter Three, Section 2.1).

2.1.2 Culture is Learned

Culture is learned through interaction, observation, and imitation as well as through several social institutions of the culture, for instance, school, workplace, or church (Haviland et al., 2013). Julia Wood (2015) states that in interacting with others, people come to understand the beliefs, values, norms, and language of their own culture.

> When an infant is born, he or she enters a cultural environment in which many solutions already exist to the universal problems facing all human populations. The child merely needs to learn or internalize those solutions to make a reasonable adjustment to his or her surroundings (Ferraro and Andreatta, 2014, p. 32).

From the moment of birth, an individual seeks to make sense of the world. It is culture that provides the tools for this sense-making process. Thus, culture is, for instance, learned through narratives and stories. Narratives are mainly intended to transmit the important messages a culture wants to teach its members. Stories about the past also shed light on social orders and daily life. They reveal how families were organized, how political structure operated, how religious ceremonies felt to the people who took part, and how power was divided between the members of a society. Therefore, these stories about the past are not only for entertainment; they teach the members of a cultural group about its cultural values and attitudes. They give concrete form to a set of beliefs and traditions linking today's people of a culture to their history (Erdoes and Ortiz, 1984).

Nowadays, culture is also transmitted and learned through media like television. "Mass media shape our attitudes, values, and perceptions of people, situations, places, and events" (Wood, 2009, p. 308). The media contain people's ideas about who they are and who they should be and consequently contribute to the construction of identity (Wood, 2009). Examples for the powerful influences of mass media are given in Chapter Three, Section 2.2, Chapter Five, Section 3.3, Chapter Six, Section 3.1.1 and Chapter Seven, Section 3.

2.1.3 Culture Presupposes a Collectivity

Culture presupposes a collectivity because it is not an individual phenomenon. Culture determines the identity of a social community while personality influences the identity of an individual (Hofstede, 2003; Kutschker and Schmid, 2011). Thus, culture is independent of the fate of an individual. This means, a culture can even continue to exist after its population has become extinct. For example, even though the original Celts stopped existing as a tribe or nation thousands of years ago, Irish people today refer to being the ancestors of the Celts (please see 'Celtic Renaissance ' in Chapter Three, Section 2.3) (Keller, 1982).

2.1.4 Culture Influences Behavior

Culture has great influence on behavior. From the moment of birth, the customs into which an individual is born shape his or her behavior. The individual becomes a creature of his or her culture and by the time he or she grows up, the individual adapts and modifies his or her behavior to that of other group members (Benedict, 2005). Sharing a similar construction of reality influences the behavior of group members in a similar way (please see Chapter Three, Section 2.4) (Keller, 1982).

2.1.5 Cultures are Dynamic Systems

Cultures are dynamic systems, interwoven with their environment. The systems are dependent on influences within and around them. When one element within the system changes the entire system strives to adjust. This also happens when an outside force applies pressure (please see Chapter Three, Section 2.5). Cultural behavior adjusts to the environment people live in (Keller, 1982; Kutschker and Schmid, 2011; Haviland et al., 2013). A possible explanation for the mutual influences is found in Bronfenbrenner's social ecological model which is explained later in this dissertation (please see Chapter Two, Section 3 and Chapter Three, Section 2.5).

2.2 Manifestation of Culture – The Onion Model

Many aspects of culture reveal themselves in visible elements. Hofstede, one of the best known and most cited researchers in this area, chooses symbols, heroes, and rituals together with values from the broad spectrum of terms applied to describe visible manifestations of culture and in this way, manages to cover the total concept quite accurately (Søndergaard, 1994; Hofstede, 2003; Hofstede et al., 2010). Culture occurs on different levels of depth – some levels are easier to perceive and therefore more visible while other levels are more hidden. Hofstede (2003) illustrates the visible manifestations of culture as the layers of an onion, beginning on the outermost layer with symbols, because they are the most superficial, while the core of the onion consists of values. Values remain invisible until revealed in behavior (Hofstede, 2003; Hofstede et al., 2010).

"Culture could be defined as the interactive aggregate of common characteristics that influence a human group's response to its environment" (Hofstede, 2003, p. 10). Thus, to understand a human group's response to its environment or human behavior, it is important to understand the elements in which culture reveals itself (Brislin, 1993). Examples related to Ireland are found in Chapter Three, Section 3.

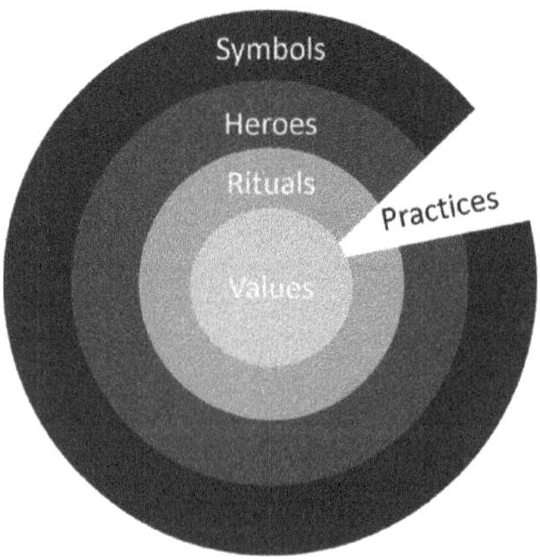

Figure 1: Hofstede's 'Onion Diagram' Illustrates How Culture Appears at Different Levels of Depth (Hofstede, 2003, p. 11)

2.2.1 Symbols

Objects, pictures, or other concrete representations of ideas, concepts, or other abstractions, such as words, gestures, and acts, are the symbols of a group or a society. These symbols frequently transmit a multifaceted meaning recognized as such only by those who share the culture. The symbols themselves are visible to outsiders. Yet, for them they are ambiguous in that they offer a variety of disparate meanings (Hofstede, 2003; Hofstede et al., 2010). When people grow up in a specific culture, they learn the meanings attached to certain symbols. Sentiments and emotions arise in members who understand the meaning of these symbols (Cohen, 1974). Culture is a learned and shared interrelated set of symbols whose meanings provide a variety of orientation guidelines for the members of a society. These guidelines represent solutions to problems that all societies face (Terpstra and David, 1991). Kenneth Burke, an American literary theorist notes the importance of "the tiny sliver of reality each of us has experienced firsthand" when his students talk to each other. While "the whole overall 'picture' is but a construct of our symbol systems" (Burke, 1968, p. 5). He further states that by using symbols human beings hold on to "a kind of naïve verbal realism that refuses to realize the full extent of the role played by symbolicity in his notions of reality" (Burke, 1968, p. 5). The ability of symbolization is a very important characteristic of humans because it helps them to identify, sort, and classify things, ideas, and behavior. Symbols can help to store the experiences of past generations. The shared meaning of a group's or society's culture enables its members to interact with one another with the least amount of ambiguity and misunderstanding. In this way, communication is facilitated and as a consequence, symbols help tie the members of a group together (Ferraro, 2008). New symbols develop quickly and easily and old ones may disappear. Symbols can also easily be adopted by other cultural groups. Therefore, they are located in the outermost layer of the onion diagram to illustrate their superficiality (please see Chapter Three, Section 3.1) (Hofstede, 2003; Hofstede et al., 2010).

2.2.2 Heroes

Heroes are characters, alive or dead, real or imaginary, mythological or legendary, sometimes of divine descent, and gifted with special skills and abilities, who have characteristics that are highly valued in a culture and thus, serve as models for behavior (Hofstede, 2003; Hofstede et al., 2010). Heroes are not a phenomenon of bygone times. Joseph Campbell, a professor of literature, argues that "[t]he bold and truly epoch-making writings of the psychoanalysts are indispensable to the student of mythology; for, whatever may be thought of the detailed and sometimes contradictory interpretations of specific cases and problems, Freud, Jung, and their followers have demonstrated irrefutably that the logic, the heroes, and the deeds of myth survive into modern times" (Campbell, 2008, p. 2). Culture is learned through the legends and myths in which the respective heroes face their challenges. Thus, legends and myths transmit what is important and what is right or wrong in the eyes of a culture. The stories are passed on from generation to generation and are used to stress moral messages (Samovar et al., 2013). For instance, the heroes in the legends who triumph do so because of their noble characteristics and admirable behavior while characters who behave in socially inappropriate ways receive the punishment they deserve. The stories consist of the existential questions of human beings, such as where they come from, why they are here, and how to make sense of the world (please see Chapter Three, Section 3.2) (Ferraro and Andreatta, 2014).

2.2.3 Rituals

Rituals are collective activities that in theory are unnecessary to the achievement of desired ends, but that within a culture are considered socially essential, keeping the individual bound within the norms of collectivity. Therefore, rituals are conducted for their own sake. Some examples for rituals are ways of greeting and paying respect to others. They can be revealed in business and political meetings by the way they are organized, as well as in social and religious ceremonies (Hofstede, 2003; Hofstede et al., 2010). Collective rituals are not impulsive or based on individual creativity reflecting certain attitudes. Instead, for the majority of people participating in rituals, they play an important role in shaping specific attitudes. When these rituals are adopted by a group, they are no longer subjective or individual but become objective in the way that rituals become the collective representations of a group (please see Chapter Three, Section 3.3) (Cohen, 1974).

2.2.4 Practices

Symbols, heroes, and rituals are summarized under the expression 'practices'. In this regard, they are visible to an outside viewer. The course of action is observable to non-members. However, their cultural meanings are invisible and lie exactly and exclusively in the ways these practices are interpreted by the members of the group. This interpretation reflects a society's value system, which is at the core of a culture. The closer a cultural layer is to the core, the less consistency and consequences are obvious (Hofstede, 2003; Hofstede et al., 2010).

2.2.5 *Values*

Values develop from religious convictions, historical experiences, and traditions. Values can, for instance, be defined as expressions of a desirable state or as individual, relatively abstract conceptions of a desirable state. A value may also be defined as a durable belief that an explicit manner of behavior or end-state of existence is personally or socially preferable to another (Rokeach, 1973). Values are a learned system of regulations for making choices and helping to overcome conflicts. They determine what is helpful, good, right, or wrong, what to endeavor for, how to live one's own life, and even what to die for. A value system represents what is commonplace or hoped for, compulsory or prohibited. Values offer a set of criteria by which behavior is judged and sanctions are applied. Each individual has an exclusive set of his or her own values (Samovar et al., 2013).

There are also values which tend to permeate a culture. These are called 'cultural values'. They are copied from the larger philosophical issue, which is part of a culture's environment and transmitted by a variety of sources, for instance, family, media, school, church, state, and history. Consequently, these cultural values tend to be broad-based, enduring, and relatively constant (Hofstede, 2003; Hofstede et al., 2010). Cultural beliefs and cultural values are deeply rooted motivations or orientations; they affect a person's perception and therefore, values lead to human actions. An understanding of cultural values supports the appreciation of the behavior of other people (Halman and Vloet, 1994; Samovar et al., 2013).

A look at the large number of instruments designed to measure human values shows that human values as a whole are not clearly defined. Instead, each researcher has subjectively selected from this unknown whole with little consensus in the research community. Consequently, Hofstede (2003) states that the content validity regarding measurements of values is inevitably low.

2.3 Stability and Change of National Culture

It is hotly debated in the research community whether it is possible to actually talk about national culture (Eringa, Caudron, Rieck, Xie, and Gerhardt, 2015). For instance, Brendan McSweeney (2002) asks "[d]o nations have cultures?" (McSweeney, 2002, p. 89). He argues that it is doubtful whether a connection between national culture and social causality actually exists and rejects the notion of a mono-causal link between national cultures and actions within nations. He states that the extent of uniformity of actions, structures, institutions, and so forth, within a nation still remains an open question (McSweeney, 2002). Further, Witchalls and Meyer argue in favor of (Witchalls) and against (Meyer) the categorization of culture by national entities (Meyer, 2004; Witchalls, 2012). Newman and Nollen (1996) in contrast take the existence of a national culture for granted in their analysis. Hofstede's model and the GLOBE Study, for instance, are even based on the idea of a national culture (Hofstede, 2003; House et al., 2004).

There are different opinions regarding the categorization of culture. McSweeney (2002), for instance, questions the view that every individual in a nation shares a common national culture because he rejects the idea that a 'national norm,' or 'central tendency,' or 'average national tendency' exists. His viewpoint is supported by the research of Fahey, Hayes and Sinnott (2005). They argue that Ireland and Northern Ireland are culturally more similar to each other than Northern Ireland is to Britain. This example shows that regions can be culturally different from the nation into which they are incorporated.

Depending on the different viewpoints of how culture is defined and categorized, different questions can be posed and therefore, only fragmented parts of the whole are revealed when attempting to answer these specific questions. Thus, if culture is categorized according to national entities, this will never represent the complexity of all viewpoints. Further, researchers, such as Meyer (2004), argue that cultural similarities are no guarantee for similarities or overlaps in value profiles.

Categorizing culture by national entities is just one option. Indeed, some factors support a categorization of national culture, such as the fact that a culture is influenced to a great extent by the representative who distributes information within that culture and the attitudes and influences on that specific representative. Witchalls (2012) argues that information is spread, among others, by the church, the state, and mass media. It is decisive that the messages of the national church, politics, and the media are consumed predominantly by the national residents. Thus, nations, for the most part, continue to consume information from national sources, e.g. because of language barriers. These national sources are crucial for maintaining continuity, enabling reproduction of existing ideas, and sustaining the cultural memory (Witchalls, 2012).

The researchers Newman and Nollen (1996) wrote that "[n]ational culture is defined as the values, beliefs and assumptions learned in early childhood that distinguish one group of people from another". Further they state that "[n]ational culture is embedded deeply in everyday life and is relatively impervious to change" (Newman and Nollen, 1996, p. 754). Culture only exists through comparison with other cultures. Hofstede treats "culture as the collective programming of the mind that distinguishes the members of one group or category of people from another" (Hofstede, 2003, p. 9). Differences and similarities in cultural patterns have ancient historical roots, going back thousands of years. Hofstede (2003) speculates that there are mechanisms in societies that permit the maintenance of stability in cultural patterns across many generations. He suggests that such mechanisms operate as illustrated below:

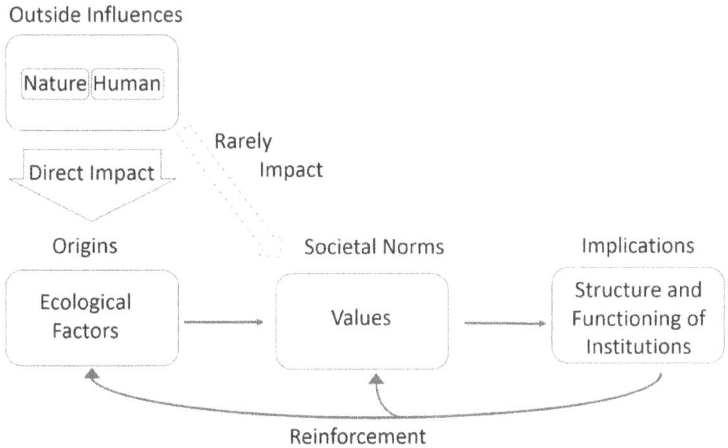

Figure 2: The Stabilizing of Culture Patterns Based on Hofstede (Hofstede, 2003, p. 12)

The origins of societal norms lie in a variety of ecological factors, such as history, economy, geography, and technology which affect the physical and social environment. A system of societal norms is at the center consisting of the values systems shared by the majority of the society. These societal norms lead to the development and pattern maintenance of institutions in a society with particular structures and ways of functioning, such as family patterns, education systems, legislation, and political systems. When these institutions are established, they reinforce the societal norms, as well as the ecological conditions that led to their creation (Hofstede, 2003).

Hofstede (2003) believes that cultural change occurs through changes in ecological conditions. Outside influences of nature and human beings have a direct impact on the origins. Changes occur through forces of nature, such as climate changes or spread of diseases. But they are also triggered by human efforts, such as trade, conquest, technological inventions, and economic domination. Kunkel (1970), who deals with the economic development of societies, supposes "that the major problem of economic development is not the alteration of character, values, or attitudes, but the change of those selected aspects of man's social environment which are relevant to the learning of new behavior patterns" (Kunkel, 1970, p. 76). However, as mentioned previously when one element within the system changes, the entire system strives to adjust. Therefore, it is arguable that not only the social but instead the whole environment is affected in the case of change.

Hofstede (2003) argues that societal norms rarely change through direct adaption of outside values except if the outside influences are extremely violent, for instance, in the case of a natural catastrophe on a grand scale or a military invasion.

Moreover, he determines that cultural differences cannot be understood without the knowledge of the history of a society, because history becomes apparent in culture, in the body of thoughts, convictions, and behavior of the present generation. There are cultures in history that have maintained their identities over time despite significant change, such as a loss of independence and/ or a loss of language. Other cultures, with comparable conditions, decayed or disappeared, for instance, the culture of the Sumerian, the Akkadian, or the Maya (Brasse, 2014; Diamond, 2014; Selz, 2016). Researchers assume different reasons for this decay. Power struggles between the different Mayan tribes, drought periods that led to famine and last but not least conquerors from Spain who brought diseases which diminished the native Maya are some of them. Also the Spanish subjugated the population in bloody warfare. In 1697, the last great free principality was conquered which for the most part ended the history of this independent and unique culture (Brasse, 2014; Diamond, 2014).

The strength of the existing self-regulation, as the model shows, and the strength of the outside forces have played important roles in these cases (Hofstede, 2003). Cultures are dynamic as they do not exist in a vacuum and thus are constantly subject to new influences from outside – still, cultures tend to persist. Minkov (2011) argues that culture is both stable and changeable. For instance, the spread of Christianity did not homogenize the affected societies – instead, these societies adapted the new faith to their own cultural traditions (Barnlund, 1989).

3 Identity

The word 'identity' has its origins in the Latin *idem* (Eisenberg and Schneider, 2011). Researchers from different disciplines have tried to provide an interpretation of identity which fits their respective opinion best. Consequently, it is not surprising that a huge variety of approaches exists, each having its own theories and models to define identity. In general, identity is abstract, multifaceted, dynamic, and socially constructed (Oetzel, 2009). As a result, it is problematic to find a single, summarizing description suitable to all fields of research (Samovar et al., 2013).

As explained below, identity and, in particular, the negative sides of identity, such as stereotypes, also called the dark side of identity here, provides basic knowledge in order to gain a better understanding of Chapter One, Section 1.2, Chapter Three, Section 2, Chapter Five, and Chapter Seven.

3.1 Characteristics of Identity

The concept of identity influences the attitude and behavior of people in many ways (Sen, 2007b). Identity has various characteristics. The characteristics provide explanations for how people create, negotiate, challenge, and renegotiate identities when interacting with other people. Characteristics of identity are, for instance, that it is multifaceted, that it consists of social and personal identities, that it is salient and can be strong or weak, and that it is both stable and changing, avowed and ascribed (Oetzel, 2009).

An individual's identity is composed of multiple dimensions. This composition determines who a person is. This is explained in the following Sections 3.2.1 to 3.2.4. Further, although an individual holds multiple identities, not all identities are equally important. Thus, identity salience refers to the degree to which an identity is prominent in a given situation, for instance, when an individual travels to another country. The strength of identity refers to the degree of importance of a particular identity. Identity is both stable and changing which means it can change or endure depending on a variety of historical, political, and social influences. Identity can be both avowed and ascribed. Avowal refers to the identity someone expresses or states directly toward others, e.g. wearing clothes that are associated with a certain tradition or stating that he or she is, for instance, Catholic, Irish or Nationalist. Ascription refers to the identity that is ascribed to someone by other people, i.e. the identity someone should have in the opinion of the other person. For example, an Irish person living in the southern part of the Republic of Ireland should be Catholic (Oetzel, 2009).

When someone perceives only a single identity of another person this may lead to conflict (Sen, 2007b).

3.2 Categories of Identity

Identity can be categorized into different types, such as personal identity, social identity, gender identity, political identity, ethnic identity, regional identity, national identity, cultural identity, and organizational identity, just to mention a few.

Hecht, Warren, Jung and Krieger (2005) state that individuals belong to different social categories and form identities based on the membership to these categories. Consequently, every individual has multiple identities. An individual's overall identity is made up of a numerous overlapping aspects and sub-identities depending on the situation or environment he or she is located in (Imahori and Cupach, 2005). Four categories of identity – personal, social, cultural, and national – are introduced below.

3.2.1 Personal Identity

According to Turner, Oakes, Haslam and McGarty (1994), personal identity defines "the individual as a unique person in terms of his or her individual differences from other (in-group) persons" (p.454). Whereas the psychologists Oerter and Montada (2002) see personal identity as a unique combination of personal characteristics that someone is self-conscious about and that is presented to others. Self-awareness and self-formation form a person's identity (Oerter and Montada, 2002). Additionally, identity "is about who we are and who others think we are" (Martin and Nakayama, 2013, p. 162). Martin and Nakayama (2002) state that identity is a core issue for most people. The umbrella questions are 'who am I?' and 'what do I want?' (Oerter and Montada, 2002). The necessity of an individual to understand the meaning of his or her identity is crucial, because identity development plays an important role in the individual's psychological comfort (Samovar et al., 2013). As a result, someone who fails to achieve a stable identity faces identity confusion, because of a lack of clearness about who he or she is and his or her role in life (Phinney, 1993). During an individual's life cycle, he or she experiences various identities, continually adapts new identities and sets aside some old ones. Thus, a person has more than one identity. On the one hand, a person identifies himself or herself differently during different periods of his or her life (Samovar et al., 2013). For instance, someone is single first, then he or she gets married and is a husband or a wife, and later on, he or she may also become a parent. On the other hand, a person shows his or her partial identity depending on the setting, for example as a parent, member of a sports club, or as a politician. Consequently, personal identity is an interwoven construct of various partial identities based on the context or situation.

3.2.2 Social Identity

Social identity defines "the individual in terms of his or her shared similarities with members of certain social categories in contrast to other social categories" (Turner et al., 1994, p. 454). The sociologists Tajfel and Turner developed the 'social identity theory' which explains social identity as a way to explain intergroup behavior. They define a group

> as a collection of individuals who perceive themselves to be members of the same social category, share some emotional involvement in this common definition of themselves, and achieve some degree of social consensus about the evaluation of their group and of their membership in it (Tajfel and Turner, 1986, p. 15).

Thus, people who are perceived to be in the same social category are considered as in-group, while people who are not included in an individual's own group are considered out-group. Social identity is one part of an individual's self-concept derived from the membership in a social group (Turner and Oakes, 1986). The sense of identity can make an important contribution to the strength of people's relationships with each other, for instance, members of the same community or followers of the same religion (Sen, 2007b). Identity, as a sense of belonging to a community, can enrich the bonds between these people, i.e. in-group members. At the same time, that sense of identity can exclude many other people. A well-integrated community, in which residents help each other, can be the very same community in which the residents violate people who move into the region from elsewhere. Consequently, identity can be a source of cohesiveness, cooperation, and support for the ideas, activities and goals among the group members. At the same time, it can be a source of violence and terror toward others (Tajfel and Turner, 1986; Sen, 2007b). The motivation of people to adapt a social identity by joining a group is to derive positive self-esteem from their group memberships (Tajfel and Turner, 1986; Smith and Mackie, 2007). Social identities are based first, on a person's demographic features, such as nationality, ethnicity, gender, age, and social class. Second, on his or her position in a group, for instance, as student, professor, employee, parent, and so on. Third, on the affiliation to formal or informal associations, such as political parties, religion, organizations, and social clubs. Fourth, on a person's vocation, for instance, scientist, artist, or gardener. And finally, on the fact whether a person belongs to groups considered outside of the main group by the majority of people, such as homeless or disabled people (Gudykunst, 2004). It is decisive to recognize that human beings hold various identities and therefore belong to more than one social group (Sen, 2007b).

3.2.3 Cultural Identity

All types of identities, or categories of identity, or aspects of one's numerous identities presented above, are influenced to a certain degree by culture (Samovar et al., 2013). According to Ting-Toomey (1999), all humans are integrated as members of a larger cultural group. This cultural dimension of identity is also the focus of the researchers Fong and Chuang. They state that culture and cultural identity "subsume racial and ethnic identity" (Fong and Chuang, 2004, p. 6). Fong and Chuang define

> cultural identity as the identification of communications of a shared system of symbolic verbal and nonverbal behavior that are meaningful to group members who have a sense of belonging and who share traditions, heritage, language, and similar norms of appropriate behavior. Cultural identity is a social construction (Fong and Chuang, 2004, p. 6).

Ting-Toomey (1999) states that cultural identity is the emotional meaning that a person attaches to his or her sense of belonging or connection with the larger culture. According to Oerter and Montada (2002), cultural identity defines the membership to and orientation to the culture someone grows up in, also known as enculturation. In other words, enculturation is the imperceptible growing into the particular culture that someone belongs to (Bailey and Peoples, 2014).

3.2.4 National Identity

National identity refers to nationality. In general, a person holds the nationality of the country he or she is born in. However, national identity can also be adopted by immigration. People who obtain citizenship in a country other than their birthplace possibly begin to adopt aspects of a new national identity, depending on the strength of their attachment to their new homeland. Further, people residing permanently in another nation possibly retain a strong connection to their homeland, for instance Irish people who immigrated to the USA (Samovar et al., 2013).

National identity is influenced, for instance, through environmental surroundings, such as mass media. "Mass media, too, are expected to make an important contribution to nation-building and to the formation of a national and cultural identity" (Heidt, 1987, p. 142) (please see Chapter Three, Section 2.2).

3.3 The Dark Side of Identity

Identity is about similarities and differences. Neither makes sense without the other (Jenkins, 2008). Human beings have a psychological need to categorize and classify because the world is too big, too complex, and too dynamic to grasp all of its details (Samovar et al., 2013). Classification of people and situations accompanies human beings every day. Neuropsychologists of the Ruhr University Bochum state that without pigeonhole thinking a secure existence would not be possible. The researchers found that classifying people and situations helps an individual to make quicker decisions that are needed for survival. Pigeonhole thinking has two levels. The first level is the mechanism which is predetermined. It depends, among other things, on the age and probably the plasticity of the brain. The second level deals with concrete contents which the brain divides into different categories. These contents change with age and the individual life situation and are learned (Smiljanic, 2016). People identify with something as a result of preference, understanding, familiarity, or socialization. Consequently, it is likely that a person will have greater tolerance toward the people and situations he or she prefers, understands, and recognizes as familiar. This preference for understandable and familiar things can influence the perception of and attitude toward new and different people and situations. If this occurs in an adverse way it can lead to stereotyping, ethnocentrism, prejudice, and racism (Samovar et al., 2013). However, a clear-cut differentiation is not always possible because the transitions can be fluent.

3.3.1 Stereotypes

Stereotypes are characteristics that are descriptive of, attributed to, or associated with a particular group of people (Stangor and Lange, 1993). When people are confronted with a lack of familiarity or similarity, they tend to use stereotypes. Stereotyping is a way of dealing with the unknown. It is a form of categorization that mentally organizes the experiences of an individual with, and guides his or her behavior toward a particular group of people. It is a person's approach to organize his or her perceptions by categorizing a group as a whole through oversimplified impressions of characteristics. However, problems may arise through this kind of categorization due to overgeneralization. Stereotypical pictures can distort perception because the individual is focused on information that is consistent with the picture already held by him or her. Stereotypes can be positive or negative and problems can occur when negative evaluations are directed toward members of particular groups (Adler and Gundersen, 2008). When stereotypes are consensually shared within a society, their consequences become much more intricate, because they affect entire groups of people in the same way (Macrae, Stangor and Hewstone, 1996). Stereotypes are learned in a variety of ways, for instance, through parents, friends, colleagues, mass media, etc. beginning in early childhood and continuing through a person's socialization process (Stangor and Lange, 1993).

3.3.2 Ethnocentrism

Being ethnocentric means someone sees his or her own ethnic group or culture at the center of his or her worldview and it refers to the inability to believe that other cultures suggest feasible alternatives for organizing reality (Webster, 1996). These judgements can permeate every aspect of a culture's existence.

Sumner (2014) describes ethnocentrism as the technical name for the point of view in which a person's own group is seen as the center of everything, while all other groups are measured and judged with reference to this group. Other cultures in which alternative customs are valued and obeyed are despised. Although individuals are not able to actively recognize their own in-groups, except in contrast to out-groups, the in-groups remain a psychological primary.

Samovar and his colleagues (2013) define three levels of ethnocentrism. At the first level, an individual or a group gives their own culture higher priority compared to others. Samovar and his colleagues consider this level natural because individuals base their personal identity and many of their beliefs on their native culture. At the second level, ethnocentrism begins to take on an evaluative dimension through the belief of an individual, or group that their personal beliefs and values are indisputably correct and that therefore their own culture is at the center. Thus, other cultures should be measured and rated by their cultural standards (Samovar et al., 2013; Nanda and Warms, 2014). At the final level, ethnocentrism not only means that an individual's culture is considered the most valid and useful. It also means that the individual or group believes their values and customs should be adopted by other cultures (Samovar et al., 2013). Aggression toward out-groups helps to strengthen their own sense of belonging – even though it is not necessary, as the familiar is always favored anyway. What is unfamiliar is regarded as in some ways minor and less 'good' – still, this does not necessarily result in unfriendliness toward out-group members. As a result, while a certain amount of liking is unavoidable in all in-group memberships, the shared attitude toward out-groups may vary strongly (Allport, 1979). In case of a conflict between in-group and out-group members, Tajfel and Turner (1986) state

> that the more intense is an intergroup conflict, the more likely it is that the individuals who are members of the opposite groups will behave toward each other as a function of their respective group memberships, rather than in terms of their individual characteristics or interindividual relationships (p.8).

Whenever social stratification is based upon an unequal division of limited resources, for instance, power, prestige, and wealth, and when for this reason there is a conflict of interests between social groups, the social situation is possibly characterized by pervasive ethnocentrism and out-group resentment between the opposing groups (Tajfel and Turner, 1986). Consequently, in case of conflict, individual characteristics and individual relationships take a back seat and strengthen intergroup thinking and ethnocentrism.

3.3.3 Prejudice

In a broad sense, prejudices are deeply held negative feelings and attitudes belonging to a particular group. These moods can include anger, fear, aversion, and anxiety (Samovar et al., 2013). "When a negative attitude toward an out-group is translated into action, the resulting behavior is called *discrimination*, defined as the process of treating individuals unequally on the basis of their ethnicity, gender, age, sexual orientation, or other characteristics. Prejudice is an *attitude*, while discrimination is overt *behavior*" (Rogers and Steinfatt, 1999, p. 56). Prejudice is expressed in a variety of ways and its intensity can be illustrated as ascending steps based on the research of the psychologist Allport (1979). Firstly, it can be expressed through verbal rejection – Allport refers to antilocution, which involves talking about a member of the target group in a negative manner. Secondly, it can be expressed through discrimination meaning the denial of equal treatment on the basis of group membership. This includes avoidance by shunning the disliked group, for example in the form of restrictive covenants, boycotts, neighborhood pressure, or legal segregation. Thirdly, a person or a group of people can be physically attacked. These physical attacks result in extermination when the objective is the elimination of a particular group of people (Allport, 1979; Dovidio, Glick and Rudman, 2005). Prejudice is caused by various factors, such as scapegoating (making others responsible for one's own failure), negative circumstances, social competition, and the amount of interaction of a person with members outside of his or her own cultural group (Oetzel, 2009).

3.3.4 Racism

"*Racism* categorizes individuals on the basis of their external physical traits, such as skin color, hair, facial structure, and eye shape, leasing to prejudice and discrimination" (Rogers and Steinfatt, 1999, p. 268). Ferraro and Andreatta (2014) argue that "[a] race is a group of people who share a greater statistical frequency of genes and physical traits with one another than they do with people outside the group" (p.7). However, no anthropologist commits to the notion that races are fixed biological entities, the members of which all share the same physical features. Despite the effort to classify people into distinct racial categories during the twentieth century, most anthropologists do not consider these categories to be particularly useful. Contemporary studies show that the amount of genetic variation is much greater within racial groups than between different racial groups. As a result, most anthropologists consider the racial typologies defined in the early-twentieth century as mostly an oversimplification of the present state of genetic knowledge (Ferraro and Andreatta, 2014).

"Race is a social construction – an attempt to give social meaning to physical differences" (Rogers and Steinfatt, 1999, p. 56). The premise of racist thinking is the division of humankind into categories called 'race' on the basis of e.g. skin color, shape of the nose, or any other physical difference. In reality, only one *Homo sapiens* species exists with no subspecies (Nanda and Warms, 2014). Racists believe that their particular 'race' is superior and thus deny the idea of basic equality of all human beings. This conviction gives racists the justification to mistreat people who are different. Racism is expressed in a variety of ways, for instance through job discrimination or racial harassment (Blum, 2002).

3.4 Conclusion

It is assumed that the identification with a group, and at the same time partly giving up personal interests in favor of conforming to the group, is the basic process underlying group phenomena, i.e. intragroup cooperation and selflessness within the group, emotional empathy and the emergence of social norms but also, for instance, stereotyping and ethnocentrism (Turner and Oakes, 1986).

Stereotypes, ethnocentrism, prejudice, and racism are permeating because they are often learned early in life and, like much of culture, become part of a person's worldview. Consequently, these attitudes are very powerful, have lasting impact, and tend to be resistant to change (Stangor and Lange, 1993).

3.5 Distinction between Culture and Identity

"Culture is not the same as identity" (Hofstede, 2003, p. 10). Identities are based on people's answer to the question of where they belong. Further, they are based on shared images and stereotypes, as well as on emotions linked to the outer layer of Hofstede's 'Onion Model' explained above. Relevant are symbols, heroes, and rituals – not values which are located in the inner circle of the model.

An example for this is the Northern Ireland conflict, also known as 'The Troubles,' which took place from 1969 to 1998 but has roots in Irish history dating back to 1169. The warring parties shared Christian and other congruent values, but had different perceived identities (Hofstede, 2003). Fahey, Hayes, and Sinnott's (2005) book *Conflict and Consensus: A Study of Values and Attitudes in the Republic of Ireland and Northern Ireland*, based on the data provided by the EVS, presents a detailed comparison of cultural values and attitudes in the Republic of Ireland and Northern Ireland. The authors state that the two ethnonational traditions (Catholic nationalists and Protestant unionists) are divided by a cleavage in collective identity and political orientation. At the same time, however, Protestants and Catholics on the island of Ireland are culturally more similar to each other than to any other national population in Europe, including Britain (Fahey, Hayes and Sinnott, 2005). A shared identity presupposes a shared 'other'. When abroad, Irish people may feel as Irish citizens, but at home in Ireland, they may feel associated with the city or region they were born in or chose to live in (Hofstede, 2003).

Chapter 2: Presentation and Examination of Different Theoretical Frameworks on Culture

Minkov (2011) argues that for many people 'culture' seems to be an easy topic so that even without training they feel qualified to express a competent view in this area. In his opinion, this is true because many people are aware of the fact that different societies often have different cultures. He argues that this consciousness has been around for a long time and cites Julius Caesar who described the Celtic tribes in terms of peculiarities that he perceived through his Roman eyes and mind (Caesar, 2005; Minkov, 2011). In the second half of the later 20th century, it became increasingly clear that cultural differences can be found even between groups – some researchers categorize them as nations – that live closely together (Minkov, 2011). When humans meet and interact with one another, they are confronted with the differences in their values, beliefs, attitudes, and behavior. As the world is becoming increasingly interconnected, for instance due to the spread of the availability of internet access which promotes globalization, it also becomes more and more important to understand these differences (Kutschker and Schmid, 2011). However, 'culture' is not an easy topic at all and many people form an opinion about culture without training and only based on assumptions (Minkov, 2011). An example for this could be the misinterpretation of gestures. When a Japanese person wants to beckon someone to come closer, the hand is held in front of the body in Japan with the fingers downwards and swung back and forth. This looks like the sign to tell someone to go away in Germany (AHK Japan, 2018). Thus, a German could interpret this Japanese gesture as a not very polite request to leave while the Japanese person wanted to be friendly and beckon him or her. Such assumptions can create negative feelings toward members of another culture and this can lead to a generalization of the members of the foreign culture. However, this does not help to understand each other and can cause confusion and failures. These attitudes can have far-reaching consequences, for instance, in business or political issues.

In the following Sections 1 and 2, the dissertation discusses some cultural models starting with the question which influences have an impact on behavior and decision-making processes, based on the assumption that no human being grows up and lives in a culture-free area and that therefore, culture has a decisive impact on behavior. Then, some data collection models are presented that reveal the values of a society. Since the data collections take place intermittently, these models are suitable for the detection of changes but do not provide explanations for these changes. Therefore, after the introduction of these two frameworks, a third model will be presented which allows deeper insights into a culture and offers the possibility to explain changes. This third model consequently aims at resolving questions that are left unanswered by the first two frameworks.

1 Cultural Anthropological Models

Researchers have devised a number of typologies that can be used to analyze key behavioral patterns found in nearly every culture (Bond and Hofstede, 1988). There are many possibilities for classification because the number of dimensions to be considered is virtually unlimited (Kutschker and Schmid, 2011). Nationality can be a suitable indicator, as already discussed in Chapter One, Section 2.3. Further subdivision is needed though for more detailed analysis (Hofstede et al., 2010).

1.1 Overview of Cultural Models

Although this dissertation recognizes the weaknesses of distinguishing cultures by division into nations, with reference to Witchalls (2012), it is assumed that the division into nations is still valid. Thus, when assuming that a national culture (meaning the values and behaviors shared by a majority or economic majority) exists, it is necessary to define criteria that distinguish one culture from the other in order to enable the analysis of a nation's culture and compare the cultures of different nations to each other. Some of the most prominent works in the field of cultural values are the studies by Parsons and Shils (1951) in their book *Toward a General Theory of Action*, and several works by Edward Hall, such as *The Silent Language*, 1959, *The Hidden Dimension*, 1966, and *Beyond Culture*, 1976 (Hall, 1959; Hall, 1990; Hall, 1989). Also among the most notable books is *Variations in Value Orientations* by Kluckhohn and Strodtbeck (1961). Several works by Geert Hofstede, such as *Culture's Consequences, International Differences in Work-related Values*, 1980, and its revised edition *Culture's Consequences: Comparing Values, Behaviors, Institutions and Organizations Across Nations*, 2001, should also be mentioned (Hofstede, 1980; Hofstede, 2003). Furthermore, Fons Trompenaars,' *Riding the Waves of Culture: Understanding Cultural Diversity in Business*, is of importance (Trompenaars, 1993). Finally,

House, Hanges, Javidan, Dorfman and Gupta's *Culture, Leadership, and Organizations: The GLOBE Study of 62 Societies*, first published in 2004, should be mentioned. This book presents results based on the European Values Study (House et al., 2004). Many of the works bear strong reference to management as especially in this field, a fundamental difficulty of working effectively with people of another culture lies in understanding basic differences in the other person's worldview. Without this understanding, it is easy to come into unnecessary conflict. In any case, all approaches are based on meaningful values which can be found in all cultures.

As explained in the beginning, the motivation for the topic of this dissertation initiated from the global economic crisis in 2007, or rather the recurrence of the phenomenon of economic crises. The question arose why economic crises occur repeatedly, for example triggered by speculative bubbles, although research on the functioning of economic systems has progressed significantly since the first well-documented speculative bubble in the Netherlands in the 17th century (Garber, 1990; Reinhart and Rogoff, 2009). Thus, the idea came up to not investigate the economic instruments but instead the human factor, meaning the economic actors who create and use these instruments. Further, this dissertation assumes that human behavior is most significantly influenced by culture because culture consists of, among other things, the shared and transmitted values of a society. For instance, values generate behavior and values are reflected through this behavior (Haviland et al., 2013).

On the assumption that humans are significantly influenced by culture, it makes sense to apply cultural-anthropological models because cultural anthropology deals with human beings while taking into account culture. The next step is to investigate whether these models can provide explanations for the behavior of the economic actors which in turn led to the global economic crisis. For this reason, some of the best-known models, as mentioned above, of Kluckhohn and Strodtbeck, Hofstede, and the GLOBE Study are briefly discussed below.

1.2 Discussion of Selected Cultural Models

For instance, the model of Kluckhohn and Strodtbeck (1961) distinguishes between five basic orientations which they call 'Human Nature Orientation,' 'Man-Nature Orientation,' 'Relational Orientation,' 'Time Orientation,' and 'Activity Orientation'. The first value orientation, 'Human Nature Orientation,' deals with the innate nature of a human being and determines whether he or she is evil, good, neutral, or, as may be the case, a mix of the two by birth. On the one hand, it deals with the question whether human nature is unchangeable and consequently determined by heritage, religious or philosophical beliefs, genetic code, or social environment. On the other hand, if human nature is changeable, what determines whether an individual is perfectible, bad, corruptible, or good? The second dimension, 'Man-Nature Orientation,' assumes that there are three possibilities for a human's relationship with nature. First, there is 'subjugation to nature' which means that the human being has the impression that natural, or, in general, outside forces control him or her and that he or she has to accept these forces. Second, 'harmony with nature' refers to the concept of humans not controlling or trying to conquer nature but rather, both humans and nature living together as one and accepting each other's forces. Third, 'mastery over nature' implies humans' intent to control nature. The dimension 'Relational Orientation' deals with the definition of the human being's relation to others, meaning the way in which people interact with each other. The three integral parts of this value orientation include: individualistic, that means humans are autonomous and should have equal rights and control over their destiny, collateral, that means humans are individuals as well as group members joining in collective decisions, and lineal orientation, that means group goals again have primacy. Fourth, 'Time Orientation' refers to the question, whether a culture focuses primarily on the past, present, or future. Finally, the 'Activity Orientation' centers exclusively on the problem of the nature of humans' mode of self-expression. Consequently, this dimension deals with the question, whether a society values the importance of 'being,' 'being-in becoming,' or 'doing'. "In the 'being' orientation the preference is for the kind of activity which is a spontaneous expression of what is conceived to be 'given' in the human personality" (Kluckhohn and Strodtbeck, 1961, p. 16). "The 'being-in-becoming' orientation emphasizes that kind of activity which has as its goal the development of all aspects of the self as an integrated whole" (Kluckhohn and Strodtbeck, 1961, p. 17). Members of 'doing' cultures favor the kind of activity that results in accomplishments that are measurable by standards (Kluckhohn and Strodtbeck, 1961; Kutschker and Schmid, 2011).

These dimensions reflect basic assumptions about the human being that are at the core of every culture and thus, reflect the specific form of worldview. Every individual – regardless of his or her culture – has to deal with five universal questions, also referred to as 'value orientations'. These orientations guide the members of a culture. All people use their culture to help them answer the same five basic questions (Kluckhohn and Strodtbeck, 1961). Kluckhohn and Strodtbeck do not insist that these dimensions are the only five orientations but state that they are useful to understand cultural differences (Gallagher, 2001).

Some of the features, although differently named, are similar to the ones discussed by Hofstede, a Dutch social psychologist (Smith, Fischer, Vignoles and Bond, 2013). His study is one of the most frequently cited and therefore also one of the best-known works, particularly in the field of business and management (Kutschker and Schmid, 2011). Hofstede (1980) designed a model to explain, by means of his defined dimensions, the cultural differences between countries. The model's dimensions refer to non-visible behavior, for instance, the acceptance of uncertainty in life by a member of a specific culture. Initially, Hofstede formulated four dimensions. His first dimension, 'Power Distance,' represents the extent to which the less powerful members of a society expect and accept that power is distributed unequally. The second dimension, 'Uncertainty Avoidance,' refers to the intolerance of uncertainty and ambiguity. The third dimension, 'Individualism versus Collectivism,' describes the degree to which individuals are integrated into the society, and finally, 'Masculinity,' stands for preferential treatment within a society for achievement, assertiveness, and material rewards for success. The opposite pole, 'Femininity,' stands for modesty and caring. After in-depth research of Asian countries, initially carried out by Bond, Hofstede formulated a fifth dimension called 'Long Term Orientation' which refers to the degree to which a society prefers to maintain time-honored traditions and norms (Bond and Hofstede, 1988; Minkov, 2011). In 2010, Hofstede published a revised version of his concept, now called 6D model, expanded by another dimension called 'Indulgence versus Restraint' which was revealed by the research of Minkov (Minkov, 2011; Hofstede, 2011). This dimension refers to the degree to which a society allows relatively free gratification of basic and natural human drives related to enjoying life and having fun. Hofstede's extensive data collection and the well-formulated dimensions enable an applicable categorization and make it possible to compare national cultures in a clear and simple way. However, Hofstede's work was also criticized by several researchers in the field of anthropology and communications, such as Müller and Gelbrich, McSweeney, Venaik and Brewer. Please see their objections below in this section (Hofstede, 1980; McSweeney, 2002; Müller and Gelbrich, 2004; Hofstede, 2006; Hofstede et al., 2010; Kutschker and Schmid, 2011; Venaik and Brewer, 2016).

The GLOBE Study (Global Leadership and Organizational Behavior Effectiveness), developed by Robert House and his colleagues, focused on nine cultural dimensions derived from earlier works of Kluckhohn and Strodtbeck (1961), Hofstede (2011), and other researchers. It is one of four major cross-cultural research projects, besides the World Values Survey, expanded from a

European Values Study (House et al., 2004). The dimensions are explained in the following table:

Table 1: The Nine Cultural Dimensions of the GLOBE Study (House et al., 2004)

The Nine Cultural Dimensions of the GLOBE Study and what they mean:		
1	Avoidance of Uncertainty	Represents "the extent to which members of an organization or society strive to avoid uncertainty by relying on established social norms, rituals, and bureaucratic practices" (House et al., 2004, p. 11).
2	Power Distance	Signifies "the degree to which members of an organization or society expect and agree that power should be stratified and concentrated at higher levels of an organization or government" (House et al., 2004, p. 12).
3	Collectivism I or Institutional Collectivism	Characterizes "…the degree to which organizational and societal institutional practices encourage and reward collective distribution of resources and collective action" (House et al., 2004, p. 12).
4	Collectivism II or In-Group Collectivism	Denotes "…the degree to which individuals express pride, loyalty, and cohesiveness in their organizations or families" (House et al., 2004, p. 12).
5	Gender Egalitarianism	Embodies "…the degree to which an organization or a society minimizes gender role differences while promoting gender equality" (House et al., 2004, p. 12).
6	Assertiveness	Describes "…the degree to which individuals in organizations or societies are assertive, confrontational, and aggressive in social relationships" (House et al., 2004, p. 12).
7	Future Orientation	Deals with "…the degree to which individuals in organizations or societies engage in future-oriented behaviors such as planning, investing in the future, and delaying individual or collective gratification" (House et al., 2004, p. 12).
8	Performance Orientation	Refers to "…the degree to which an organization or society encourages and rewards group members for performance improvement and excellence" (House et al., 2004, p. 13).
9	Humane Orientation	Refers to "…the degree to which individuals in organizations or societies encourage and reward individuals for being fair, altruistic, friendly, generous, caring, and kind to others" (House et al., 2004, p. 13).

The GLOBE Study extended the dimensions by including the personal desires, i.e. values, of the participants and what they considered as appropriate in their societies, i.e. actual practices. The study seeks to understand culture's influence on leadership and how cultural values are related to organizational practices, conceptions of leadership, the economic competitiveness of societies, and the human condition of a culture's members, and therefore, 62 cultures from all over the world were involved (House et al., 2004; Javidan, House, Dorfman, Hanges and Sully de Luque, 2006). GLOBE adopted the first five dimensions of Hofstede and expanded them to a total of nine dimensions which served as basis for the questionnaire. They kept the terms 'power distance' and 'uncertainty avoidance,' however, not necessarily their original meaning. The GLOBE Study divided 'collectivism' into 'institutional collectivism' and 'in-group collectivism' and further 'masculinity – femininity' into 'assertiveness' and 'gender egalitarianism'. The dimension of 'long-term orientation' was renamed 'future orientation'. The dimensions 'humane orientation' and 'performance orientation' were added to the study (House et al., 2004).

Hofstede (2006) criticized the model because the questionnaire items used did not, in his opinion, measure what the researchers had intended them to and further, because many of the GLOBE items at country level could be seen as conveying hidden meanings not intended and understood by their designers. In addition to this, he thought the questions to be formulated at a high level of abstraction, rather far from the respondents' daily concerns, and therefore he questioned the interviewees' interpretation of the questionnaire (Hofstede, 2006; Hofstede et al., 2010).

The researchers of GLOBE defended their work by pointing out that there was no theoretical or empirical basis for Hofstede's criticism that GLOBE's measures of values were too abstract or for his contention that national and organizational cultures were phenomena of different order. They also emphasized a limited understanding on Hofstede's side concerning the relationship between national wealth and culture, and state that Hofstede's reanalysis of the GLOBE data is inappropriate and produces incomprehensible results (Javidan et al., 2006).

As mentioned above, other researchers, such as Müller and Gelbrich (2004), McSweeney (2002), or Venaik and Brewer (2016), Blom and Meier (2017), and Lang and Baldauf (2016) state that the models of Hofstede and GLOBE involve fundamental problems.

Müller and Gelbrich (2004) criticize, among others, the atheoretical approach. First, the data was collected and then the dimensions were formulated. McSweeney (2002) states that "in any event a closer examination of the number of questionnaires used by Hofstede reveals that the average number per country was small, and that for some countries it was minuscule" (p.94). Further, he criticizes the idea of a national culture (please see Chapter One, Section 2.3) in the work of Hofstede for being defined as territorially unique. In McSweeney's view, the population of a nation can be differentiated on various grounds. He rejects Hofstede's idea that regardless of these divisions every national population somehow shares a unique culture. He cites as an example the state 'Great Britain' which is composed of at least three nations (England, Scotland, and Wales) and is treated as a single entity with a single national culture by Hofstede (McSweeney, 2002).

Venaik and Brewer (2016) criticize, among others, that the national culture scores for similar dimensions across the models of Hofstede and GLOBE for the same countries are either unrelated or negatively related, and that for dissimilar dimensions they are often more strongly related than for the similar dimensions. A lack of convergence weakens the credibility of the dimension scores for the representation of the cultural phenomena that they claim to represent. Therefore, using these scores to infer the broader characteristics of societies, individuals and organizations is invalid and the recommendations for action based on such research are misleading (McSweeney, 2002; Venaik and Brewer, 2016).

Blom and Meier (2017) point out that Hofstede disregarded the economic environment, such as inflation and level of income. They argue, for instance, that material incentives (an indicator for masculinity) are more important in countries with low income and/ or a low level of public welfare. Consequently, the economic environment has significant influence on Hofstede's cultural score. Another aspect concerning Hofstede's model is mentioned by Lang and Baldauf. They argue that the data is outdated because cultures evolve over time (Lang and Baldauf, 2016). Another aspect to keep in mind is that Hofstede's original study was limited to IBM employees but he used the results to draw conclusions about the entire population of the different countries. Due to the high level of qualification required of employees, it can also be assumed that IBM employees in most countries were not representative of the 'average' citizen in terms of education, wages, etc. Therefore, some results from this study may be distorted and deviate from the average population (Towers and Peppler, 2017).

Despite the criticism, no scientist has yet managed to design a model commonly accepted by the whole research community. Some of the criticism seems to be comprehensible, for instance, when regarding the classification in national entities. In this specific case, when comparing the Republic of Ireland and Northern Ireland, their cultural values are more similar as opposed to the values of Northern Ireland and Britain (Fahey, Hayes and Sinnott, 2005). Other points of criticism seem to be untenable, such as a weakening in correlation. Studies correlating the old country scores of Hofstede's model with related variables available on a year-by-year basis in many cases find no weakening of the correlations (Hofstede, 2011).

1.3 Review and Conclusion of Cultural Models

Researchers focused on different goals while creating their models. Kluckhohn and Strodtbeck, E. T. Hall, as well as F. Trompenaars focused on basic assumptions about the human being as composing the core of every culture while Geert Hofstede focused on values instead. The GLOBE Study involves dimensions based on basic assumptions, as well as dimensions based on basic values. There will always be points of friction between the different cultural studies and it is unlikely that a study will ever exist that is accepted by all researchers (Kutschker and Schmid, 2011).

The cultural models mentioned above provide approaches to distinguishing the cultures of different countries. However, no concept is able to cover the whole cultural complexity. The presented models show different approaches to categorizing culture but in fact, the amount of possible dimensions to identify differences between cultures is basically unlimited (Kutschker and Schmid, 2011). Consequently, no cultural model is able to include all influencing factors.

Further, the data collection, for instance, of Hofstede's models, took place within a temporally limited period around 1968 and around 1972 (please cp. Hofstede in *Culture's Consequences*, 2003, p. xv), with the exception of the additional Asian study in the 1980s, while the GLOBE Study's data collection period was from 1994 to 1997 (Kutschker and Schmid, 2011). This implies that the models may be able to compare cultures, however, they do not display the cultural change of the investigated countries over time. Hofstede (2003) argues, however, that since culture only changes little by little, his study can be considered up-to-date.

The authors of GLOBE acknowledge that their study has limitations. Some points mentionable in this respect are cultural diversity within societies, as well as the fact that culture not only changes over time but also disperses geographically via emigration and multicultural coexistence. They concede that due to dramatic changes, for example a profound economic crisis during the collection of the GLOBE data, some distortions of the findings are likely. They admit that in times of crisis, values may shift toward a stronger idealization of values. Consequently, this may affect the stability of the findings for countries that underwent considerable change during the data collection period (Chhokar, Brodbeck and House, 2007).

Inglehart and Oyserman (2004) argue that basic cultural orientations are not static attributes of given societies but reflect socioeconomic change. They emphasize that economic development facilitates cultural shifts, e.g. increased emphasis on individual freedom-focused values and reduced focus on traditional hierarchies. Consequently, these cultural shifts are, for instance, conducive to the emergence and flourishing of democratic institutions.

The country scores according to Hofstede's dimensions are always relative, and therefore only exist interdependently. Hofstede (2003) assumes that the forces that cause cultures to change tend to be global. This means that they affect many countries at the same time, and thus, cultures change together and their relative positions remain stable. Exceptions to this rule are developments that occur very rapidly in one country in comparison to other countries (Hofstede, 2003). Thus, cultural models are not an appropriate tool for examining changes within a single culture as these models cannot record any changes due to the one-time data collection.

2 Dynamics in Changes of Basic Orientations

As mentioned before, culture, as it is used in this dissertation, consists of the shared and transmitted ideas, values, and perceptions, which are used to make sense of experience. These parameters generate behavior and are reflected in that behavior (Haviland et al., 2013). The previous section introduces cultural-anthropological models, discusses the strengths of these models, but also addresses the criticisms of some of these best-known models. The cultural models provide indicators, such as dimensions, to reveal and compare values. However, as explained, forces that cause cultures to change affect many countries at the same time, and thus, cultures change together and their relative positions remain stable. Further, the models are not able to detect any changes due to the one-time data collection. This leads to the conclusion that cultural-anthropological models are not suitable to reveal changes in value orientation.

Therefore, this section of the dissertation considers a concept of intercultural comparative studies. There are research programs aiming at finding changes in the parameters of the people of a country, such as their values and attitudes, e.g. the European Values Study (EVS), established in 1981 and the European Social

Survey (ESS), established in 2001. Both studies use repeated questionnaires (Halman, Sieben and Zundert, 2012; ESS, 2015; European Values Study, 2015a).

In the following, the studies are presented in detail. However, some of the domains are also given special attention in the analyzing chapters.

2.1 The European Values Study (EVS)

Inglehart (2007) argues that globalization is pervasive. Thus, it could be assumed that the world's cultures are converging into one homogenized global values system. However, this is not true as the following data collection models show. Inglehart states that the cultural heritage of societies also plays a significant role. Religious and other historical differences continue to shape human values (Inglehart, 2007).

The EVS was initiated by an informal group of academics, abbreviated as EVSSG (European Value Systems Study Group) in the late 1970s. Today, the EVS has emerged as a network of social and political scientists who have made high standards in data creation and processing their goal. The study is a large-scale, cross-national, and longitudinal survey research program for examining the ideas, beliefs, preferences, attitudes, values, and opinions of the inhabitants of many countries which geographically belong to Europe. It is aimed at exploring the moral and social values underlying European social and political institutions and governing behavior by interviewing thousands of citizens through standardized questionnaires. The survey provides insight on how people in Europe think about life, family, work, religion, politics, and society. The survey examines value differences, similarities, and value changes and sheds light on the question how the European society is developing. The special feature of this study is that it is repeated every nine years hitherto from 1981 to 2008. Thus, the survey takes into account changes in the respective answers of the interviewees over time (European Values Study, 2015b).

The research domains, i.e. life, family, work, religion, politics, and society and the respective topics, for instance, political interest for the domain politics that they deal with are introduced briefly below.

2.1.1 Life

The domain 'life' deals with the topics well-being, happiness, life satisfaction, and locus of control. Whether a nation is predominantly happy or unhappy can be explained by the differences in living standards between countries. However, there are also some poor countries that judge themselves as being happy.

Well-being or happiness is the individual judgment of the total quality of an individual's life. It is the result of weighing the personal mental and health state against the own aspirations and expectations. However, there are controversial discussions about the term 'happiness' because personal happiness can be considered as being either too complex to understand or a too individualistic matter. Some researchers have argued that people are just born happy or unhappy, for instance, they argue that the Irish are optimistic by nature. Others have debated that happiness basically depends on comparison with others so that well-being or happiness has no absolute value. An individual cannot be happy 'enough,' however, an individual is able to adjust to unhappiness. Things that make people happy can differ from time to time, and from place to place. The results of the study show that happiness is greater in nations characterized by rule of law, freedom, civil society, cultural diversity, and modernity, such as schooling, technology, and urbanization. These factors plus material comfort explain almost all differences in happiness across nations. Additionally, the results show that people are happier when they have the impression that they have some control over the way their life turns out, which is referred to as 'locus of control' by psychologists. This is considered an important aspect of an individual's personality. People with an 'external' locus of control believe that life is guided by external circumstances, such as fate or luck. The individual's behavior does not matter very much because he or she has no influence on what happens. On the contrary, individuals with an 'internal' locus of control believe that life is steered by their own personal decisions and efforts. They have direct influence on their fate (European Values Study, 2015c).

2.1.2 Family

The domain 'family' deals with the topics marriage, children, unconditional love, the role of women, and transmission of values.

For instance, one of the outcomes of the survey is that only a few Europeans today have the traditional gender role allocation with a male breadwinner, a female housekeeper, and several children. However, Europeans mostly hold on to conservative family values. Thus, 'married-with-children' is the preferred lifestyle for the great majority of the interviewees despite the liberating sixties, emancipation, and individualization. Children are not an economic necessity any more. They are not needed to care for their parents later, nor are they a duty to God, instead having children, and the amount of children, are a matter of personal and free choice. Europeans invest a lot in their own children in the form of physical belongings and education, as well as through intense emotional involvement. The results of the study show that where once the male breadwinner stood at the center of the family, the center of the family has now slowly shifted to the children. Most Europeans are convinced that parents should do their best for their children and put them before their own interests and well-being. Further, the prevailing view of the Europeans is that both parents are necessary for a child to grow up happily. Consequently, when it comes to children, individualism is put aside. The outcome of the survey implies that the offspring's well-being has become an important, if not the most important, issue for Europeans (European Values Study, 2015d).

The domain family is given additional consideration in the analysis of Chapter Five, Section 1.1 and Chapter Seven.

2.1.3 Work

The domain 'work' deals with the topics importance of work, work qualities, job satisfaction, work ethos, and obedience to one's superior.

Work ethos or work ethic reflects how strongly interviewees place work at the center of their lives. Individuals with a strong work ethic regard hard work as intrinsically good and almost as a moral duty. In contrast, they consider leisure time as potentially harming to society. The level of work ethos for each European country can be calculated using the Europeans' opinions on five statements which are 'someone needs a job to fully develop his or her talent,' 'it is wrong to receive money without working for it,' 'without work, people become sluggish,' 'pursuing a job is a duty toward society,' 'work takes precedence'.

Work can be a necessity or not, and an individual's attitude toward work, for example, by considering work as a form of self-actualization (in accordance with Maslow's hierarchy of needs), is likely to play an important role (McEwen and Wills, 2014). In any case, the results of the survey show that work is 'very important' for 70% of all Europeans and that it is therefore a central part of their lives (European Values Study, 2015e).

2.1.4 Religion

The domain 'religion' deals with the topics church attendance, confidence in the church, importance of God, and traditional beliefs.

The results indicate that Europe has become a secularized continent because church attendance in Europe has declined and fewer Europeans state that they believe in God. However, about half of the interviewees claim to pray or meditate at least once a week. In any case, there are more people who consider themselves to be religious than people who attend church. The outcomes of the EVS show that the amount of people attending church services is on the decline, especially in the western part of the European continent. Consequently, the traditional religious institutions have lost their status over the last decades, even though people who consider themselves to be atheists are a small minority.

Sociologists describe this phenomenon as a 'church-free spirituality' because choosing religious beliefs, doctrines, and practices, and then mixing and matching them, is a kind of believing without belonging. Europeans remain religious, even though their approach has become eclectic (European Values Study, 2015f).

The domain religion is considered in more detail in the analysis of Chapter Five, Section 2 and Chapter Seven.

2.1.5 Politics

The domain 'politics' deals with the topics political interest, willingness to join in political actions, left-right placement, post-materialism, and support for democracy.

The results of the EVS show that the majority of Europeans agree with the point of view that democracy – even though not considered perfect – is better than any other form of government. Further, the researchers of the EVS argue that democracies in Western Europe, especially in Norway, Iceland, Denmark, and Greece have existed longer than in the eastern parts of Europe, such as Estonia, Latvia, Lithuania, and Belarus. Establishing confidence in a democratic system is a process which takes time. In Eastern Europe, the endeavor to join in political actions is weaker than in Western Europe. Consequently, the support for democracy is stronger in western and weaker in the eastern parts of Europe. For the people who live in a communist regime and are not happy with it, the system of democracy may offer an alternative without these people really knowing what democracy can achieve. A change of the political system does not solve all problems immediately but needs a long period of transition. Thus, people in Eastern European countries may not be aware of the advantages of a democracy and may hold on to political circumstances that impede the transition to a functioning democratic system (European Values Study, 2015g).

The domain politics is given more attention in the analysis of Chapter Five, Section 3, Chapter Six, Section 2 and Chapter Seven.

2.1.6 Society

The domain 'society' deals with the topics social networks, confidence in others, solidarity, tolerance, and permissiveness.

The results of the EVS show a tendency toward a decline of civic life, a weakening of social bonds, and a loss of social cohesion. The researchers of the EVS state that these arguments were listed by politicians and religious leaders as causes of modern social problems, such as a high level of crime and social isolation.

Further, the study reveals that tolerance is a characteristic European value. Basically, tolerance means accepting the way other people live their lives even when not agreeing with the others' lifestyle. For 70% of all Europeans, tolerance is an important value which they also consider important to teach their children. Sociologists agree that tolerance is an important value in a society because the more tolerant people are of the rights of others, the more secure the rights of all are. In addition to this, tolerance encourages a peaceful coexistence between the people of a society. Intolerance may be widespread within a society but is often hidden and remains undiscovered. However, tolerance is not an absolute value, there are variations in the degree of tolerance.

The EVS measures the tolerance of the Europeans by challenging their environment. Questions, such as 'What kind of people do Europeans not like to have as neighbors?' were designed. Possible answers are, for example, heavy drinkers, large families, different skin color, immigrants, and gay people. There is a large deviation among European nations regarding the tolerance towards homosexual people. The general trend shows that the northern and western countries are the most tolerant and that the southeastern countries are the least tolerant toward gay people (European Values Study, 2015h).

The domain society is given more consideration in the analysis of Chapter Five, Section 1 and Chapter Seven.

2.2 European Social Survey (ESS)

After the introduction of the European Values Study in the previous Section 2.1 which focuses on values and attitudes of Europeans, this dissertation now considers another very important survey. As the name European Social Survey (ESS) implies, the survey aims at revealing social change, for instance, among policy makers. The ESS was established in 2001. The ESS measures the attitudes, beliefs, and behavior patterns of diverse populations in more than thirty nations. The years covered so far include the period from 2002 to 2014. ESS data is usually released in October of the year after fieldwork takes place, e.g. October 2017 for ESS Round 8. The interviews are repeated every two years (ESS, 2015).

2.2.1 Main Objectives of the Study

The survey's basic aim is to chart stability and change in social structure, conditions, and attitudes in Europe and to interpret how Europe's social, political, and moral fabric is changing, based on face-to-face interviews. The aim of the ESS is to make social-scientific data available to all interested users in a transparent, high-quality, and free of charge form. Thus, students or scientists do not have to use their own financial resources. Consequently, the ESS improves the visibility and access of data on social change among academics, policy makers, and the wider public (ESS, 2015). Tajfel and Turner use social change "in the sense of changes in the mutual relations, behavior, and attitudes of large-scale human groups that have been distinctly different in status in the past", particularly, when the processes of change become very fast (Tajfel and Turner, 1986). Since the survey is conducted every two years, rapid social change can be revealed. Therefore, the ESS is an adequate survey to find out not only if, but also at which speed, social change occurs in contrast to the EVS which is only repeated every nine years.

2.2.2 Research Modules

Ireland has participated in each ESS wave since the beginning of the study. The ESS main questionnaire consists of the core modules, which are interrogated in almost each wave, and are assigned to the rotating modules that cover more specific topics. In the case of Ireland, for instance, the core module questions were in the fields of 'television watching and social trust,' 'politics, including political interest, trust, electoral and other forms of participation, party allegiance, socio-political orientations,' and 'subjective well-being, social exclusion, religion, perceived discrimination, national and ethnic identity, and immigration'. Further, the socio-demographic profile was recorded, such as household composition, sex, age, marital status, type of area they live in, education and occupation of respondent, partner, parents, union membership and income (ESS, 2015).

Rotating modules in the Irish questionnaire of round number 7, which took place in 2014/ 2015, were 'immigration, including attitudes, perceptions, and policy preferences' and 'health, including health conditions, fruit, vegetable, and alcohol consumption as well as smoking behavior'. The supplementary question was about human values, such as 'importance to be rich, have money, and expensive things' and 'importance that people are treated equally and have equal opportunities'. Finally, administrative variables and user-defined variables were recorded.

These indicators of national progress were introduced based on the interviewee's perceptions and judgements of key aspects of their respective societies (ESS, 2015).

2.3 Review and Conclusion of the Presented Intercultural Comparative Studies

There are similarities and differences between the two studies. For instance, both studies contain identical questions, such as 'how happy are you?' Further, both studies collect their data according to nations. This is, in particular, a point of criticism of the cultural models, as there are different opinions in the research community whether one can even speak of a common national culture, as already discussed in Chapter One, Section 2.3. However, in contrast to the ESS (which covers Ireland and the United Kingdom), the EVS also conducts a separate study for Northern Ireland. Consequently, the EVS makes it possible to compare the Republic of Ireland with Northern Ireland.

The presented surveys are intercultural comparative studies even though it is also possible to record deviations within a country due to the repetition of the surveys. However, the deviations in the data of the EVS and ESS need to be interpreted because the data merely shows what has changed but does not indicate why basic orientations, such as values, attitudes, and behavior, have changed.

The mere detection that something has changed in a basic orientation does not explain which influencing factors existed. However, it is also possible that the questionnaires had different outcomes even though there was no actual change but instead the legislation or economic situation had changed. For instance, concerning the marital status in Ireland, there were no divorces before 1996 because up to this year divorces were prohibited by law (Mayer and Schwepcke, 1995).

A low divorce rate after 1996 can be explained by legal reasons. Although divorce was possible since 1996, the respective legislation still made it extremely difficult. In addition to this, there were economic reasons because a divorce is extraordinarily expensive in Ireland. Thus, the decline of the divorce rate after the Celtic Tiger period did not occur due to a change in values but instead was a result of the associated significant costs (please see Chapter Seven) (Holmquist, 2015a; Holmquist, 2015b).

Therefore, it is important to consider other influencing factors, such as the political, legal, and economic environment to understand changes in the data.

In conclusion, the analysis in Chapter Five, Six and Seven aims at detecting changes in social structure, conditions, and attitudes in Ireland and also intends to interpret how Ireland's social, political, and moral fabric is changing. Thus, the holistic approach of this dissertation can provide additional explanations for change and is therefore a valuable contribution to the EVS and ESS.

However, as shown in Sections 1 and 2 above, neither the cultural-anthropological models nor the surveys EVS and ESS were able to fully reveal the values, value changes, or provide an explanation for changes that generate human behavior. Therefore, a third model should be introduced to examine change in values and provide an explanation for this change.

3. Methodology – The Social Ecological Framework

All human behavior takes place within different interrelated contexts. Any given interaction is not just between two people. A wide variety of factors shape that interaction, including past history, cultural values, personal values, attitudes, biases, emotions, the media, current political settings, the natural environment, and many more (Oetzel, 2009). No interaction is completely unaffected and the following sections are intended to help gain an understanding of the factors that may influence and shape these interactions. Because most issues are too complex to be sufficiently explained by individual behavior alone, a model – that is more integrated and complex – is needed in order to comprehend the various factors that influence individual behavior (Stokols, 1996). The social ecological framework offers a more comprehensive approach to better take into account the influences of social and cultural contexts and of environments on human behavior.

The sociologist Hawley (1986) states that "[e]cology is the study of the relation of organisms to their environment" (Hawley, 1986, p. 1). However, there are differences in how the major parameters are defined and how the relations between the parameters are treated. For instance, there are significant differences in the approaches ranging from some that have very specific environmental features to some that use a very broad definition of environment. The approaches can also treat organisms either individually or view them as collectivities. Finally, the approaches work either with an ontogenetic perspective (referring to an individual's entire lifespan) or a phylogenetic (including the genetic lineage) perspective (Haeckel, 1906; Hawley, 1986; Bubolz and Sontag, 2009). The social ecological model is based on the proposition that organisms – including human beings – are connected to their physical and social surroundings. It considers interdependencies between human development throughout the life span and the changing environments in which the individual actually lives (Bronfenbrenner, 1977). The model thus considers the dynamics of these interrelations from different perspectives depending on the precise demarcation of the major influencing factors.

Human development refers to the understanding of how and why human beings change over the course of their lives, whereby "'development' connotes progressive structural and functional change over time…" (Bronfenbrenner, 1975, p. 439). Researchers from various disciplines, such as medicine, psychology, sociology, theology, and anthropology, are investigating this subject in-depth.

The changing relations between the individual and the environment are comprehended in terms of systems within the social ecological model. A system is a set of parameters which are connected with each other in some form of coherent relationship. The systems will be discussed in more detail below. The concept of a system allows the visualization of a set of related parameters that are organized according to a coherent structure or coherent function. The coherence of these parameters signals persistency and stability to a certain degree. However, change is also possible because the parameters contained in a system do not exist in isolation but relate to each other in some manner. Change and activity in one part of the system have an impact on, and affect, other parts of it. Consequently, a system can be described as a defined structure consisting of interacting, interrelated, or interdependent factors that form a whole (Bronfenbrenner, 1977; Hawley, 1986; Rogoff, 2003; Wong and Candolin, 2015)

To comprehend any occurrence, it is necessary to understand the single parts in relation to the whole. Societies consist of complex systems of persisting and ordered relations. Each system defines the limits of a specific level of organization and the structure within those limits. The economy, for instance, is such a system (Susser and Susser, 1996; McLaren and Hawe, 2005). Therefore, it is crucial to examine how an individual and his or her related parties develop and change within their respective ecological surroundings (Rogoff, 2003).

3.1 Description of the Concept

In order to gain a better understanding of the ways in which the social and cultural environment influences human development, the developmental psychologist Urie Bronfenbrenner created the ecological system approach. His framework focuses on the subsystems of the human ecological surroundings, as well as on the ways in which these subsystems interact with and influence each other. The subsystems can be illustrated as a series of layers (Bronfenbrenner, 1979).

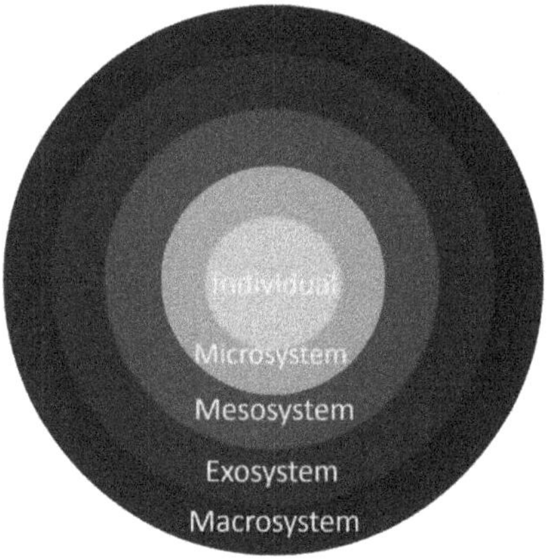

Figure 3: Illustration of the Layered Approach Based on Bronfenbrenner's Ecological System Theory of Human Development (Tregaskis, 2015)

3.1.1 The Individual

The individual is at the center of Bronfenbrenner's model and is affected by his or her physical characteristics, such as gender, age, or health. Age, for instance, plays an important role because people who are in their developmental years and are confronted with new ideas are more likely to adapt and accept these and also to share them in the future (Fogarty, Ryan and Lee, 1984). In which period of life an individual is, is also decisive for how strongly an experienced event will influence him or her. These factors receive more attention in the chronosystem, explained in 3.1.6 of this chapter. Bronfenbrenner later engaged in self-criticism for neglecting the role the individual plays in his or her own development. Therefore, the individual is specifically the focus of a reconceptualized developmental perspective called the 'bioecological model' (Bronfenbrenner, 1979; Bronfenbrenner and Ceci, 1994).

3.1.2 The Microsystem

The microsystem is the layer closest to the individual and contains the structures with which the individual has direct contact. It represents the complex of relations and interrelations between the developing individual and his or her environment, meaning the direct setting containing that individual, for instance, home, school, place of work, church, neighborhood (Bronfenbrenner, 1977; Rogoff, 2003). In addition to the contact to other persons in the immediate environment the microsystem also includes physical objects, such as toys and technology, which influence the individual. These physical objects can have an impact on the individual's physical and intellectual performance in later years (Martin and Fabes, 2009).

A setting is defined as a place with specific physical characteristics in which the participants take part in specific activities in specific roles. For example, one person can be a daughter, a parent, a member in a sports club, a teacher, a peer, and an employee for specific periods of time. The factors of place, time, physical characteristics, activity, participation, and role represent the characteristics of a setting (Bronfenbrenner, 1977). The influences in the microsystem are the strongest and therefore have the greatest impact on the individual.

3.1.3 The Mesosystem

The mesosystem encompasses the interrelations between two, three, or more important settings that contain the individual during a specific period of time in his or her life. In brief, the mesosystem is an 'in-between level' because an individual participates in more than one microsystem during a certain period of time (Ting-Toomey, 2011). It represents the relations between the microsystems in which an individual is involved. There are overlaps and communication between the settings and there is information in each setting about the other ones. An example for this are harmonizing or clashing practices at home and at school. For instance, at home a child may never prays but at school he or she takes part in morning prayer with the rest of the students. This is a reference to Ireland where in 2011, 92 percent of the country's primary schools were under the direction and control of the Catholic Church (Frerk, 2017). In contrast, in many U.S. homes a child will pray daily, but never in a public school due to the separation of religion and state (Green, 2014). Each example represents mesosystems. Thus, a mesosystem is a system of microsystems (Bronfenbrenner, 1977; Rogoff, 2003).

3.1.4 The Exosystem

The exosystem is an extension of the mesosystem – it includes other social structures that do not themselves contain the individual but have an effect upon or encompass the direct settings of the individual and therefore influence what happens (Bronfenbrenner, 1977). In other words, exosystems interconnect the microsystems in which the individual is involved to settings in which the individual does not have an active role. As a consequence, even though the individual's immediate environments in which he or she participates directly are the most powerful influences on him or her, the settings not directly experienced by the individual are of great influence too (Rogoff, 2003).

They include the working environment, the mass media, agencies of government, the distribution of goods and services, communication and transportation facilities, and informal social networks. For instance, financial problems within the family, job loss of a related party, or the help of friends and family may affect an individual although the respective individual is not involved directly. All these factors are part of the exosystem (Bronfenbrenner, 1977; Rogoff, 2003).

3.1.5 The Macrosystem

The macrosystem is the outermost layer of the individual's environment. It refers to the all-encompassing patterns of a culture or a social group of which the different systems or layers are tangible manifestations. These general patterns – for example, economic, social, educational, legal, and political systems – characterize a culture (Bronfenbrenner, 1979).

Macrosystems are conceived and examined in structural terms and as carriers of information and beliefs that, both explicitly and implicitly, provide meaning and motivation to specific organizations, social networks, roles, activities, and their relationship to each other (Bronfenbrenner, 1977; McLaren and Hawe, 2005). The macrosystem includes the culture, as well as the subculture, historical change, social policies, and the economic system in which the other settings are embedded (Martin and Fabes, 2009). It includes cultural beliefs and cultural values, public policies and programs, as well as social norms that influence how individuals manage their everyday matters. Also belonging to the macrosystem are socioeconomic status and ethnicity (Miller, Lerner, Schiamberg and Anderson, 2003).

Some macrosystems exist in explicit form as written laws and rules. However, most macrosystems are implicit and internalized in the minds of the members of a society as beliefs and cultural values made visible through practice in everyday life (Bronfenbrenner, 1977). Human behavior is impacted by the culture in which an individual is born and raised, and culture, in turn, is an integrated system. Hall expresses it this way: "you touch a culture in one place and everything else is affected" (Hall, 1989, p. 16). Ferraro and Andreatta (2014) state that most changes occurring in cultures tend to be linked changes. They also consider cultures as systematic wholes, the parts of which are interconnected. Consequently, changes in one part of the culture would be likely to bring about changes in other parts (Ferraro and Andreatta, 2014). This description of the system 'culture' shows why the social-ecological model can be helpful to understand the impact of culture on people's behavior.

A macrosystem differs significantly from the previously mentioned systems in that it does not refer to the specific contexts affecting the life of an individual but instead, to general models existing in the culture or social group that set the pattern for the structures and activities taking place at other levels. The macrosystem surrounds the remaining systems and is mutually influenced by all of them. The members of a culture may share a common set of values but, for any particular value system to have any influence on a developing individual, the values have to be experienced within one or more of the microsystems in which that individual is found. The macrosystem can be seen as a context – encompassing culture, subculture, or other extended social structure whose members share values and/ or beliefs, resources, threats, lifestyles, and patterns of social exchange (Tudge, Mokrova, Hatfield and Karnik, 2009).

3.1.6 The Chronosystem

Bronfenbrenner later supplements his model by adding the chronosystem which refers to how the individual and the environments change over time. The system 'time' opens up a third dimension for the environment. For human development 'time' is not merely a feature of the growing human being, meaning chronological age, but also a feature of the surrounding environment and its changes across historical time. This means that the chronosystem encompasses change or consistency over time not only in the characteristics of the person but also of the environment in which that person lives. Examples are internal changes, such as physiological changes that occur with human aging, and external changes, such as changes during the life course in family structures, socioeconomic status, employment, place of residence or historical events. These historical circumstances affect contexts at all other levels (Bronfenbrenner, 1994). The external changes can also refer to changes in the macrosystem (please see Chapter Seven, Section 2).

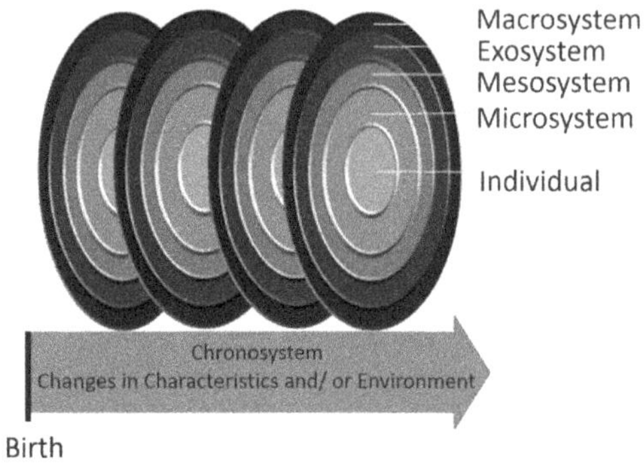

Figure 4: Illustration of the Chronosystem Based on Bronfenbrenner's Ecological Framework for Human Development (Bronfenbrenner, 1994)

3.2 Relationship of the Layers to Each Other

As shown above, the social ecological system consists of five subsystems that visualize the influences of social and cultural contexts or environments on human behavior. Also mentioned earlier, is the mutual influence of the systems. To be more specific, each system depends on the interrelations of the individual's life and offers a continuously growing variety of options and sources as explanation of the individual's behavior. Moreover, within and between the systems bidirectional influences exist. These bidirectional influences imply that relationships have an impact in both directions – away from the individual and towards the individual. Not only does each of the mentioned subsystems of Bronfenbrenner's model affect behavior, but the subsystems themselves may also change as their members are replaced or altered. Therefore, "an ecological perspective implies reciprocal causation between the individual and the environment" (McLeroy et al., 1988, p. 354).

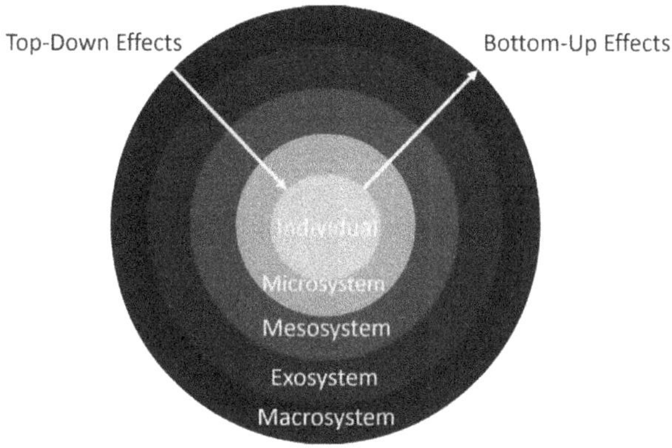

Figure 5: Illustration of the Layers Based on Bronfenbrenner's Ecological System Theory of Human Development Extended to Include Top-Down and Bottom-Up Effects (Tregaskis, 2015)

3.2.1 Bottom-Up Effects

Bottom-up effects show the influence that the inner layer (the individual) has in the direction of the cultural layer at the outer circle. They can be understood as the impact of an individual through personal relationships on the following layers up to the layer of culture and thus show the power of the individual to effect changes in culture. Specifically, this is evident through men and women in history who shaped the fate of a country through their actions. It shows that it is possible for individuals to reinforce and recreate culture through individual behavior (Oetzel, 2009). Examples for such an individuals were Charles Stuart Parnell or Éamon de Valera whose followers regarded them as outstanding representative in the struggle for a free Irish state against oppression and social injustice (please cp. Chapter Three, Section 3.2.4 and 3.2.5).

3.2.2 Top-Down Effects

In contrast, thc top-down effects describe the impact of the outermost layer in the direction of the inner circle. They illustrate the influence of the cultural and societal layers, such as cultural values and mass media, on the individual's behavior. In particular, the cultural layer affects the organizational layer, such as the workplace or the school, which in turn shapes the interpersonal layer, such as peers or classmates, and then has an influence on the individual (Oetzel, 2009).

3.2.3 Interactive Effects

Bottom-up and top-down effects suggest some sort of cumulative effect passing either up or down from one level to the next in a systematic fashion. The 'interactive effects' in contrast take into account simultaneous and mutual processes that take place at multiple contextual levels. For instance, the effects of one level, such as economy, influence the outcomes at another level, such as society (Zhang and Ting-Toomey, 2014).

3.3 Genetic Inheritance in Ecological Perspective

Homo sapiens is probably unique in its capacity to adapt to, tolerate, and especially to create the ecologies in which he or she lives and grows up. Human nature is diverse. Different environments produce distinguishable differences in individuals, across but also within societies, regarding talent, temperament, human relations, and particularly the ways in which each culture brings up the next generation. The process and product of making human beings human significantly varies by place and time (Bronfenbrenner, 1979).

Bronfenbrenner took genetic inheritance into account in his ecological perspective. Heritability is highly influenced by events and conditions in the environment. For instance, Bronfenbrenner and Ceci mention that human growth depends on nutrition. Thus, if members of the same genetic decent grew up in different regions having different diets their growth could be different (Bronfenbrenner and Ceci, 1994). Daly (1997) explains in her essay "*Revisionism and Irish history: The Great Famine*" that statistics show that Irish military recruits in pre-Famine times were taller than their English counterparts, which she attributes to the fact that the Irish diet was dependent on the potato. The potato is the only staple crop which does not carry the risk of a deficiency disease (Daly, 1997).

This fact finds consideration in the bioecological model. This is a model that takes into account the interactions between genotype and the environment for human development (Bronfenbrenner and Ceci, 1994). Consequently, the model considers the impact that environment has, in addition to biology, on human development.

The bioecological model is an extension of Bronfenbrenner's social ecological approach and it is also a model that considers the entire lifespan. Bronfenbrenner's social ecological theory favored aspects of context. However, he regularly took note of the changing nature of his theory (Tregaskis, 2015). Therefore, he later recognized that his theory focused too much on context and that the role of the individual in his or her own development had been neglected.

Thus, he continuously worked to further develop his model until his death in 2005 (Tudge et al., 2009). His more recent records include processes of human development. The bioecological model introduces a more stable approach for the microsystem. It emphasizes the distinct contribution to development of proximal processes involving interaction with people but also with objects and symbols (Bronfenbrenner and Morris, 1998). In Bronfenbrenner's opinion the 'process' could offer a possible explanation for the connection between some aspect of the context (for instance culture) or some aspect of the individual (for instance gender) and an outcome of interest. He points out that 'proximal processes' are the key factor in the development of the individual (Bronfenbrenner and Ceci, 1994; Bronfenbrenner, 1994). In this model, development is defined as the phenomena of stability and change in the biopsychological characteristics (these are the effects of biological factors, for instance neuronal, hormonal, and biochemical influences on behavior) of human beings, both as individuals and as groups (Bronfenbrenner and Morris, 2006; Kirschbaum, 2008).

Bronfenbrenner's theory in its mature form brings up the interrelations among the four defining properties of the bioecological model – process, person, context, and time – abbreviated as 'PPCT Model' which is introduced in the following (Bronfenbrenner and Morris, 2006).

3.3.1 Process

Process is at the core of the model, as proximal processes that occur over time are considered the principal mechanisms producing human development (Bronfenbrenner and Morris, 2006).

Through active interaction with other persons and the environment individuals are able to make sense of the world and understand their place in it. Proximal processes mean that a lot of an individual's learning during his or her development from childhood to adulthood happens through imitation of the beliefs, behavior, etc. of the people surrounding him or her. An example for this is the way in which humans learn to speak their mother tongue. Bronfenbrenner summarizes it in two central propositions which are theoretically interdependent and subject to empirical test. His first proposition states that:

> Especially in its early phases, but also throughout the life course, human development takes place through processes of progressively more complex reciprocal interaction between an active, evolving biopsychological human organism and the persons, objects, and symbols in its immediate external environment. To be effective, the interaction must occur on a fairly regular basis over extended periods of time. Such enduring forms of interaction in the immediate environment are referred to as proximal

> processes (Bronfenbrenner and Morris, 1998, p. 996; Bronfenbrenner and Morris, 2006, p. 797; Bronfenbrenner and Ceci, 1994).

The second proposition defines that:

> The form, power, content, and direction of the proximal processes effecting development vary systematically as a joint function of the characteristics of the developing person, the environment — both immediate and more remote — in which the processes are taking place, the nature of the developmental outcomes under consideration, and the social continuities and changes occurring over time through the life course and the historical period during which the person has lived (Bronfenbrenner and Morris, 2006, p. 798; Bronfenbrenner and Ceci, 1994).

This means that processes work in different ways depending on the specific person and the respective context.

3.3.2 Person

Bronfenbrenner considers the relevance of biological and genetic aspects of the individual and concentrates on the individual's characteristics which are brought along into any social situation (Bronfenbrenner and Ceci, 1994). He identifies three characteristics that influence proximal processes:

Demand characteristics are, for instance, age, gender, skin color, or physical appearance. These attributes set processes in motion and influence the first interactions due to the expectations that instantly arise. For example, it is likely that the act of communicating with a child will differ from the act of communicating with another adult (Bronfenbrenner and Morris, 2006).

Resource characteristics take into account mental and emotional resources, such as past experiences, knowledge, and skills, next to social and material resources, such as stable social surroundings, access to good food and health care, accommodation, and educational opportunities. These attributes are not immediately apparent and may be influenced by the demand characteristics (Bronfenbrenner and Morris, 2006).

Force characteristics refer to variations of temperament, motivation, and persistence amongst others. For instance, despite having equal resource characteristics, two individuals can develop in different ways because of their different motivations to cope with challenges (Bronfenbrenner and Morris, 2006).

Actually, all three characteristics appear twice within the bioecological model. First, they are mentioned as one of the four elements influencing the form, power, content, and direction of the proximal process. Second, they are developmental outcomes which are qualities of the developing person that emerge at a later point in time as the result of the common, interactive, mutually reinforcing effects of the preceding four principal components of the model. Consequently, the characteristics of the person function indirectly as producer and at the same time as a product of development (Bronfenbrenner and Morris, 2006; Lerner, 2012).

There is a mutual influence and change between persons and ecology. This means that individuals are active in their own development through selective patterns of attention, actions, and responses while in contact with their environment (Ceci, 2006; Barnes and Rowe, 2013).

3.3.3 Context

Bronfenbrenner develops five interrelated systems, the microsystem, mesosystem, exosystem, macrosystem, and chronosystem — explained above — to categorize influences on human development. Context includes four of them:

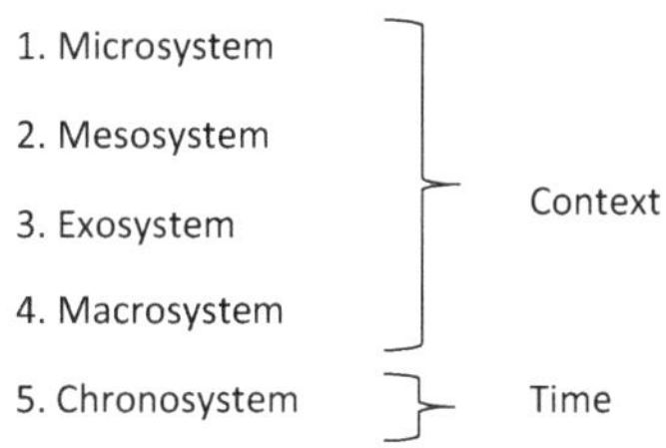

Figure 6: Bronfenbrenner's Five Systems That Influence Human Development (Tudge et al., 2009)

Bronfenbrenner delivers a convincing approach for the explanation of individuals' roles in changing their context. The change can be rather passive. This is the case when an individual changes his or her environment merely by taking part in it to the degree that others react to him or her in a different way on the basis of demand characteristics. Alternatively, the change can be relatively active. The ways in which the individual changes the environment are related to his or her resource characteristics. Finally, the change can be very active. This refers to the degree to which the person changes the environment and is partly linked to the respective person's will and ambition to do so – the so-called force characteristics (Bronfenbrenner and Morris, 1998; Tudge et al., 2009).

Bronfenbrenner also introduces concepts and criteria that differentiate between those features of the environment that support or interrupt the development of proximal processes.

On the one hand, the development of proximal processes is supported by interaction not only with people but with objects and symbols. On the other hand, the development of proximal processes can be interrupted by increasing hecticness, instability, and disorder (Bronfenbrenner and Morris, 2006; Bronfenbrenner and Morris, 1998).

3.3.4 Time

The fourth element of the PPCT model is time. Time has an important role and is organized on three successive levels: (1). micro-time, (2). meso-time, and (3). macro-time.

Firstly, micro-time refers to continuity versus discontinuity during the occurrence of the proximal process — or more simply, what happens during the course of particular activities or interactions of the proximal process (Bronfenbrenner and Morris, 1998; Bronfenbrenner and Morris, 2006). Secondly, meso-time refers to the extent to which the processes occur in the individual's environment, such as over the course of days, weeks, months, or years (Bronfenbrenner and Morris, 2006). And thirdly, macro-time, or the chronosystem, refers to the fact that developmental processes are likely to vary according to the specific historical events occurring while the developing individual is at a certain age. These changes affect and are affected by processes and outcomes of human development over the life course (Bronfenbrenner and Morris, 2006).

For instance, each individual experiences the effects of an event, such as an extraordinary economic upturn or downturn with its subsequent historical consequences, completely differently because they experience each of these events at a different point in their lifetime.

Time and timing are in the same way important because all aspects of the PPCT model can be understood of in terms of relative steadiness and change. A culture or cultures are continuously going through times of change, even though some periods of historical time have higher rates of change than others.

3.4 History and the Social Ecological Framework

The social ecological framework additionally considers the influence of history (Oetzel, 2009). The layered perspective includes the effects of other contexts. Factors, such as historical incidents and the economic system, have an impact on the individual's behavior. The layered perspective shows synthesis and synergy, creates links and loops, and consequently, sheds light on reciprocal contextual influences (Klein, Tosi and Cannella, 1999). Thus, history shapes individual behavior, and individual behavior can change history.

The cultural-historical approach integrates an individual's development into a social, cultural, and historical context. The approach assumes that individual development must be understood within, and cannot be separated from, it's social and cultural-historical context. The efforts of individuals are not isolated from the activities in which they take part or the institutions in which they are integrated. Humans in their earliest developmental stage, as children, learn to use the tools for thinking, provided by culture, through their interaction. They learn to transform the tools of culture for their own purpose. Culture is dynamic. It is formed by the efforts of people's interactions using and adapting material and symbolic tools provided by predecessors and by the process of creating new ones. Consequently, individual development constitutes and is constituted by cultural-historical activities and practices. In the socio-cultural perspective, culture is not something that influences individuals, but instead people contribute to the creation of cultural processes and vice versa. Thus, the individual and cultural processes mutually define each other (Rogoff, 2003; Vygotsky and Cole, 1978).

The individual's development over his or her whole life is influenced by the historical development of human beings and cultural communities. Development occurs in different time frames: the pace of species change, the historical changes within a society, the individual lifetimes, and finally the individual learning moments. These four developmental levels provide a helpful tool to investigate the interrelating nature of cultural and biological processes and the changing nature of culture itself (Rogoff, 2003).

Bronfenbrenner (1992) states that the human species on the one hand, by virtue of its unique capacity to use tools and symbols, continuously creates and elaborates its own environment in the form of culture. On the other hand, the evolution of culture is seen as a historical process that has taken different forms across both time and place. Moreover, humans are not only culture-producing, they are also a product of culture (Bronfenbrenner, 1992).

3.5 Review and Conclusion of the Social Ecological Approach

Bronfenbrenner's approach of a layered perspective was initially used in studies which examined child development. However, this model of a layered perspective can be transferred to various other fields. The social ecological framework helps to explain the interplay between the individual and his or her environment in a variety of areas (Bronfenbrenner, 1979). For instance, researchers, such as Stokols, used the approach to examine causal connections between human behavior and public health programs (Stokols, 1996).

Research that aims to explain human behavior tends to focus on the individual. However, other factors, such as history, geography, or economic systems which shape an individual's behavior, are then usually not taken into consideration (Oetzel, 2009). Thus, studies that focus on just one level will, by definition, underestimate the effects of other contexts (Ting-Toomey, 2011). When taking into account the surroundings of an individual, the possible impacts on the individual are considered too. In this way, human behavior is not merely viewed as a series of individual choices – instead, other factors place the individual's behavior in a context. It should be noted critically that individual responsibility is not removed, but that the approach highlights other explanatory factors as well. In addition to this, a layered approach helps to identify how certain contexts support or inhibit behavioral change (Oetzel, 2009).

Cultural models can explain human values and human behavior by focusing on culture. Consequently, different behavior of individuals can be explained by the affiliation to different cultures. These models compare cultures by evaluating a certain aspect of a culture in comparison to another culture (Hofstede, 2003). However, such models seem to be an inappropriate tool for examining cultural change during a period of time within only one culture. In contrast, the social ecological approach is able to foster synthesis and synergy, creating links and loops and making reciprocal contextual influences within one culture visible (Ting-Toomey, 2011). It allows the creation of a complex picture of the aspects human behavior, human values and the change of values over time which have an impact on someone's culture. Consequently, it explains how history shapes individual behavior and how individuals can change history (Oetzel, 2009).

The layered perspective poses challenges and burdens at the same time. The model is very complex and instead of focusing on a single issue, it requires a lot of ecological details and the consideration of a large number of factors, concepts, and issues. Consequently, it can be challenging to determine and evaluate all relevant data for a study. Another difficulty is that a layered approach takes into account multiple issues, and because everything is connected in loops and links, one can assume that every issue matters – even though, in a given situation certain factors matter more than others. These factors need to be emphasized. A study with a layered framework must be limited, because it is not based on a linear perspective. Therefore, such a study must be well-organized beforehand with a clear definition of where to begin and where to end. Consequently, the design of the study reflects, as is probably the case in other studies too, the biases of the researcher (Oetzel, 2009).

Chapter 3: History, Cultural Characteristics and Manifestation of Culture Illustrated by the Example of the Republic of Ireland

The island of Ireland is located in northwestern Europe. The island is surrounded by the North Atlantic Ocean to the north and to the west, the Celtic Sea in the south-east, and the Irish Sea to the east. Currently, the island of Ireland is politically divided into Northern Ireland, which is part of the United Kingdom, and the Republic of Ireland.

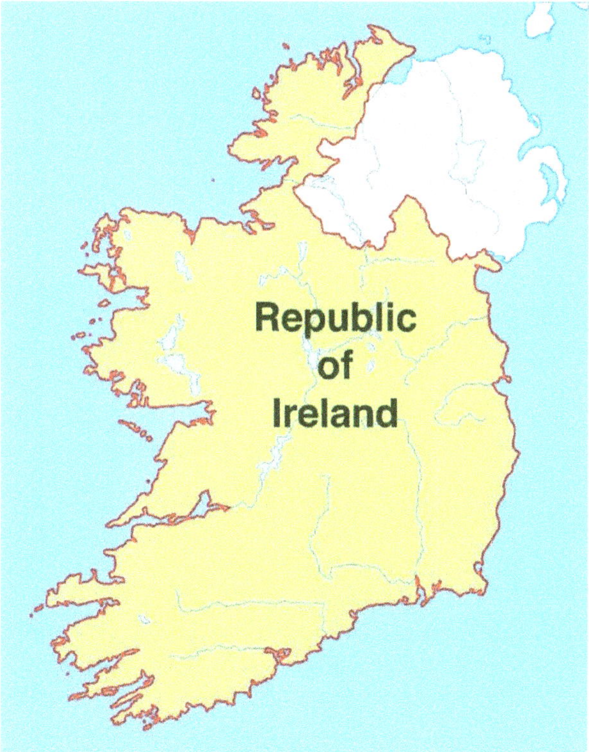

Figure 7: Map of Ireland: Republic of Ireland defined by Red Borders (Koczy, 2019)

1 The Historical Development of Ireland

History includes, among other things, Ireland's legends of great battles and heroes, the stories told by its poets and the people's perception today of their history. This perception is shaped by recent events and events from the distant past. History is also important for today's Ireland. As mentioned in Chapter One, Section 1, history provides collective memories, and people who share collective memories usually share cultural identities. History is a central element of culture and culture is shaped by history. Examining Irish history more closely helps to shed light on the collective memory and cultural identity of the Irish which in turn helps to explain Irish culture. Because culture has a deep impact on behavior and decision-making processes, historical events are investigated to reveal influences on behavior and decision-making processes, and this can provide explanations for economic and societal development. Therefore, the history of ancient Ireland gives us some understanding of the foundation of the country and of the development and characteristics of Irish society. A brief overview of selected events is given below in chronological order to illustrate which events had an impact on Irish identity. The main focus of attention will be on significant turning points that influenced the country's destiny in order to illustrate which events shaped the Irish society of today.

An examination of Irish history explains, for instance, the roots of the Northern Ireland conflict which influences the economy and politics until today, also in the Republic of Ireland.

The analyzing part in this dissertation aims at answering the research questions by means of the theoretical model of the layered perspective. This model was introduced in Chapter Two, Section 3, and then applied to Ireland. Various links are drawn to historical events that offer explanations for the attitudes and values, and consequently, the generated behavior of, for instance, Irish households, as illustrated in Chapter Six, Section 1.

1.1 The Beginnings

In the most recent glacial period in Europe, which began approximately 115,000 BC, Ireland was covered by a layer of ice hundreds of meters thick. From 10,000 BC onwards, Ireland was definitely suitable for settlement (McCaffrey and Eaton, 2002). During the Bronze and Iron Age, the people who settled on the island of Ireland, made technological progress (Waddell, 1998). They figured out that tools and weapons made of metal were more efficient than those made of stone. This helped them to improve their agricultural techniques as well as their crafting skills. People in Ireland were not an isolated cultural enclave at this time. They exported copper and things made of copper, mainly axes and knives, wind instruments, and jewelry. Irish copper- and goldsmiths were highly skilled. Nowhere else than in Ireland was there more jewelry to be found (McCaffrey and Eaton, 2002). These examples show that the Irish were already a highly developed culture which contradicts the cliché which the Normans later spread about them being a backward tribe.

In the late 19th and early 20th century, the Irish aristocratic society referred to the Celtic past of the Irish people. This movement is also called the 'Celtic Renaissance'. The Celts were not one homogeneous nation, but instead consisted of various tribes or tribe alliances from Middle and Western Europe who also settled in Ireland approximately 600 BC (Birkhan, 1997). From a current point of view, it is legitimate to label the Irish people of that time as Celts (Kuckenburg, 2010). However, the definition of the 'ancient Celts' is a recent construct according to the current point of view. It is questionable whether the peoples called 'keltoi' by the Greeks ever considered themselves as belonging to one ethnically identifiable group (Waddell, 1998).

From 700 to 1150, the Christian faith became popular and the Irish monasteries gained great wealth and affluence. This great wealth led to power struggles within the country while the monasteries also became targets for plunderers, especially from a group of people known today as the Vikings who gained more and more influence and power in Ireland at the time. The political conditions remained unstable and were characterized by various alliances and breakages of these alliances between Irish kings among themselves on the one hand and alliances between Irish kings and Viking kings on the other hand. Occasionally, Irish kings agreed to alliances with Viking kings to fight against other Irish rival kings over power and wealth. There were quarrels, conflicts, and wars on a regular basis during these years (Ó Corráin, 2008). The Battle of Clontarf became legendary because Viking influence faded following the defeat of the Vikings by High King of Ireland Brian Boru, at Clontarf in 1014. Brian Boru was the only king who ever ruled the entire country of Ireland and although he actually existed and the Battle of Clontarf actually took place, he was glorified as a folk hero, cultural patron, glamorized protector and defender of the early Christian attainments of Ireland (please cp. Chapter Three, Section 3.2.3). In fact, however, his principal opponents were not the Vikings but the King of Leinster who did not want to surrender to Brian Boru. The Battle of Clontarf did not put an abrupt end to the power and influence of the Vikings (Duffy,

2014a; Duffy, 2014b). It was rather that the presence of the Vikings as individuals faded gradually as they assimilated through intermarriage and conversion to Christianity (Logan, 1992). Though the army of Brian Boru won the Battle of Clontarf, Brian and his son lost their lives on April 23, 1014. Brian Boru's successors failed to establish a unified Irish kingdom. The temptation of gaining power over the entire country sparked enduring territorial disputes and struggles for the throne between the kings who wanted to become the next High King of Ireland. This dissention ultimately led to the Norman Invasion in 1169 (McCaffrey and Eaton, 2002).

1.2 The Normans

The descendants of the Vikings who settled in Normandy later became the Normans. In the 11th century, the Normans crossed the sea to England. They defeated Anglo-Saxon King Harold of England in 1066 at the Battle of Hastings and took control of the English throne and the country itself. There had been some indication that the Normans planned to invade Ireland but things turned out differently.

The King of Leinster, Dermot MacMurrough, as one amongst others, also had strong ambitions to become the next High King of Ireland in succession of Brian Boru who had been killed. However, he was defeated by another Irish king as an act of revenge for an earlier lost battle. Dermot lost his throne and was forced to flee. To recapture his throne, he asked English King Henry II for help. Henry II sent some mercenaries with him, and Dermot was able to re-establish himself as king. But the story did not end there. The Anglo-Normans arrived and the call for help justified an invasion of Ireland. The Anglo-Norman conquest of Ireland was carried out with the explicit permission of Pope Adrian IV. The Pope's intention was to gain power and influence for Rome in Ireland. In return for the English support, Dermot promised the hand of his daughter to an English earl who went down in history as Strongbow. He also bequeathed his kingdom to him after his death which was against Irish laws of the time (Mackie, 1907; McCaffrey and Eaton, 2002; McCaffrey, 2006). King Henry II named his son 'Lord of Ireland' in 1177 upon approval by Pope Alexander III who was Pope Adrian IV's successor. Since then, this title is incorporated into English monarchy. The later King of England, Henry the VIII – who broke with the Roman Catholic Church to appoint himself Supreme Head of the Church of England and determined the dissolution of the monasteries in England – ensured in 1541 that the Irish Parliament declared him 'King of Ireland' (Scarisbrick, 1997; McCaffrey, 2006). Naturally, there was opposition in Ireland against a non-Catholic king. When his daughter, Elizabeth I, acceded to the throne, she faced considerable resistance in Ireland and a time of war (1570 to 1607) for supremacy in Ireland ensued. However, only the northern part of Ireland, i.e. Ulster, remained under the authority of the English crown. In 1609, the English began to pursue their 'policy of plantation' in Ulster. To ensure loyalty to the crown, Protestant families from England and Scotland moved to Ulster and settled down there whereas Irish natives were expelled from their lands. This treatment of Catholic people led to uprisings in 1641. In the 17th century, the Penal Laws were introduced. They strengthened Protestant land ownership on Irish land and prevented Catholics from sitting in the Irish or British parliament. They outlawed Catholic clergy, withheld higher education from Catholics and contained many more retrenchments of rights. From this time on, sectarian conflict became an issue in Irish history (McCaffrey, 2006).

1.3 The Union

In 1782, pressured by the threat of another Irish uprising, the British government conceded to greater legislative independence for the Parliament of Ireland. However, the British Parliament still controlled most of the political processes in Ireland. Consequently, Irish nationalists felt that constitutional methods alone were insufficient to succeed in the political arena (McCaffrey, 2006). During the 1790s, the political conditions in Ireland became increasingly unstable. The independent Parliament of Ireland was causing disturbance in the British government through its constant administrative challenges to the overriding power of Westminster. Ideas of a self-governed Ireland attained through military means were strengthened in the wake of the American and French revolutions. The party of the 'United Irishmen' wanted to create a free Ireland using force of arms. In 1798, a rebellion against the British rule in Ireland arose. Although the United Irishmen had stated non-sectarian aims, the rebellion ended in bloody intercommunal religious violence. The British managed to crush the rebellion and regained control of Ireland. In 1800, the Irish Parliament was dissolved by the passing of the 'Act of Union' which came into effect on January 1, 1801 and united Ireland politically with Britain. The act was an attempt to set limits to the political freedom of constitutionalists and to reduce the risks from insurgents (Cronin and Adair, 2006).

The Act of Union contained eight articles. Article one to four dealt with political matters, such as creating the 'United Kingdom of Great Britain and

Ireland'. The fifth article dealt with the unification of the Church of Ireland and the Church of England. The sixth article established free trade between Ireland and Britain but also included duties on certain goods. The seventh article provided for the financial systems of the two countries to remain separate. The eighth article declared that all laws and the jurisdiction of all courts at the time of the passing of the Act of Union should remain as they were before (Crown, 1800; 2002).

Irish Protestants had become passionate supporters of the Union, which they regarded as their only protection against the Catholic majority and further gave them a distinct claim on preferential treatment by the government. They tended to judge every policy concerning Ireland which the government pursued by its effect on their own position and influence (Beckett, 2008). Real integration of the two countries did not take place. The power to pass a bill had moved from Ireland to Britain, but the same Protestant ascendancy remained in control of the central and local government in Ireland. From a religious perspective, the Act of Union further vilified the Catholic faith in Ireland (Macinnes, 2011).

By the end of the 18th century, Ireland experienced a period of economic expansion. Irish farmers had found an expanding market in the growing non-agricultural population of industrializing Britain. The war between Britain and France from 1793 to 1815 had pushed up demand and limited imports from continental Europe at the same time. During the years of war, the prices for Irish cereals, meat, and dairy products rose significantly. However, this economic success was based on a fragile concept. The defeat of France in 1813 led to a downturn in demand while it also reopened the British market to continental traders. From the end of the war on, the prices for grain, meat, and butter on the Dublin market fell by 50% on average. The consequences for all classes of countryside society were catastrophic. Landlords struggled with falling payments from tenants and the farmers were not able to pay their rents (Kinealy, 2006; Ó Corráin and O'Riordan, 2011).

In 1824, the Irish economy was shocked by the collapse of the wool and cotton industry. The Irish industry in the late 18th century had thrived because of import duties. The Act of Union provided a cancelation of all such duties by 1824 in favor of creating a free trade area within the United Kingdom. The sudden cancelation of protection was a hard blow for the Irish economy. Widespread business failures in Ireland followed and the Irish were now dependent on English and Scottish imports for the bulk of their cotton and woolen cloth. On the other hand, technical inventions had made possible the industrial processing of linen yarn. The traditional home of the linen industry in Ulster transferred resources from a declining cotton trade into an increasingly profitable linen production and Belfast became the center of this new industry. Consequently, the North separated economically from the southern parts of Ireland in which agriculture and small-scale handicrafts still played an important role (Ó Corráin and O'Riordan, 2011). The act paved the way for the development of a common market and also became an issue of economic historians' debate: one side argues that the Irish economy was weakened by the Act of Union due to over-taxation and duties, while the other side questions whether a native Irish parliament would have fared any better (Pašeta, 2003).

It is important to view this economic development parallel to indicators of social and cultural change at the time. The intervention in primary education in Ireland by the state began during the 16th century when the Tudors became the ruling power in England and Ireland. In the early part of the 18th century, the so-called 'hedge schools' emerged, a very unusual type of informal education with classes supposedly taking place outdoors near hedges. These schools were independent of any kind of authority. At the end of the 18th century, the ban on Catholic schools was removed from the statute books, but hedge schools still continued to flourish (Lyons, 2016; Coleman, 2009).

Significant progress was made in the field of education. In 1806, 200,000 children received school education in contrast to 560,000 children who received school education in 1824. As a consequence, the educational background also improved. The statistics show that in 1841, 60% of all males born between 1821 and 1830 were able to read and write. However, the proportion of children who were able to speak Irish had fallen from 45% to 28% during that period. Thus, access to higher education not only led to a rise of literacy but also to language change and resulted in the remarkable growth of a sophisticated new style of popular politics. Although living standards were lower in comparison with Britain in the first half of the 19th century, the Irish had a successful economy, good education, and good living-standards measured on the basis of health. None of this is congruent with the stereotypical image of a society immersed in poverty and economic stagnation (Ó Corráin and O'Riordan, 2011). However, things changed by the ensuing tragedy of the Great Famine.

1.4 The Great Famine

The potato was brought to Europe from South America by Spanish sailors in the 16th century. There is evidence that at the beginning of the 17th century, the potato was cultivated in Ireland and that by the end of the 17th century, the potato had developed to the staple food of the Irish people, providing them with a highly nutritive, if monotonous, diet (Massard, 2009a; Massard, 2009b).

When potato blight infested the potato crops throughout Ireland during the years 1845 to 1847, a human catastrophe occurred. Potatoes became inedible and the Irish people died of starvation and the impacts of malnutrition.

Historians are divided over how the British government managed the Famine and whether more could or should have been done to take countermeasures against the tragedy (McCaffrey, 2006). However, there seems to be a common agreement among historians that the British government of that time acted amiss. Some historians state that Ireland was considered the eyesore of Britain (Coogan, 2012). Therefore, the British government grasped the 'opportunity' of the Famine to modernize Ireland's economy, politics, and religion by refusing help to the Irish people (Kelly, 2012). Other historians argue that British politics contributed to the disaster: Although hundreds of thousands of people were suffering from extreme hunger, Ireland was forced to export plentiful harvests of wheat and dairy products to Britain. The British military protected the food transports from Ireland against Irish people who tried to gain access to the food. Between 1845 and 1851, 1.5 million people died and another million people emigrated from Ireland, mainly to the United States of America. The population never reached its pre-Famine level of approximately eight million people until the early 21st century (Kinealy, 2006).

The unexpected failure of the potato crop was a violent external shock to the people and had far-reaching consequences for the economic development. Without the potato blight the population could have stabilized at around eight million people, with cheap labor sustaining a large and still profitable agricultural sector and gradually rising living standards (Ó Corráin and O'Riordan, 2011). However, the most crucial effect of the Famine was that they were morally destroyed by the catastrophe.

1.5 The Home Rule

Since the policy of plantation in the beginning of the 17th century, the land had been in the hands of English landlords. However, the Irish who survived the Famine began to fight for more rights and a fairer division of land. The aim was the right of self-governance within the United Kingdom, also called Home Rule. Ireland formed a constituent part of the United Kingdom from 1801 to 1922 but Britain's control of Irish politics was weakened by the achievements of the politician Charles Stewart Parnell (McCaffrey, 2006).

Parnell developed a strategy of punishment which later became famous as 'boycotting' (please see Chapter Three, Sections 2.4 and 3.2.4). Parnell's method of enforcing his ideas became very famous and successful. The British realized that very little could be done to counteract it. Therefore, the British government decided to pass a bill for land reform which guaranteed, among other things, fixity of tenure and fair rents. What is more, after hundreds of years, land ownership was finally returned to Irish farmers (Turner, 1917; Kinealy, 2004; McCaffrey, 2006).

McCaffrey (2006) reveals that there was opposition to Home Rule from the Catholic Church. The bishops had become very powerful and feared they might lose power to politicians who could introduce a nonsectarian school system. Catholic schools had been established under the British government which also supported the Catholic University financially. Moreover, the Irish movement encountered opposition by Pope Leo XIII himself. The Pope urged the Irish people to refrain from boycotting in his decree ‚*Saepe nos* – Encyclical of Pope Leo XIII on boycotting in Ireland' (Leo XIII, 1888). The British, who had broken with Rome since Henry VIII and his Reformation, sought support against Home Rule. They made promises to Rome concerning Catholic education which probably influenced the Pope's attitude towards Home Rule (McCaffrey, 2006).

The province of Ulster – where the majority of people were Protestants – feared they could become a Protestant minority and be discriminated against in an independent Ireland (Turner, 1917). Consequently, they favored the union with Britain and threatened with military steps for a separate Northern Ireland if independence were to be granted to Ireland. At the same time, Irish nationalists also started arming themselves in order to bring freedom and, if necessary, by military means.

The Home Rule Bill was passed, yet it never became legally effective. The act was postponed because of the outbreak of World War I in 1914 when both Unionists and Nationalists joined forces with Britain. Many Irish assumed that Home Rule would be approved after the war if they supported and fought for the British Empire. Others, however, did not trust the British government. This led to a crucial event in Irish history: the Easter Rising in 1916 which attempted to end British rule over Ireland (McConnel, 2011).

1.6 The Path to Independence

Soon after the outbreak of World War I on August 4, 1914 – when British soldiers were stationed in Belgium to support their alliance partner against German troops – Irish nationalist militants saw their opportunity to start a rebellion against Britain. "England's difficulty was Ireland's opportunity" (Fanning, 2015, p. 34). They chose the Easter event to disguise their activities in the form of maneuver and parades. Ceremonial deployment during an important

Christian festival would not arouse suspicion. And therefore, this event went down in history as the Easter Rising.

On Easter Monday, April 24, 1916, armed Irish groups occupied key locations in Dublin and set their headquarters at the General Post Office in Dublin's city center where they declared an Irish Republic independent of Britain. However, the rebellion was brutally put down by the British army and many Irish civilians lost their lives too. The rebellion finally ended on April 30 when the rebels were arrested. At first, the majority of the Irish people had actually been opposed to the rebellion. However, public opinion turned when it became generally known that the British government responded by executing many of the leaders and participants of the rebellion without a fair trial. This behavior of the British government fueled anti-British sentiments among the Irish. Although this violent attempt to gain independence from Britain was a military failure, the event marks a turning point in Irish history which in the end did lead to the country's independence (Coogan, 2001).

In 1917, Éamon de Valera – who had been a military commander in the Easter Rising in 1916 – became President of Sinn Féin, a republican party whose main interest was an independent Ireland and who, if necessary, enforced their interests violently. The frustration of the people about the British treatment of the leaders of the Rising and the frequent postponement of Home Rule resulted in the victory of Sinn Féin at the General Election in 1918. However, the members of Sinn Féin refused to take their seats as Members of Parliament in Westminster (and still do). Instead, they seceded and assembled in Mansion House in Dublin to form a 'rebel' (from a British point of view) parliament called 'Dáil Éireann,' proclaimed an independent Ireland and established a government under Éamon de Valera. The British Prime Minister of the time declared the new party illegal (Fanning, 2015).

In the following war which is known as the War of Independence, the army of the recently declared Irish Republic – called Irish Republican Army (IRA) with roots in 1916 – waged a guerilla war against British forces from 1919 to 1921 (McCaffrey, 2006). In July 1921, a cease-fire was bargained between the Irish and the British forces. The official end of the War of Independence is marked by the signing of the Anglo-Irish Treaty in December 1921. Twenty-six counties achieved formal independence from Britain and formed the Irish Free State. However, the six counties in the North – where the majority of the population was Protestant – remained within the United Kingdom as an option offered by the British government (Kinealy, 2004). Thus, the division of the country was confirmed.

The division of the country had far-reaching consequences and the foundation was laid for decades of violence in Northern Ireland. The supposed political stability after World War II collapsed in the late 1960s. In the period that followed nationalists and republicans seeking a united Ireland clashed in Northern Ireland with loyalists and unionists declaring continued loyalty to the English Crown. This period of continued violence, generally known as 'The Troubles,' was stressful for all of Ireland and only ended with the Good Friday Agreement of April 10, 1998 (Keating and Martin, 2007).

The Anglo-Irish Treaty of 1921 did not truly create an independent Irish state but rather an Irish dominion of the United Kingdom. Consequently, the treaty triggered divided opinions within Ireland's major political parties. Next to the division of the country, the treaty also determined the constitutional connection to the British monarch as Head of State, as well as limits to sovereign power. Sinn Féin and Éamon de Valera rejected the dominion solution.

As a consequence, the Irish Civil War followed from 1922 to 1923 between pro-Treaty and anti-Treaty parties (Fanning, 2015). Today, the two largest political parties in Ireland have their origins in the opposing sides of the Civil War. The pro-Treaty party won the war and de Valera was imprisoned for one year. However, he continued to pursue his political aims and organized a republican party called Fianna Fáil in 1926. His party took office in 1932 with him as Head of Government for the next 16 years.

De Valera promoted the secession from Britain. He induced a stop of annual land payments – the return of loans from contracts from the turn of the century – to the British government. In return, the British government heavily taxed agricultural imports from Ireland and introduced a quota system. De Valera levied taxes on British goods in response. The disputes spawned the Economic War of 1932 to 1938. As a result, trade between Britain and Ireland was significantly reduced.

In 1937, a revised constitution was introduced in which the state was declared a sovereign, independent, and democratic republic called Ireland – or Éire in Irish language – and Ireland's first president was installed. In accordance with Ireland's independence from Britain, it remained neutral during World War II (1939 to 1945). The consequences of World War II were an enlargement of the political and economic division between the northern and southern parts of Ireland as well as between Éire and the United Kingdom (Kinealy, 2006).

As a result of the Republic of Ireland Act in 1948 which ended the formal role of the British monarch, Ireland was officially declared a republic in 1949 and the president became sole representative of the state (Kinealy, 2006). After World War II, the economic development only continued sluggishly in the new republic. However, in the 1960s, the political parties strove for economic growth motivated by the pursuit of joining the European Economic Community (EEC) – which was the predecessor of today's European Union (EU). The economic development of the Republic of Ireland is explained in detail in Chapter Four.

Ireland and Britain enacted a free trade agreement and in 1973, the Republic of Ireland and the United Kingdom both joined the EEC. The economy of the Republic of Ireland was positively influenced by the accession: Irish farmers were granted subsidies and price protection, the EEC supported the improvement of the infrastructure, and the Irish industry gained access to European markets. As a result, the income of Irish farmers rose and the Irish economy was less dependent on Britain. In 1979, the Republic of Ireland – unlike the United Kingdom – joined the European Monetary System (EMS). In the following years, Ireland became an esteemed member of the EU with a good reputation. Economic reforms in the 1980s created one of the world's highest economic growth rates in Ireland (Kinealy, 2006).

Increasing prosperity influenced other areas of life, such as house building and employee benefits while the economic growth was also reflected in societal and cultural change. The population was steadily growing and Ireland became attractive for the tourist industry. In the 1990s, Ireland – which had long been considered a country of emigration – now became a country of immigration. This period went down in history as the 'Celtic Tiger'.

2 Characteristics of Irish Culture

Assuming that culture has a significant impact on behavior and decision-making, this section offers a deeper analysis of Irish culture following the aforementioned characteristics of culture according to Keller (1982), such as visible and invisible elements of culture, to provide possible explanations and contribute to the holistic model of a layered perspective. Given the fact that the characteristics of culture are innumerable, only some selected examples will be explained.

2.1 Irish Language as a Cultural Element

Language is visible or at least noticeable. However, the transmitted meaning may be invisible to outsiders of a social group. As Huntington (1996) states, language is at the heart of a culture.

Today, most Irish people speak English although there are still some small regions, called Gaeltacht, where the inhabitants predominantly speak Irish Gaelic as testimony to the past. The question arises whether another language was ever spoken there before Gaelic respectively or an earlier version of it.

There are myths and legends about pre-Celtic people but no assured facts about them (Macalister, 1921). The archaeologist Peter Harbison (1988) defines the arrival of the Celts as the point in time when an ancestor language of modern Gaelic was first spoken in Ireland. There is no evidence for the languages of the first people in Ireland. Indeed, prehistory literally means 'before recorded history' (c.f. Thomsen's Three-age System in Heizer, 1962). Therefore, prehistory is the timespan since *Homo sapiens* first appeared but before the development of writing systems which enabled history to be recorded. Consequently, prehistoric archaeology cannot provide information on which languages were spoken at any time before written records emerged.

According to Harbison (1988), there is no evidence in the archaeological records for invasions massive enough to have brought about Celticization which makes it unlikely that a completely different language other than an ancestor of modern Gaelic was spoken at the time. Further, he states that there are just two historically known invasions. First, the invasions by the Vikings, which only had minor effects on the language of the country. Second, the Norman invasions, which for centuries only managed to change certain parts of the country regarding the use of the Norman language (Harbison, 1988). Consequently, Irish history illustrates that these invasions did not have the impact of a total language replacement. For many researchers today, the emergence of a Celtic language in Ireland was the culmination of a long process of social and economic interaction between both Ireland and Britain and parts of continental Europe (Waddell, 1991; Kuckenburg, 2010).

From 1366, speaking Irish was prohibited and punished by the English authority (Asch, 1994) Irish Gaelic speakers decreased continuously and nearly disappeared during the Great Famine in 1845. The Irish language then again regained importance due to the 'Celtic Renaissance' in the 19th century. Since the 20th century, the constitution of Ireland – *Bunreacht Na hÉireann* – determines in article 8 section 1 that "Irish language as the national language is the first official language" (Department of the Taoiseach, 2010, art. 8, sec.1). Section 2 further declares that "[t]he English language is recognised as a second official language" (Department of the Taoiseach, 2010, art. 8, sec.2).

The census of 2011 carved out that less than half of the interviewees, namely 41.44% of the people aged 3 years and older, were actually able to speak Irish. Further, just 2% of the respondents said they spoke Irish on a daily basis outside of the education system. Still, the constitution defines Irish as the first official language. It is remarkable that a language spoken only by a small minority in the country is important enough to hold the status of the first official language. This clearly shows the importance of the Irish language and implicates that language provides identity (Wade, 2012; Central Statistics Office, 2012).

2.2 How Irish Culture is Learned

Culture is, among other things, learned through narratives and stories. The visible elements of a culture can be revealed in its mystical and legendary narratives. Myths (from the Greek *mythos* meaning 'story'), sagas (meaning 'retell'), and legends (meaning 'written word') are stories, sometimes based on historical events, potentially embellished, or purely invented. The mystical and legendary narratives in their primary sense are the cultural beginning of human's relationship with the environment and are a fundamentally important aspect of mentality (Waddell, 2014). These stories are narrated by family members, friends, neighbors, and other people and transmit their knowledge from one generation to the next. The settings for narration may be schools, churches, or other places of social interaction. The sense of these narratives is to instruct, encourage, or caution the members of a group, and to pass on the invisible values of a society (Wahl, 1997). Narratives link the people of a culture of today with their history (Erdoes and Ortiz, 1984). Every culture is a concept shaped by mutual influences and changes. In the form of oral, visual (e.g. monuments, historical buildings, etc.) and written records, cultures preserve these changes as history, imaginative or real, and this is embedded in language. History is passed on through oral and written transmission from one generation to the next and thus, the past pervades human consciousness through generations (Konner, 2011). The narratives and stories are also an important instrument for preserving language and cultural memories and serve as a valuable instrument in the process of socialization by teaching people how to interact with other people and by communicating the values of a society (Rodriguez, 1999).

In ancient Ireland, the priests of the Celts, called druids, and the bards had the task to retell Ireland's greatest myths, sagas, and legends throughout the centuries. There are no written documents by the ancient Irish people. They did have Ogham script, however, these characters were said to have magical power and the script was not intended to set out in writing something which should persist alive in human memory. Therefore, Ogham was only rarely used. However, with the establishment of monastery and convent schools where monks copied psalms and the Testament, it also became common to write down the Irish myths, sagas, and legends. The writers mixed up the appearance of the mythological heroes and saints in the first centuries AD although there were hundreds of years between their appearances. It seemed to be important to the people that the mythological heroes and saints knew and liked each other (Dühnfort, 2012). These tales contain a good set of people, places, events, and miracles and are often described as "cultural history" (Yolen, 1986, p. 3).

Today, culture is also learned through mass media, such as radio, television or multi-media devices. They transmit, for example through advertising campaigns, the messages which shape the attitudes, values, and perceptions of their audience. According to Wood, mass media transmit people's ideas about who they are and should be and consequently contribute to the construction of identity (Wood, 2009).

In return, mass media can reproduce a 'learned' image of a culture which is not confirmed by the culture in question. The respective culture's identity has no connection to the transmitted attributes. An example for this is the advertisement of an American fast food chain in which social media managers published their idea of Irish culture via the U.S. Twitter page. The fast food chain was mocked on social media for this advertisement showing a mint-flavored milkshake dyed green, popular since the 1970s and sold in March to celebrate St. Patrick's Day. The commercial featured a red-haired man, dressed in Scottish tartan with the English prehistoric monument Stonehenge in the background (Lonergan, 2017; Mulraney, 2017).

Figure 8: American fast food chain advertisement for a green-dyed, mint-flavored milkshake, published in 2017 (Lonergan, 2017; Mulraney, 2017)

The scene shows the man 'playing' the milkshake as if it were Great Highland Bagpipes which are native to Scotland (in contrast to the Uilleann Pipes which are native to Ireland). Social media strongly criticized the advertisement and denoted it as 'insensitive'. The aspect that was most strongly criticized in the social media community was apparently not the inclusion of Scottish symbols but rather the use of the distinctive English monument Stonehenge. Eventually, the company issued an apologetic statement and assured their respect for the Irish culture. The advertisement was promptly deleted by the company (Lonergan, 2017; Mulraney, 2017).

This example shows that mass media are able to communicate identity and can therefore also shape and reinforce a group member's identity. However, if an identity conveyed through mass media is inconsistent with the identity of members of the respective culture, this can lead to outrage and hurt feelings.

2.3 Irish Collectivity

Culture represents a collectivist or social phenomenon. Further, culture determines the identity of a social collectivity (Hofstede, 2003; Kutschker and Schmid, 2011). Culture is independent of the destiny of an individual. Thus, a culture can even continue to exist after its population has become extinct (Keller, 1982).

As with many cultural groups, the Irish have also experienced traumatic events during their history, such as the Great Famine. Traumatic events have direct effects on the individual experiencing them him- or herself or indirect effects if his or her ancestors experienced them because historical traumata affect all people within that cultural group. Oetzel (2009) states that there is evidence that traumatic events from as long as 400 years ago have mental and physical impact on people in the present and this is called historical trauma. The historical trauma of the Great Famine led, among other things, to a loss of identity of the Irish people.

The common habit of connecting the Irish language with the word 'Celtic' is actually rooted in the 19th century and describes a change in Irish society also known as the 'Celtic Renaissance' (McCaffrey and Eaton, 2002; McCaffrey, 2006). This is a literary and cultural movement of Irish activists striving to establish a sense of identity for the Irish people at a time when the country was in a deep identity crisis. The reasons for the crisis were hundreds of years of English occupation and denunciation. Already at the beginning of the 14th century, speaking Irish and wearing traditional Irish clothes, as well as jurisdiction according to Brehon law as an expression of ethnic-cultural identity, were prohibited and punished by the English conquerors (Asch, 1994). Besides the stigma imposed on the Irish by the British public, the forced union of Ireland and Britain was both an economic and political catastrophe. Moreover, the Famine resulted in a dramatic population decline caused by emigration on the one hand and mass mortality through starvation and disease on the other hand. "The Famine was to leave deep psychological scars on the Irish memory" (McCaffrey and Eaton, 2002, p. 52). It took decades for the Irish to be able to talk about the human tragedy and to cope with the events by commemorating them and it also took decades for the British government to give an official statement of its role at that time (Marks, 1997).

The Irish politician Stewart Parnell, who started his political career in 1875, gave the 'Celtic Renaissance' impetus to regain identity. During the 1890s, some of the most famous Irish writers made the re-establishment of national pride their business. They investigated the history of the country and tried to discover the origins of Irish civilization. In their writings, they describe an idealized notion of a homogenous Celtic-Irish ethnicity – that possibly never existed – with the purpose of creating and reclaiming a sense of identity and self-respect for the Irish people (McCaffrey and Eaton, 2002; McCaffrey, 2006). It was Éamon de Valera's merit that the Irish language regained popularity due to being embedded in the Irish Constitution after having been nearly wiped out during the Great Famine (Fanning, 2015). Irish traditions also experienced a revival, such as the sports game hurling (*iomáint* in Gaelic) (Mac Mathúna, 2006). The earliest written record of hurling was found in the Brehon Laws of the 5th century, the old Irish form of civil law before the Anglo-Norman occupation. It is assumed that hurling came to Ireland with the Celts and therefore predates Christianity. The Normans prohibited hurling, however, this sports game was revived during the Celtic Renaissance when foreign visitors noted its position within Irish culture. This revival climaxed in 1884 with the founding of the Gaelic Athletic Association (GAA). This association supports, among other things, Irish cultural activities like hurling, Gaelic football, and Irish music and dance (Humphries, 2003). Even though the Celts were not the first human beings on the Irish isle, they are considered to be its native people. Although they do not exist in their original nature anymore a kind of Celticization has recurred.

2.4 The Influence of Irish Affiliation on Behavior

Culture has great influence on the behavior of its members because a single member will adjust his or her behavior to that of other group members (Benedict, 2005). For instance, the Irish politician Stewart Parnell stirred the masses into ostracizing the English landlords to punish them for mistreating their

Irish workers. It is assumed that ostracism was the traditional punishment imposed by druids to those who threatened the community. One of the first English landlords who suffered this treatment was Mr. Boycott who evicted some tenants for non-payment of rent. Soon after that, he and his family were outcast by the entire community (McCaffrey, 2006). Bernard Becker, a renowned journalist, traveled through Mayo, Galway, Clare, Limerick, Cork, and Kerry during 1880 and described his experiences with Mr. Boycott as follows:

> Farm labourers, workmen, herds-men, stablemen, all went long ago, leaving the corn standing, the horses in the stable, the sheep in the field, the turnips, swedes, carrots, and potatoes in the ground, where I saw them yesterday. Last Tuesday the laundress refused to wash for the family any longer; the baker at Ballinrobe is afraid to supply them with bread, and the butcher fears to send them meat. The state of siege is perfect (Becker, 1881, p. 15).

He further describes the situation of Mr. Boycott:

> [H]e can neither sell his crop to anybody else, nor [...] "win" it for himself. There remains in the ground at least five hundred pounds worth of potatoes and other root crops, and the owner has no possible means of doing anything with them. Nor, I am assured on trustworthy authority, would any human being buy them at any price; nor, if any such person were found, would he be able to find any labourer to touch any manner of work on the spot under the ban (Becker, 1881, p. 16).

When Mr. Becker wanted to visit Mr. Boycott, his driver refused to drive him to Mr. Boycott's home (Becker, 1881). Eventually, Mr. Boycott and his family left Ireland (Marlow, 1973). This treatment became commonly known as 'boycotting,' named after the Boycott family (McCaffrey, 2006). Ostracism is traditionally anchored in Irish culture. There seems to be a common agreement with regard to how people should be treated who are perceived as a threat by the majority of the members of a culture. This is an example of how a single member of a culture adjusts his or her behavior to that of other group members.

2.5 The Dynamics of Irish Culture

Culture is a dynamic system, interwoven with its environment. The system is dependent on interior and exterior influences. When one element within the system changes the whole system strives to adjust. This also happens when an outside force applies pressure (please see Chapter One, Section 2.3). Cultural behavior adjusts to the environment that people live in (Keller, 1982; Kutschker and Schmid, 2011; Haviland et al., 2013). Environmental influences on an individual are taken into account by Bronfenbrenner in his social ecological model (please see Chapter Two, Section 3).

3 The Irish Onion

Hofstede (2003) states that culture reveals itself in different levels of depth. He illustrates this manifestation of culture in his 'Onion Model' the theoretical structure of which is explained above (Hofstede, 2003). His concept is now applied to Irish culture in this chapter.

3.1 Symbols

Symbols are the visible characteristics of a society. In the following, some of these representations of ideas, concepts, words, gestures, and pictures which shape Irish identity are explained.

3.1.1 The Harp

The harp is probably the most significant symbol of Ireland. Ireland is the only nation which has a musical instrument as a national emblem (DJEI, 2016). The harp can also be found on the envelope of the Irish passport and is integrated into the logos of Irish companies, such as Ryanair Ltd., an Irish low-cost airline. Further, the harp appears as logo of Ireland's most famous beer Guinness which today, however, is part of the British Diageo beverage group, headquartered in London. However, due to the harp – as a significant symbol of Irishness – Guinness still appears to be Irish.

Figure 9: Guinness Uses the Harp Symbol on Their Beer and Merchandising Products (Photos Taken by the Author, 2017)

The symbol of the harp already appeared in Ireland on coins in 1207 (Kinealy, 2004). In 1534, under the rule of English King Henry VIII, Irish coinage shows a plain harp surmounted by a crown. This symbolizes an Ireland under English rule (O'Donnell, 2015a; O'Donnell, 2015b). With the introduction of the Euro in January 2002, the harp is displayed on all Irish Euro coins.

The image of the harp used today in official matters is based on the oldest extant Irish harp, also known as the 'Brian Boru' or 'Trinity College' harp kept by Trinity College in Dublin (TCD). Visitors can view the harp there in the Long Room Library (TCD, 2014). This kind of harp is also called Brian Boru harp because the oldest known image of this kind of harp which appears on the *Breac Moedoc*, or shrine of St. Moedoc, dates back to the 10th century which is also the time when Brian Boru lived (please see also this chapter, Section 3.2.3) (Chatterton Newman, 2011; Wall, first published 1905, reprinted 2015).

The Irish harp has been essentially tied to Irish culture for centuries. Irish people granted a high social status to harpists, because "[h]arps were valuable, for they were constructed by an expert and the woodwork was often elaborately carved" (Rimmer, 1964, p. 196). Therefore, the harp is a masterpiece of knowledge and handcraft. Someone who had the technical ability to play the harp was assigned to the aristocratic upper class. The English authorities viewed the harp with suspicion (O'Donnell, 2015a; Rimmer, 1964). However, the English who considered the Irish to be underdeveloped did have high esteem for the skills of the Irish harpers. This contradiction of an uncivilized race fostering such an advanced culture was difficult to reconcile (O'Donnell, 2015b).

After a period of war in the 1920s, and in times of political change when the Irish Free State was founded in 1922, it was necessary to recreate political and social stability. National symbols, such as the Irish harp, were important unifying devices in these years. While the country was transformed from a dominion to a democratic republic, the Irish harp survived as a prominent image of continuity (O'Donnell, 2013).

Since the 1990s, however, the Irish harp underwent modifications in its design. As O'Donnell (2013) states, the transformations of the Irish harp emblem during the Celtic Tiger era reflect changes in political, social, and cultural values during this period.

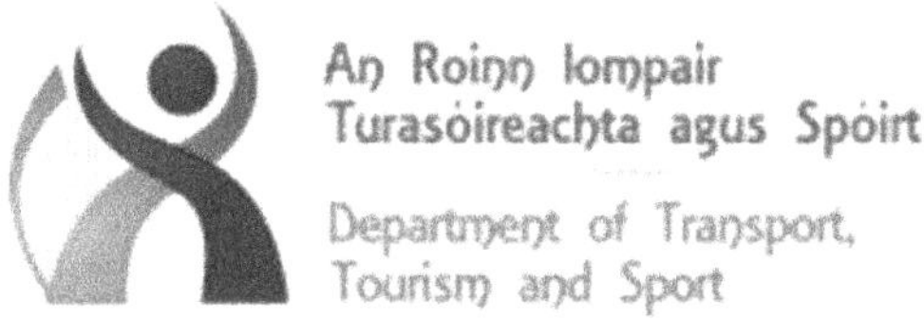

Figure 10: Examples for the Transformations of the Irish Harp Emblem by Different Government Departments, for Example The Department of Transport, Tourism and Sport (DTTAS, 2013)

Figure 11: Examples for the Transformations of the Irish Harp Emblem by Different Government Departments, for Example The Department of Agriculture, Food and the Marine (DAFM, 2016)

The government departments viewed themselves more and more in corporate terms and as a commercial brand rather than as a political unit serving its citizens (O'Donnell, 2013). O'Donnell blames these transformed images to be "disconnected metaphors commenting on contemporary Irish society, politics and culture" (O'Donnell, 2012, p. 35).

3.1.2 The Shamrock

The shamrock is one of the most popular symbols associated with Ireland (Mulvihill, 2012). Early sources already contain reports mentioning the shamrock, for instance, the journal of the English topographer Thomas Dineley who traveled through Ireland in 1680 and documented his observations in 'The Journal of Thomas Dineley' which was published in 1681. The original manuscript of his excursions can be viewed in the National Library of Ireland. In 1856, 'The Journal of the Kilkenny and South-East of Ireland Archaeological Society' published some pages from his journal under the title 'Extracts from the Journal of Thomas Dineley, Esquire, Giving Some Account of His Visit to Ireland in the Reign of Charles II'. These are some lines with his observations regarding the feast in honor of St. Patrick, the national saint of Ireland:

> The 17nth day of March yeerly is St Patricks, an immoveable feast, when ye Irish of all stations and condicons were crosses in their hatts, some of pins, some of green ribbon, and the vulgar uperstitiously wear shamroges, 3 leav'd grass, which they likewise eat (they say) to cause a sweet breath (Dineley, Shirley and Prendergast, 1856, p. 183).

This is the first mentioning of shamrocks being worn (Mulvihill, 2012). The shamrock as a symbol is tied to the national saint and hero St. Patrick, as who is said to have picked a shamrock from the ground and to have used it to explain the Holy Trinity with its three leaves and single stem (Moran, 1913). Other sources indicate that this is only one of the myths surrounding St. Patrick invented at the beginning of the 18th century, for there are no other sources mentioning the shamrock as explanation for the Holy Trinity before this time (Mulvihill, 2012).

Today, commercial firms which ship shamrocks for St. Patrick's Day as 'authentic shamrock – grown in Ireland' send the three-leafed yellow clover to their customers as the true shamrock in accordance with the myth that was used by St. Patrick to convert Ireland to Christianity (Milmo, 2006).

Today, the shamrock is also a state emblem. Using the shamrock in connection with any business must be approved by the Minister of Jobs, Enterprise and Innovation. In case of misuse that would misleadingly indicate that the goods labeled with the shamrock are of Irish origin, the Minister is authorized to take legal action. The shamrock is used as a badge by Irish sports teams and as a part of the logos of some Irish state organizations and companies, both parastatal and private. It is also displayed on the uniforms of Irish troops serving abroad (DJEI, 2016).

Thus, the shamrock is a symbol that transmits the idea of Irishness and Irish pride – not only on St. Patrick's Day – within Ireland and throughout the world.

3.1.3 The Flags

There are references in an armorial from the 13th century indicating that the Irish harp is a symbol of Ireland. This French roll of arms cited a golden harp on a blue background as the arms of the king of Ireland (O'Donnell, 2015a). In *The Handbook to English Heraldry* by Charles Boutell (1914), the harp of gold with silver strings on a blue field is described as a device and badge of Ireland (Boutell, 1914). Indeed, the color blue was associated with Ireland before the color green. The English king Henry VIII claimed to be King of Ireland in the 16th century, and his coat of arms showed blue and red fields. Therefore, a blue flag with a harp symbol decorates the presidential flag (Waxman, 2017). The official emblem shows a harp with vertically oriented strings and placed at a slight angle to show off the body and its design. Next to being the official seal of the President's office, the harp is also used in general by government departments and offices (Department of the Taoiseach, 2016).

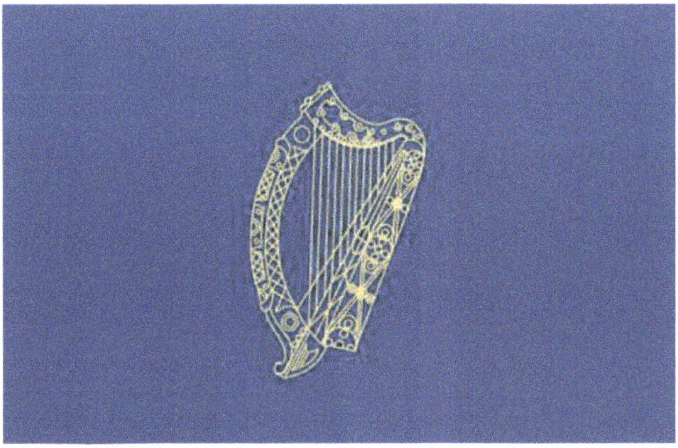

Figure 12: Presidential Standard (Mayes, 2013)

A green flag with a gold-colored harp is a symbol going back at least to confederate Ireland in the 1640s. It was unofficially used as the flag of Ireland by the Catholic majority who wanted to free Ireland from the British rule. It was also widely employed during the period of 'The Union' and in 1798 when the rebellion against the British rule in Ireland took place (Department of the Taoiseach, 2016). During the Easter Rising in 1916, a green flag featuring a golden harp was prominent on many of the rebel strongholds (O'Donnell, 2013).

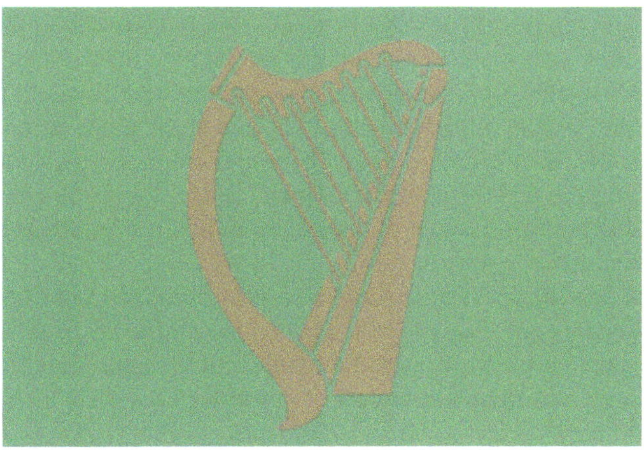

Figure 13: Green Flag with a Golden Harp (Department of the Taoiscach, 2016)

Inspired by the French Revolution (1789–1799), the Irish also created a tricolor, modeled on the French flag, with the Irish tricolor consisting of green, white, and orange (Department of the Taoiseach, 2016).

Figure 14: The National Flag of Ireland: a Tricolor with Green, White, and Orange (Department of the Taoiseach, 2016)

The green color is based on the traditional green flag with the golden harp and stands for the older Gaelic tradition and the majority of the Catholic people of Ireland. During the rebellion in 1798, the green color was applied politically. Green was adopted for garments and uniforms were made of green fabric (Cahill and Casey, 2015). The orange color represents the members of the Protestant minority loyal to the British Crown and founders of the 'Orange Order' in 1795. They founded this order to defend their interests and named it after King William III of Orange who became Protestant King of England by defeating the Catholic King James II of England at the Battle of the Boyne in 1690. Therefore, their color is orange. The white color is a symbol for peace in between the green and the orange (O'Donnell, 2012). The colors symbolize the inclusion and hoped-for union of the people of different traditions in Ireland (Department of the Taoiseach, 2016).

Nevertheless, until the Easter Rising in 1916, the green flag with the harp was indisputably the flag of Ireland. On Easter Monday 1916, a tricolor flag was hoisted over the General Post Office. In the aftermath, the tricolor achieved great encouragement as the national flag because of its association with separatism and as a symbol used during the Easter Rising of 1916, the event which paved the way for the foundation of the Irish Free State. In 1922, the flag was employed as the official flag of the Irish Free State. After the War of Independence (1919–21) and the Irish Civil War (1922–23), it was crucial to recreate political and social stability. National symbols, such as the tricolor flag, were important unifying devices (O'Donnell, 2012). In 1937, its status as national flag was defined by the newly established constitution in article 7.

In contrast to the harp and the shamrock, the national flag is not a state emblem but it is protected by the Irish Constitution (Department of the Taoiseach, 2016).

3.1.4 The National Anthem

'The Soldier's Song' or 'Amhrán na bhFiann' in Irish was written in English by the Irish political activist and freedom fighter Kearney and was later translated into Irish by O'Rinn. The song was first published in the newspaper 'Irish Freedom' in 1912. However, it did not become popular until the Easter Rising of 1916, when it was sung at the General Post Office, the headquarters of the rebellion. The song became an important unifying device in the early years of the new state. The chorus was officially adopted as the national anthem in 1926 (Cumiskey, 2003; Department of the Taoiseach, 2013). When the national anthem is played in the presence of the national flag, all present are asked to face the flag, stand to attention and salute it, remaining at the salute until the last note of the music (Department of the Taoiseach, 2016).

3.1.5 The High Cross

Distinctive visual symbols of Irish monasteries are the gigantic High Crosses erected between the 9th and 12th century, sometimes also referred to as Celtic Crosses. High Crosses are free-standing stone crosses, probably painted in bright colors in earlier times, with a ringed cross head, and mounted on a stepped base (Kuckenburg, 2010; O'Brien and Harbison, 1996). The cross is a significant symbol of Christianity. It is first found as a Christian symbol around the 5th century (Steffler, 2002).

Figure 15: High Cross, Clonmacnoise, Co. Offaly (Photo Taken by the Author)

High Crosses can still be widely found in Ireland in the vicinity of ruined monasteries. The fine stone craftsmanship was common in Ireland at a time when stone carving was rare in the rest of Europe. The crosses are carved with sequential scenes from the Bible but also show abstract design and ornaments. The meaning of the ring design is highly debated among researchers. There are various interpretations ranging from static reasons over boundary markers to a religious background. Some experts speculate that the ring is connected with pagan belief and assume that it represents the pagan icon of the sun (Powell, 2007; Stalley, 1994).

Other researchers think the design of the High Crosses is connected to present-day Egypt. In his book *The Forgotten Hermitage of Skellig Michael*, Horn and his colleagues present a tapestry weave unearthed in Egypt as evidence. The fabrication of this cloth is dated to the 5th or 6th century AD (Horn, Marshall, Rourke, O'Leary and Snodgrass, 2002).

Figure 16: Coptic Curtain, 5th/ 6th Century, Linen and Wool Tapestry Weave (Minneapolis Institute of Arts, 2016)

The curtain was made by a Christian Egyptian weaver to be used as a sanctuary curtain in a Coptic Church or monastery. With its many symbolic images, this curtain is among the most important early Christian fabrics surviving to this day. The combination of a wreath, traditionally awarded to winners of competitions, and the Latin cross, referring to Christ's crucifixion, symbolizes victory over death and the joy of everlasting life (Minneapolis Institute of Arts, 2016).

The cloth is sewn with a richly decorated ring cross, a design that became common on Irish cross slabs and High Crosses until the 8th century AD. Consequently, although the occurrence and the widespread popularity of High

Crosses are a distinctively Irish phenomenon, it is questionable whether the idea of the High Crosses actually has its origin in Ireland.

Another reference of a connection to the Mediterranean region is the find of 'The Faddan More Psalter' in 2006. It is a medieval Christian psalter (prayer book), which was discovered in the peat bog in Faddan More, in the north of the county Tipperary in Ireland (National Museum of Ireland, 2016a).

Figure 17: The Faddan More Psalter (National Museum of Ireland, 2016a)

Experts state that its papyrus-lined cover is direct evidence for the interlinkage between Ireland and the Mediterranean region 1,200 years ago. They argue that papyrus, a writing material produced out of reeds, was grown in the Eastern Mediterranean, especially in Egypt (Parsons, 2010; National Museum of Ireland, 2016a).

3.1.6 Saint Patrick's Bell

According to the National Museum of Ireland, the bell is reputed to have belonged to St. Patrick who supposedly lived at the end of the fourth or in the fifth century and who is probably the most famous saint in Ireland (please also see this chapter, Section 3.2.2) and is frequently mentioned in written sources.

Figure 18: The Bell of St. Patrick, AD 8th/ 9th Century, Armagh, Co. Armagh (National Museum of Ireland, 2016b)

The bell is made of iron and bronze and is stored in a valuable artistically designed shrine made of gold and silver.

Figure 19: Shrine of St. Patrick's Bell, Front View, Side View and Back View, Approximately AD 1100, Armagh, Co. Armagh (Paor, L. de, 1978)

The shrine is decorated with a ringed cross and elongated beasts intertwined with ribbon-bodied snakes which makes it an authentic relict of Irish Christian metal work with excellent Celtic style artwork (Paor, L. de, 1978; National Museum of Ireland, 2016b).

Some sources state, that this or a similar kind of a bell could have been used by St. Patrick and buried with him in his grave. The Annals of Ulster for the year AD 552 record that three relics from St. Patrick's tomb were removed, one of them being a bell (Paor, L. de, 1978). However, the Museum of Ireland dates the bell for the 8th/ 9th century and therefore not less than at least 200 years after St. Patrick's death.

Nevertheless, this bell and its shrine is such important because about many artefacts, e.g. as the 'Faddan More Psalter' do not exist proven facts about who crafted them, who used them, or how they came to be hidden away for centuries before their discovery. However, Saint Patrick's Bell and Bell Shrine is one noteworthy exception. The bell shrine has a documented history. The inscription on the shrine shows the names of the craftsmen, the keeper of the bell, and the king who commissioned the shrine and lived between AD 1094 and AD 1121 and thus, indicates that it was manufactured around AD 1100. Moreover, the history can be clearly traced because since the putative date of manufacturing of the shrine, it has never been lost sight of. These artefacts had a comprehensively keepers in succeeding generations its custody was continued in the same family until the end of the 19th century (National Museum of Ireland, 2016b).

3.2 Heroes

Some heroes, who are highly important in Irish culture and thus provide guidelines for a generally recognized concept of morality in Irish society, and other characters, who have contributed significantly to influencing Irish history through their work, and therefore can also be considered as heroes, are briefly introduced in the following.

3.2.1 The Mythological Hero Cú Chulainn

Irish legends tell the story of the mythical warrior Cú Chulainn who is a well-known and famous hero in Ireland. Cú Chulainn was the son of a god. When he was born his name was Sétanta. When he was a little boy, he slew a guard dog that had attacked him. This dog belonged to a smith called Culann. When the smith lamented the loss of his dog, Sétanta offered to assume the protection of the smith in lieu of the dog and was henceforth called Cú Chulainn – Irish for 'hound of Culann'. He was trained by Scáthach, a supernatural warrior princess, who made him invincible. His outstanding skills in the use of arms, his supernatural skills, as well as his exceptional courage enhanced his status as a hero. Cú Chulainn boasted with his supernatural skills by stating "[w]hen he is weakest his strength is that of twenty" (Squire, 1910, p. 185). However, in a battle which would become his last, he was duped by his enemies and the magic of his invincibility was broken so that he was mortally wounded. With his last energy, he tied himself to a menhir so that he died in a standing position. His enemies did not realize he was dead until a crow started pecking on him (Squire, 1910; ui Ógáin, 2003).

In 1916, the General Post Office (GPO) in Dublin became the headquarters of the rebels of the Easter Rising when the proclamation of the Irish Republic was read out from its steps. Therefore, the GPO became a symbol of Irish nationalism. The bronze statue 'The Death of Cuchulainn' was installed commemorating the victims of the Easter Rising (Lalor, 2003).

The GPO is the symbolic birthplace of the republic and Cú Chulainn is one of the greatest Irish heroes. Thus, the statue was erected in memory of the fallen heroes of the Easter Rising.

Figure 20: Bronze Sculpture of Cu Chulainn in the GPO, Dublin (Lynch, 2003, p. 1090)

3.2.2 St. Patrick (4th/ 5th Century)

There are historical facts and fiction. St. Patrick actually existed but a lot of the information about him, for example about his birthplace or the year of his death, does not consist of assured facts. For instance, Binchy states that the most prominent years which were given for St. Patrick´s death, 461 and 493 AD, are both wrong and that he surely died before 431 AD (Binchy, 1962).

There are two documents which historians agree were written by him and serve as main sources. The first document is a letter from St. Patrick addressed to the British tyrant Coroticus. He and his soldiers kidnapped and killed many of St. Patrick's Christian converts (Freeman, 2014). The second document is his profession of faith written in the form of an autobiography – *Confessio*. In the latter he writes that his father is from Bannauem Taburniae and that he too lived there until the age of 16 (Saint Patrick, 2013). Unfortunately, this place is unknown today and there are cities in both Wales and Scotland with similar names. So people speculate that any of these places could be the birthplace of St. Patrick. In any case, he was not Irish but a Briton. References for this can be found in his autobiography *Confessio* where he writes that he is "again in Britain with my parents [kinsfolk]" (Saint Patrick, 2011, p. 9). He was raised Catholic but was not deeply religious in his early years. At the age of 16, he was abducted by pirates and brought to Ireland. In captivity he had to tend flocks and during this time of hardship he found God. He managed to escape, fled Ireland and started studying as a monk in a monastery. He was then ordinated and went back to Ireland as a missionary (Saint Patrick, 2011). St. Patrick is surrounded by innumerable legends and myths that have grown throughout the centuries.

The absence of snakes in Ireland led to the legend of them having been banished by St. Patrick (Robinson, 1842). The legend says that St. Patrick chased them all into the ocean after they attacked him during a 40-day period of fasting. In fact, it is more likely that in post-glacial Ireland there never were any snakes. Ireland is an island which makes it impossible for snakes to immigrate. Snakes often represent evil in Christian literature, for instance in the *Book of Genesis* in the Old Testament where a snake persuades Eve to eat from the forbidden apple. When St. Patrick is said to have driven the snakes out of Ireland it also symbolizes that he drove the pagan belief, considered evil by the Catholic Church, out of Ireland (Roach, 2014; Owen, 2014).

In the following, some reasons for his popularity are mentioned. The fact that documents exist which are agreed by many experts to have been actually written by St. Patrick himself gives him a huge amount of credibility. Further, there are more documents which are based on St. Patrick's work. The monasteries that were founded by him were places of learning. The monks were highly sophisticated and continued to constantly improve their skills. For instance, the monks created some of the most impressive books existing to this day with artistic pictures and historically valuable information about that time. The three most important books are the *Book of Durrow*, the *Book of Armagh*, and the *Book of Kells*. All of them are stored at Trinity College in Dublin today.

Another aspect why St. Patrick became extraordinarily famous is for political reasons. In the 7th century, the monasteries strived for power and wealth. The Church of Armagh wanted to become the primary center of Christianity in Ireland and its clerics supported the church in order to reach this goal. For instance, the monk Muirchú and the bishop Tírechán wrote about the life and acts of St. Patrick and at the same time fostered the interests of Armagh (Bury, 1902). St. Patrick was enhanced by assigning worked wonders and superhuman actions to him. It is also impossible that St. Patrick founded all the monasteries and churches within one lifetime as documented in the ecclesiastical annals. Consequently, the doings of other missionaries must have been ascribed to St. Patrick. Further, in the *Book of Armagh*, substantial lines were demonstrably extinguished in order to present St. Patrick as the most successful proselytizer and founder of monasteries in Ireland (Board of Trinity College Dublin, 2011). Although there is no direct evidence connecting Patrick with Armagh, the writings of clerics describe him as founder of the Church of Armagh. The foundation by a saint was meant to strengthen Armagh's divine right to religious primacy in Ireland. As Armagh rose in importance, smaller monasteries and churches paid tributes or taxes in order to place themselves under the protection of Armagh and this in turn added to the wealth of Armagh (McCaffrey and Eaton, 2002). As Armagh's power and wealth grew, its founder also became more import and famous. As a consequence, St. Patrick and Armagh were inevitably interconnected. To the present day, the Roman Catholic Church and the Protestant Church of Ireland each have their primacies there and both are named after St. Patrick and both churches claim to have descended from him.

Furthermore, religiously fortified legitimations for fragile power claims are an essential strategy in unstable times to enforce personal interests. The Uí Néill, one of the most powerful families of that time, strove for more power by expanding their territory and taking over the area of Armagh. If they were to be the dominant dynasty in Ireland, their own province Ulster would have to be the most important and in order to achieve this goal the Uí Néill strengthened the position of the Church of Armagh. History shows that they actually did become the most powerful family for the next few hundred years (McCaffrey and Eaton, 2002).

One of the answers to the question of St. Patrick's success might be that he was able to speak the language of the people as opposed to his predecessors. He also became familiar with the details of Druidism and made concessions. Instead of enforcing definite church doctrines he incorporated pre-Christian philosophies and traditions into the Christianity he preached thereby combining the religious ideas of non-Christians with Christian thinking. St. Patrick allowed non-Christians to hold onto their traditions but encouraged them to do this in a Christian way. Further, St. Patrick's tactic included Christianizing the tribal chief so that the subordinates had to follow (Moran, 1913).

Ecclesiastical documents claim that St. Patrick consecrated approximately 350 bishops and founded innumerable monasteries and churches throughout the whole country (Moran, 1913). The wandering monks traveled around in the whole county but also abroad on the European continent to convert people to Christianity. These measures ensured the continuance of Christianity in Ireland also after St. Patrick's death. In summary, he gave Christianity a steady basis in a country with unstable political conditions. Nevertheless, after St. Patrick's death, the vast majority of Ireland was still pagan (McCaffrey and Eaton, 2002).

St. Patrick is today the national saint of Ireland and a symbol of universal Irishness. The reason for the feast – St. Patrick's Day – in honor of St. Patrick, celebrated on March 17, is therefore more a motivation to celebrate national or ethnic identity than the celebration of a religious feast (McCaffrey and Eaton, 2002).

3.2.3 Brian Boru (roughly 941–1014)

Brian Boru was born in Munster in the second quarter of the 10th century as son of a king but his family was of no great distinction. He was raised in an Ireland where political power was dominated by the Uí Néill, the only great dynasty of the time. Although about half a dozen provincial rulers would have been powerful enough to achieve national supremacy, the Uí Néill were the ruling dynasty. They held exclusive rights to a place called Tara. This place was already considered sacred among the ancient Irish people and therefore had always been the center of power. This gave the Uí Néill the exclusive claim to kingship (Duffy, 2014b). All his life Brian Boru waged war against the Uí Néill in order to undermine their power, and he finally succeeded in 1002, when the Uí Néill high king succumbed to him. This event was a sensation in Irish history and catapulted Brian Boru to the status of a shining hero. Someone from outside the ruling dynasty had raised a claim to the high kingship and had not only beaten the most powerful family but also prevailed over divine right. This fundamentally altered the rules of Irish political history. Brian Boru had permanently broken Uí Néill dominance of the high-kingship in Ireland. However, his supremacy was contested and finally led to the Battle of Clontarf in which his army was victorious, but Brian Boru and his son were killed so that Ireland lost their high king. Brian Boru unified Ireland and became the only monarch who ruled over the entire country. His victory at this final battle radically changed the politics of the time and had major effects on the future of the Irish (Duffy, 2014b; Cavendish, 2014).

As mentioned above, Brian Boru fought against the king of Leinster who was supported through an alliance with the Vikings. However, in the perception of later generations of Irish people, Brian Boru became a hero because he led his people to victory over the would-be Viking conquerors. He was celebrated for securing people's freedom from foreign domination and for the unification of Ireland, even though it was not peaceful in spite of the unification (Chatterton Newman, 2011).

The Battle of Clontarf took place on Good Friday and the Irish monk and annalist Marianus Scottus wrote that Brian Boru was killed during his Easter prayer in his tent – so he died focused on God and not on the battle field (Duffy, 2014c; Grant, 2011; Chatterton Newman, 2011). As a result, Christians compared Brian Boru's death to the death of Jesus Christ who saved humankind by sacrificing his life. As a consequence, Brian became a saintly figure (Downham, 2005; Duffy, 2014a; Duffy, 2014b). In addition to this, Brian Boru received backing from the Monastery of Armagh, the most important monastery in Ireland, located in Ulster. The *Book of Armagh* states that when Brian Boru "… arrived at Armagh… [he] presented a golden ring of twenty ounces as an offering on St. Patrick's altar" (Gwynn, 1913, p. 103). This donation secured Brian the support of Armagh and enhanced his status through sacred right.

3.2.4 *Charles Stewart Parnell (1846–1891)*

Figure 21: Charles Stewart Parnell, 'uncrowned king of Ireland' (McCaffrey, 2006, p. 183)

Charles Stewart Parnell was Irish and came from a wealthy family. He was educated at English boarding schools and attended college in Cambridge. However, he bore an intense dislike and disrespect for the English. In 1874, he decided to fight for Home Rule – the right of self-governance (Callanan, 2003). He became one of the driving forces to establish the National Land League which represented the interests of the tenants whose central concerns were the fixity of tenure and fair rents. In 1875, he was elected to Parliament and 4 years later, he became leader of the Irish party. He became famous for his tactic of boycotting as already explained above (please see Chapter Three, Section 2.4) (McCaffrey, 2006).

Parnell was elevated to an iconic status. Although, Parnell never achieved Home Rule, he was honored by the Irish people. There were various attempts to counter his iconic status by the British Press, British politicians, and, above all, the Catholic Church with the aim of discrediting Parnell and destroying his good reputation. Nevertheless, he became a hero for the Irish people. His activities gave an impetus to the idea of Home Rule which would have lasting implications (McCaffrey, 2006; Kee, 2000).

3.2.5 Éamon de Valera (1882–1975)

Figure 22: Éamon de Valera in 1919/ 1920 (Fanning, 2015, picture bonuses between p. 148 and p. 149)

Éamon de Valera was born in New York, in 1882 as the child of an Irish emigrant mother who met his Spanish-born father in New York. He was taken to Ireland when his father died in 1884 and grew up in Limerick. When he made his first public appearance Ireland was part of United Kingdom. Despite his American descent, de Valera was a passionate advocate for Ireland's independence and also an ardent supporter of Irish tradition and language. For instance, he established a policy requiring the use of the Irish language wherever possible and as mandatory for state education and employment in the civil service. It is his merit that Irish is specified as the first language in the constitution (Fanning, 2015).

He took on a military role as commander in the Easter Rising of 1916 and escaped execution due to an accumulation of fortunate circumstances. One of them was that Éamon de Valera was still politically unknown at this time. His American citizenship also helped delay his execution and when the executions became public and caused growing public discontent, his execution was cancelled. So, as one of few, he managed to survive the Easter Rising and then began a career as politician.

With the Anglo-Irish Treaty of 1921, Ireland was granted partial independence as a dominion of the United Kingdom called the Irish Free State. De Valera still ardently opposed the treaty and continued to demand an independent republic. He is considered a divisive figure because his petulant rejection of the treaty enforced the Civil War of 1921–1922. In addition to this, his policy led to the Economic War (1932–1938) and his neutrality in World War II was also controversially discussed. However, with his iron will to achieve independence from the United Kingdom, he is also described as the most remarkable man in the history of modern Ireland. He is ascribed the role of the protector of Irish nationalism and creator of the Irish nation (Fanning, 2015).

In 1959, he was elected President of Ireland and in 1966, he was re-elected for another seven years. He was a skillful speaker and became an iconic leader who significantly influenced Irish politics on the country's way to independence. He dominated Irish politics for nearly 50 years. De Valera's career spanned the period of Ireland's modern cultural and national transformation with him being a key figure in this process of transformation. His supporters considered Éamon de Valera as the driving force without whom Ireland would probably not have achieved independence in such a short time making him a hero of national liberation. In retrospect, however, he is also a very controversially discussed character, not least because of his political attitude during World War II (Kinealy, 2004; Fanning, 2015; Rolleston Gwynn, 2016).

3.3 Rituals

Rituals are able to unite a social group independent of individual differences in beliefs or strength of convictions (Edles and Appelrouth, 2015). They generate and maintain the collective consciousness of the community (Durkheim, 2008). Rituals are social and religious ceremonies, as mentioned before (Hofstede, 2003; Hofstede et al., 2010). Some of the most important Irish rituals are illustrated below.

3.3.1 St. Patrick's Day

St. Patrick's Day is celebrated in Ireland on March 17 and in many other countries all over the world, especially in countries with a large number of Irish immigrants, such as the USA. A great part of those who emigrated during the years of the Great Famine migrated into the United States. March 17 is the official date of St. Patrick's death even though this date is not confirmed by assured facts (McCaffrey, 2006).

In 1607, 1100 years after St. Patrick lived, the day was listed as a saint's day in the Irish legal calendar and thus became a religious event with St. Patrick also elevated to the status of patron saint of Ireland. Although St. Patrick was acclaimed locally, the Vatican later endorsed and encouraged the worship of St. Patrick because his episcopal appointment strengthened the Pope's claim to jurisdiction over the Celtic Church. In 1631, Pope Urban VIII added the feast of St. Patrick to the calendar of the church. St. Patrick's Day established itself in the 17th century as a consensual festival – a both ecclesiastical and civil celebration with market stalls of food and drink, music, and dance. Green ribbons and shamrocks have been worn on St. Patrick's Day since at least the 1680s (Cronin and Adair, 2006).

Irish intellectuals who traveled and settled on the European continent during the centuries are referred to as having started the tradition, probably as a way of staying connected to their home country (McCaffrey and Eaton, 2002). In this way, emigrants held on to their traditions. By the end of the 17th century, St. Patrick's Day became increasingly famous as a day of feast for all ranks of society with established customs and emblems. In the wake of the Act of Union, St. Patrick's Day again became a key date in the annual social calendar because the day enabled the Irish to show united Irishness. Moreover, St. Patrick's Day represents the Irish people the way they wish to see themselves – as a pleasant, hospitable, public-spirited, and united people. Green clothes, common symbols, such as the shamrock, and vast parades suggest uniformity of sentiment and conceal divisions within the Irish community (Cronin and Adair, 2006). "Such anonymity can be advantageous: if 'everyone' is entitled to be green on St. Patrick's Day, there is less need to divide people along religious and political lines. The celebrations can, therefore, provide an annual sense of group cohesion" (Cronin and Adair, 2006, p. 249).

Even today, St. Patrick's Day is celebrated on a grand scale, extraordinarily grandiose in the USA. Rivers, fountains, and lakes are dyed green, for instance, the Chicago River. St. Patrick's Day arouses powerful emotions among the Irish around the world – no matter where they are or who they are. The feast is celebrated by those who have an Irish heritage, by those who claim to be Irish, and also by many non-Irish. It is far more than merely a Catholic festival – it is a mainstream event involving families and friends, companies, schools, civic groups, and the media (Cronin and Adair, 2006). Celebrating St. Patrick's Day has become a way to confirm ethnic identity and to create bonds of solidarity (Roach, 2014). A sentence frequently heard on the streets on St. Patrick's Day is: 'American by birth – Irish by the Grace of God'. This sentence symbolizes enormous pride, regained confidence, a sense of self, and demonstrates people's ties to their home country and their place in the world.

St. Patrick's Day has become increasingly commercialized since the end of the World War II and today is a commercially important and successful entertainment event (Cronin and Adair, 2006).

3.3.2 St. Brighid's Day

St. Brighid's Day, also called 'Imbolc,' is well-documented in the folk customs of Ireland, as well as the Western Isles and Western Highlands of Scotland. The feast marks the resumption of agricultural work after the winter season. This feast is protected by St. Brighid, the patron saint of agriculture and cattle, and is celebrated starting on the eve of the night of February 1 (Maier, 2001). St. Brighid is the second important saint after St. Patrick and probably originated from the Celtic divinity Brigantia (Ó Riain, 2003). The eve before St. Brighid's Day was marked by the same belief that households would be visited by the saint and that tokens of welcome should be put out for her. Imbolc appears as a feast but without much mysterious significance attached to it in contrast to Samhain. Imbolc was probably integrated into the Christian calendar in the form of Candlemas (Hutton, 1993).

3.3.3 Beltane

In pre-Christian Europe, most important holidays were celebrated on the eve before the actual date of the shift from one season to the next (Arnold, 2001). The 'May Day Eve' feast Beltane (of which various other spellings exist, such as Beltain, Beltainne, Beltaine, Bealtaine, Beltany, Beltine) is celebrated starting on the eve of the night of April 30 and then also on May 1. The feast marks the beginning of the summer season, the time of sowing, and the time when cattle were driven up to the pastures (Maier, 2001). It was ardently celebrated across all of the British Isles and there is evidence that in Britain it was even more important than Samhain. In general, May Day was a great folk festival from Ireland to Russia. Bonfires were more important in Ireland and the Scottish Highlands, whereas the maypole was more important in England, Wales, Cornwall, and southern Scotland. This may reflect the spread of maypoles from the continent during the middle ages (Hutton, 1993; Monaghan, 2004).

3.3.4 Lughnasadh

Lughnasadh, also Lughnasad, Lughnasa, Lugnasad, Lúnasa, was celebrated starting on the eve of the night of July 31 and then continued on August 1. It marked the end of summer and the beginning of the harvest season in which the reaping of grain took place (Hutton, 1993; Maier, 2001). The Irish came together on Lughnasadh near lakes, rivers and wells or on hills. Festive activities included eating the first meal of the year's new food crop, taking part in sports activities, and picking bilberries. The custom also existed on the Isle of Man, in Cornwall, Wales, and in northern England (MacNeill, 1982).

3.3.5 Samhain

Irish records document the distinction between winter time and summer time based on the sun year. Samhain is also called 'Night of the Spirits,' 'Feast of the Dead,' 'All Hallow's Eve,' 'Festival of the Harvest' and has been given many other names of which, however, the most well-known is 'Halloween'. The feast is celebrated on the night of October 31 (Arnold, 2001). It marks the beginning of the winter season and is one of the most important seasonal festivals on the British Isles. The classification of this feast and other important feasts, mentioned above, is linked to agriculture and consequently to climatic conditions in Ireland (Maier, 2001). Christianity assimilated the worship of the dead into the Christian calendar with 'All Saints' on November 1.

In ancient Irish belief, the feast marks not only the division of the year between summer and winter but also the division between 'this world' and the 'otherworld' which is at its thinnest at Samhain, allowing spirits to pass through the 'otherworld' into the world of the living. At this time, when the earthly world of the living becomes interwoven with the 'otherworld,' which not only contains the spirits of the departed, but also gods, fairies, and other supernatural beings, people wear costumes and masks to disguise themselves so that they are not recognized by harmful spirits (Gilroy, 2000). There is plenty of evidence for the importance of Samhain in Ireland but also, for instance, in Wales and Cornwall. In contrast, no comparable celebrations associated with October 31 existed in most of England and parts of Scotland. Presumably, it was a feast known all over the Iron Age British Isles with no equivalent among the Anglo-Saxon invaders. Irish immigrants, fleeing the Great Famine, brought this custom to the United States of America, where it was enthusiastically adopted as Halloween and the wearing of costumes and masks to ward off harmful spirits survived. From there, the custom was transferred to Britain (Hutton, 1993).

According to *Statista*, an online statistic, market research and business intelligence portal, retail spending on Halloween products, such as costumes, decorations, toys, confectionery and other food and drink items rose in the United Kingdom from 2013 to 2017. In 2017, consumers in the United Kingdom spent a total of 400 million British pounds on Halloween products (Statista, 2018).

Customs on Halloween are, for example, the collection of candy by children. In former times, the Irish believed that ghosts needed some sort of appeasement in the form of ritual offerings on Samhain. If the ghost accepted the offering it was benevolent but if the offering was withdrawn the ghost became malevolent and misfortune would befall the household in the following year. Gilroy (2000) speculated that some vestiges of this tradition survived in the modern Halloween custom of 'trick or treat'. Dressed-up children knock on a household's door and ask for treats, usually in the form of candy, and threaten to play a trick on the owner if they receive nothing. The treat represents the ritual offering whereas the trick represents the malevolent consequences of inadequately appeasing the ancestral ghost (Gilroy, 2000).

3.3.6 Bloomsday

With his novel *Ulysses*, published in 1922, James Joyce, a well-known Irish writer, created what some people regard as the greatest work of prose fiction ever written in the English language (Menand, 2012). The story is set in Dublin and describes the city as it actually was during the lifetime of James Joyce. The story tells the events of June 16, 1904 from the perspective of the main character Leopold Bloom and his experiences on that day. On Bloomsday – the feast is named after the main character – fans of the novel visit the real places in the story, sometimes dressed-up like the main character Leopold Bloom wearing his bowler hat or his wife Molly in her petticoats, or in the fashion of other novel characters. The fans reenact the actions of the characters in the book, such as buying lemon soap in Sweny's pharmacy. This pharmacy exists in the form of a non-profit organization today and is maintained by volunteers wanting to preserve the shop as it was at the time when Ulysses was written (Joyce, 2013; Kiberd, 2009). James Joyce chose June 16, 1904 as the date for the events in his novel because he connected a special experience with his girlfriend to it (Brown, 2003). Professor of Anglo-Irish Literature Kiberd (2009) speculates that the celebration of Bloomsday may be an attempt by Dubliners to reassert a lost sense of community (Kiberd, 2009).

3.4 Resume of the Irish Onion

Irish culture reveals itself in the visible elements explained above. The Irish Onion illustrates how Irish culture becomes manifest on different levels of depth. Cultural change can be fast for the outer layers, characterized as 'practices'. These are the visible part of cultures. People can learn new practices throughout their whole life, for example, when older people learn how to use the internet and acquire new symbols, such as icons, meet new heroes, and communicate through new rituals (Hofstede et al., 2010). Therefore, Irish history explains how the meaning of the harp became a symbol for Ireland. It also shows how this symbol has started to crumble in recent years. Irish heroes are honored because in the examples they fought for Ireland's independence. Irish history shows that the issue of independence is particularly important for the Irish people who have suffered centuries of oppression. The Irish festivals, such as Samhain, are based on pagan festivals but were integrated in the Christian calendar. This shows that paganism further exists even when the original pagan people have become extinct. Consequently, without the knowledge of Irish history, Irish culture cannot be understood.

Cultural change is slow for the core of the onion model. The core of the Irish Onion consists of the values of the Irish. They are learned during childhood and it is assumed that in the majority of the cases, these values are taught by the parents. Therefore, the values of a society are quite stable regardless of changes in practices. Values remain invisible until revealed in behavior (Hofstede, 2003; Hofstede et al., 2010). Thus, according to Brislin (1993), culture influences human behavior. He states that the knowledge of specific aspects of culture can help to analyze human behavior. The behavior, in turn, influences the course of history.

Chapter 4: The Economy of Ireland

There are various factors that highlight the importance of taking into consideration Irish economic history (Haughton, 1995). Looking at economic history creates awareness for the fragility of economic growth and its historical continuity of booms and breakdowns (Reinhart and Rogoff, 2009). Researchers warn against tunnel vision and state that it is important to take into account both long-term perspective and lateral linkage. Lee (1989) criticizes that often non-economic factors are excluded from economic analysis. Basic knowledge of economic development is required for the analysis in Chapter Six which revealed the environmental influences contributing to the fall of the Celtic Tiger.

1 Some Essential Macroeconomic Aggregates

Here, some important economic terms used in the following will be briefly explained.

The gross domestic product (GDP) measures the total performance of an economy. The Organization for Economic Cooperation and Development (OECD) states that the GDP is the most frequently used indicator in national accounts. Further, the organization argues that the GDP lies at the heart of the entire system of national accounts. Thus, the GDP is one of the main macroeconomic variables and is agreed to be internationally defined as

> an aggregate measure of production equal to the sum of the gross values added of all resident institutional units engaged in production (plus any taxes, and minus any subsidies, on products not included in the value of their outputs). It is also equal to the sum of the final uses of goods and services measured in purchasers' prices, less the value of imports of goods and services. It is also equal to the sum of primary incomes distributed by resident producer units (Lequiller and Blades, 2014, p. 507)

Therefore, the GDP illustrates all the output or production carried out by all the firms, non-profit institutions, government bodies, and households in a given country during a given period of time, regardless of the type of goods and services produced, provided that the production takes place within a country's boundaries. Usually, it is calculated quarterly or annually (Lequiller and Blades, 2014). However, the national accounts must distinguish whether the change in the observed monetary aggregates results from a change in the quantities produced or from a change in prices because an increase in quantity is generally good while rising prices indicate inflation (Lequiller and Blades, 2014).

The problem of changing price levels is solved by the measure of the 'real GDP'. Real GDP takes into account the fact that not only the added value can change from one period to the next, but also prices of the traded products can change from one period to the next. Real GDP is calculated by comparing the value of all goods sold at the prices of a reference or base year. The variation in real GDP shows a percentage change in the market value, based on the reference year, of all final goods and services produced within a country in a given period of time. This eliminates the distorting effect of price changes on GDP (Barro and Grilli, 1996; Hardes, Schmitz and Uhly, 2002; World Bank Group, 2017a).

The real GDP, serves as an indicator for the economic development of national economies and is therefore, the most important figure of national accounts (Statistisches Bundesamt, 2013; Lequiller and Blades, 2014).

In order to summarize a country's entire economic activity within a set of internally consistent tables, national accounts have to rely on significant estimates and adopt conventions that are sometimes arbitrary. It is necessary to be aware of these conventions, such as households' internal production, i.e. cooking and cleaning, or underground economy, such as illicit employment, which are not covered in the national accounts (Lequiller and Blades, 2014).

In the case of the Irish economy, experts argue that the official GDP statistics are artificially inflated. They claim that stated profits of multinational companies are included in Ireland's GDP and further that multinational companies artificially boost these profits through 'transfer pricing' (Haughton, 1998; Ó Gráda and O'Rourke, 1995).

Approximately two-thirds of the world's cross-border trade accounts for trade payables between legal entities within an enterprise. The financial valuation of these intercompany transactions is the transfer price. Through internationalization and globalization, the issue transfer pricing is becoming increasingly important (Rieke, 2015). The transfer price is the price for internally exchanged goods, services, licenses, and loans. It is possible to shift profits between several legal entities within a company through transfer pricing. This can be achieved by underpricing the inputs or overvaluing the exports (Haughton, 1998). Companies which operate in different countries strive to shift most of their profits into the country with the lowest tax charges (Yaropolov, 2014; Leubecher, 2014). Transfer pricing is a common and legal instrument used for tax avoidance by multinational companies. Consequently, it is a source of harmful tax competition between the European Member States (Aujean, 2001). Ireland benefit from its very low tax policy. Therefore, multinational companies have an interest in making their profits 'appear' in Ireland (Haughton, 1998).

Employment/ unemployment is also an important economic factor. The unemployment rate, expressed here in percent of total labor force, refers to the share of the labor force that is without work but available for and actively looking for employment (World Bank Group, 2017b; Horvath, 2013). The rate provides an indication of the consumer demand. For instance, a high and constant rate of unemployment is an indication of structural unemployment. This means a sustained change in demand for employees in individual industries, for instance due to the use of new technologies (Barro and Grilli, 1996; Hardes et al., 2002). Further, the emergence of a recession involves a phase of gradually rising unemployment and respectively falling employment (Barro and Grilli, 1996).

Government debt as a percentage of GDP is the amount of national debt a country has in percentage of its GDP. Government debt is the capital owed by the central government to its creditors. The lower the debt-to-GDP ratio, the more likely it is that the country will be able to repay its debt. Furthermore, the country is more likely to satisfy its debt obligations (Minter, 2013; Barro and Grilli, 1996). Thus, government debt as a percent of GDP is used by investors to measure a country's ability to make future payments on its debt. Therefore, a country's borrowing costs and government bond yields are affected (Fedec and Sousa, 2012). According to the Maastricht Treaty (Art. 126 AEUV), the government debt should be limited to 60% of the GDP (Steindorff, 2013; Barro and Grilli, 1996).

The inflation as measured by the consumer price index sheds light on the increase in prices of consumer goods. The higher the prices are, the lower the purchasing power of the consumers is. The consumer price index (CPI) measures changes in the price level of consumer goods and services in a predetermined market basket purchased by households. The price changes of consumer goods are compared periodically. The items are weighted according to their importance. For instance, the highest weights are applied to food, medical care, and housing (Barro and Grilli, 1996; Hardes et al., 2002; Jasper, 2013; World Bank Group, 2017c).

An interest rate is the cost or price of borrowing, or the gain from lending, normally expressed as an annual percentage amount (Lequiller and Blades, 2014). The real interest rate is the interest rate adjusted to inflation. The real interest rate is used in various economic theories to explain different phenomena, for instance economic bubbles. When the rate of real interest is high, i.e. demand for credit is high, money will, with all other things being equal, move from investment and consumption to savings. By contrast, when the real interest rate is low, demand will move from savings to investment and consumption (World Bank Group, 2017d). Shifts in house prices can be adequately represented by how much an individual can borrow based on the prevailing disposable income and interest rates (McQuinn and O'Reilly, 2006).

2 Background Influences

In the following, some background influences on the Irish crisis will be mentioned in order to help gain a better understanding of the global economic environment in which the Irish crisis developed.

In general, crises have existed since the invention of money and the existence of financial markets. "The monetary history of the last four hundred years has been replete with financial crises" (Kindleberger and Aliber, 2005, p. 275). There are many different types of crisis, for instance the financial crisis that recurs over the centuries until today, the banking crisis, the exchange rate crisis or the sovereign debt crisis, just to mention a few. Some types can easily be identified, such as the inflation crisis. In the case of other crises, more qualitative and judgmental analysis is required (For further discussion of crises, their definition, distinction, and detection see Reinhart and Rogoff's *This Time is Different: Eight Centuries of Financial Folly* or Kindleberger and Aliber's, *Manias, Panics, and Crashes: A History of Financial Crises*) (Reinhart and Rogoff, 2009; Kindleberger and Aliber, 2005; Laeven and Valencia, 2008).

The most recent crisis is the global financial crisis of 2007 to 2009. It is the result of a speculative bubble in the housing market that began to burst in the United States of America in 2006 and has caused ruptures across many other countries in the form of financial failures and finally led to a global credit crisis (Shiller, 2008). A seemingly endless amount of literature examining the origins and consequences of the recent U.S. financial crisis is available (For instance see *The Financial Crisis Inquiry Report* in which the Financial Crisis Inquiry Commission (FCIC) appointed by U.S. Congress determined the causes of the recent financial crisis. For consequences and recommendations of regulatory reforms see *Balancing the Banks: Global Lessons from the Financial Crisis* by Dewatripont, Rochet, and Tirole) (United States, 2011; Dewatripont, Rochet and Tirole, 2010). Many different factors that contributed to the crisis were identified in various examinations, for instance by the FCIC.

Essentially, a speculative bubble which was fostered by a policy of low interest rates and lax regulation was crucial for the occurrence and extent of the crisis. Moreover, the commission considered the rating agencies to have played a decisive role in the United States in significantly having increased the crisis potential (United States, 2011).

It is important to emphasize the international factors that played a major role in the timing of Ireland's economic downturn because in 2008 there was not merely an Irish domestic financial crisis. This event was part of the global financial crisis of 2008, which involved a near collapse of the US financial system following the bankruptcy of many financial institutions in the US, such as, among others, Lehman Brothers (Donovan and Murphy, 2014). Tens of thousands of banks, insurance companies, hedge funds, pension funds, but also small investors, churches, and counties worldwide were interlinked with Lehman Brothers (Lennihan, 2010; Brinkbäumer, Goos, Hornig, Ludwig and Pauly, 2009). It is estimated that Lehman Brothers left a US $ 200 billion debt (FTD, 2009). The consequences of the bankruptcy of Lehmann Brothers were not limited to the US. This development acutely intensified shocks to the global real economy and enormously increased worldwide financial shocks. In the wake of the crisis, banks mistrusted each other in financial dealings, resulting in significantly fewer loans being lent worldwide. Immediately, a run on the British bank Northern Rock began and progressed to the major difficulties experienced by the world's biggest bank, the Royal Bank of Scotland, a very sizeable lender to the Irish banking system. This was followed by a banking crisis in Iceland and a slowly developing property and banking crisis in Spain. At the same time, the economy in Greece also crumbled, just to mention a few examples (Donovan and Murphy, 2014).

In light of the many different factors regarding the origins, effects, and consequences of the U.S. real estate crisis, a detailed illustration would clearly go beyond the scope of this dissertation. Although there are differences between the emergence and the course of the U.S. and Irish crisis, the central trigger in both cases was a speculative bubble.

Therefore, a speculative bubble is explained below, which is then followed by a short explanation of the US economy giving basic knowledge about the contributing factors to Ireland's economic crisis.

2.1 Contributing Factors to the U.S. Housing Bubble

The fact that crises have existed for a long time is proven by the fact that one of the first speculative bubbles is historically documented by the first medium that published news on a grand scale, a newspaper regularly printed since the early 1600s. Although the record of these early newspapers is lost for the most part, it is known that it regularly reported on the 'Dutch tulip mania' from 1634–1637

(Kindleberger and Aliber, 2005; Shiller, 2000; Garber, 1990; Garber, 2000). Speculative bubbles develop under the prerequisite of the interconnection of market participants and further the emergence of a perceived economic advantage that everybody wants to benefit from. This leads to a "market-determined asset price at odds with any reasonable economic explanation" (Garber, 1990, p. 35). A bubble is basically the uncontrolled overvaluation of a commodity, worsened by opportunist manipulation, and fundamentally based on consumer's belief that the commodity's price is spiraling upward. "Bubbles always implode; by definition a bubble involves a non-sustainable pattern of price changes or cash flows" (Kindleberger and Aliber, 2005, p. 1).

In the following, an explanation of some of the factors enabling and contributing to the occurrence of a speculative bubble in the U.S. and also affecting the Irish economy is given.

One reason for the U.S. housing bubble was the growing availability of subprime mortgage credit in the mid-2000s. Households were able to borrow higher multiples of income with lower required down payments. U.S. law obligates consumers buying real estate to take out insurance when the loan-to-value ratio is over 80%. This insurance is a so-called private mortgage insurance (PMI). In order to avoid paying for PMI because of a loan-to-value ratio in excess of 80%, consumers take out a second loan, the so-called piggyback loan of which the interest is tax-deductible. Consequently, taking out a piggyback loan is often advantageous for potential home buyers compared to taking out insurance.

In general, real estate is financed with own capital plus borrowed capital. When financing real estate with a piggyback loan instead, this results in total debt financing consisting of 80% mortgage loan plus 20% piggyback loan (Dewatripont et al., 2010).

In addition to this, the lack of possibility for sanctions on the U.S. financial markets encouraged the application for mortgage loans. In many states the real estate of the borrower is the only security for the creditor. Other assets of the borrower are exempt from the creditors' attachment. The homeowner mails his or her house keys to a mortgage lender due to an inability to meet mortgage payment obligations. When property values decrease, consumers who invest no or little equity do not have an incentive to service their interest rate and pay back their rates. They only lose their comparatively low share of equity and have to accept a low creditworthiness for a short period of time (Budzinski and Michler, 2014).

Households benefit from tax deductibility of interest paid on mortgages. As a consequence, the consumers were encouraged to increase their debt in order to purchase real estate (Calomiris, 2008). The president of the US also encouraged American households to buy homes. Indeed, there was little impetus to raise alarms about the increase of easy credit that was helping President George W. Bush to meet housing goals. Lindsay, the president's first chief economic adviser, concluded that no one wanted to stop the upcoming bubble, because it would have conflicted with the president's policies (Becker, Stolberg and Labaton, 2008).

Many subprime borrowers were also given easy credits with low rates for the first few years with rates sharply increasing afterwards. Initially low interest rates, so-called 'teaser rates,' lured the households making mortgage payments seem affordable for many.

Most mortgages have a fixed interest rate. Under adjustable-rate mortgages, borrowers usually have lower initial rates but face the risk of higher payments in case the rates in the broader economy rise. Greenspan, the Chairman of the Federal Reserve at the time, argued that homeowners who closed a contract with fixed interest rates were paying as much as 0.5% to 1.2% for protection against potential rate increases. In contrast, with an adjustable-rate mortgage, many homeowners could save a lot of money (Kirchhoff and Hagenbaugh, 2004). This indicates that Greenspan expected further economic growth.

The macroeconomic situation of the USA was judged very contrarily by economists: Greenspan and the former Secretary of the Treasury O'Neill were very optimistic. O'Neill described the current account deficit as a meaningless concept and recommended that political decision-makers should pay no attention to this (Economist, 2002). In contrast, Rajan, Chief Economist and Director of Research at the International Monetary Fund (IMF), published a working paper in 2005 in which he warned of a financial crisis (Rajan, 2005).

Although his warnings were not taken seriously, he was proven right. The beginning of the crisis in the USA was characterized by falling house prices, a decrease in the demand for houses, and an increase in mortgage defaults and home foreclosures. These events affected the construction sector and the negative effects spread quickly to other sectors of the economy (Campbell and Cocco, 2011).

Not least, the performance of Irish exports was weakened because of the downturn in the U.S. economy. Demand for exports from the large and therefore important trading partner, the USA, which constituted the bulk of total exports, declined significantly. Therefore, the export-oriented sector in Ireland began to lose its formerly dominant position for economic growth (Donovan and Murphy, 2014).

2.2 Stability Mechanisms in the U.S. – The Federal Reserve System (Fed)

At this point, the stability mechanisms should also be mentioned because it is the function of the Fed to provide security and prevent crisis. It can therefore be assumed that Greenspan's assessment of the situation had a certain impact.

In 1900, there had been calls for a central bank in order to establish a more stable monetary and financial system in the United States because individual banks stood separately with no mutual bonds between them. A central bank could have established such bonds (Rothbard, 1994). A panic in 1907 gave rise to bank runs that caused chaos in the banking system. In response to this event, Congress wrote the Federal Reserve Act to address these banking panics and it was signed by President Woodrow Wilson on December 1913. The Federal Reserve Act created the basis for establishing the Federal Reserve System (Fed). It was assigned several broad responsibilities, for instance fostering a sound banking system. The Fed serves as the central bank of the United States (Fox et al., 2005).

The federal system consists of the Board of Governors based in Washington D.C. as a central, governmental authority and twelve regional Federal Reserve Banks. This structure of the Fed is intended to provide an encompassing perspective on the economy and on economic activity in all parts of the United States. Whereas the Board of Governors is an autonomous government agency, the Federal Reserve Banks are set up like private corporations (Barro and Grilli, 1996; Fox et al., 2005).

On a critical side note, despite the existence of the Fed, the worst banking crisis of the USA occurred in the years between 1930 and 1933 when approximately 9,000 out of 25,000 banks were declared bankrupt (Barro and Grilli, 1996). Researchers assert that paradoxically, the financial crisis would not have been as bad as it was without the existence of the Fed. The banks of that time relied on the Fed and its involvement in case of emergency but the Fed did not intervene. The main reason is identified by Friedman and Schwartz (1963) as "limited understanding of the connection between bank failures, runs on banks, contraction of deposits, and weakness of the bond markets" (Friedman and Schwartz, 1963, p. 358). Further, most failures were recorded among smaller banks while the influential players in the system were big city bankers who considered the disappearance of smaller banks as their advantage because the less banks there were, the more customers they had for themselves. The comparatively few large banks that failed were regarded as unfortunate cases of bad management and therefore were considered as no matter for corrective actions by the central bank (Friedman and Schwartz, 1963).

In 2005, Fox et al. listed four general responsibilities of the Fed: First, the Fed leads the monetary policy by influencing monetary and credit conditions in order to maximize employment, stabilize prices, and hold moderate long-term interest rates. Second, the Fed supervises and regulates banking institutions in order to guarantee on the one hand the safety and soundness of the banking and financial system and on the other hand to protect the credit rights of consumers. Third, the Fed maintains the stability of the financial system. And finally, the Fed provides financial services to depository institutions, the U.S. government, and foreign official institutions, including playing a major role in operating the nation's payments system (Fox et al., 2005).

As it turned out, the stability mechanisms, such as the Fed, have failed. The reasons and indicators for improvement in order to ensure their functioning in the future are left to further research. The stability mechanisms in Ireland failed too. Some reasons for the Irish case are revealed below in the analysis in Chapter Six, Sections 2 to 5.

3 Economic Development of Ireland

A significant question relates to the conditions that allowed the crisis to emerge in Ireland, the reasons why the crisis took the form it did, and why it was so profound. The social and political environments and the ways in which they are embedded in the economic environment are crucial to understanding these issues (Ó Riain, 2014).

3.1 The Economic History of Ireland

In the 19th century, Ireland was a poverty-stricken, agricultural economy that had served as a source of cheap labor for booming cities in Britain and North America as a result of Britain's political and economic control over Ireland (Honohan and Walsh, 2002). The political and economic loosening of the ties between Ireland and Britain took its course with the signing of the Anglo-Irish Treaty which established the Irish Free State in 1922. However, as mentioned in Chapter Three, Section 1.6, it was not until 1949 that Ireland reached its full independence from Britain (Kinealy, 2006). Therefore, in this dissertation, the development of the Irish economy is examined beginning with the year 1949.

The economists Barro and Sala-i-Martin explained the existence of convergence in the sense that economies tend to grow faster in per capita terms when they are below the steady-state position. This means that the economy of poor states tends to grow faster than the economy of rich states if the countries are similar regarding structural parameters of preferences and technology. The speed of convergence gives the impression to be roughly the same – around 2% per year (Barro, Sala-i-Martin, 1992). However, their assumption seems to be inconsistent, in particular in relation to Ireland (Barro, 1991). The years from 1950 on show convergence in living standards across Europe with Ireland being a clear exception (Honohan and Walsh, 2002).

Whereas in the 1950s most Western European economies grew very quickly after WWII, Ireland's economic performance remained significantly below the European average with much lower real GDP growth rates. One reason for this is that Ireland struggled with emigration on a grand scale. Ireland's state of economic underdevelopment was reflected in the small share of people who worked in higher-productivity, i.e. nonagricultural employment. In Ireland, almost a quarter of all working people were engaged in the agricultural sector. In this sector, for instance income per capita was 40% lower in comparison to the United Kingdom (Honohan and Walsh, 2002). During the 1960s, the Irish government implemented policies that led to improvements in productivity because of the upcoming goal of joining the EEC in 1973. Policies moved away from protectionist trade and focused on encouraging export-oriented foreign direct investment (FDI)[1] (O'Connor, 2007a). Moreover, in 1967, universal free secondary education was introduced. Educational standards improved quickly and made way for employment outside the agricultural sector in fields that require a higher education. Additionally, a baby boom occurred in the 1970s. Thus, the depressed Ireland of the 1980s is represented by a very large population below working age. The influence of this demographic factor gradually eased over time so that by the late 1990s, Ireland had a higher fraction of population of working age. Consequently, on the one hand, employment in the agricultural sector declined while on the other hand, productivity increased when more employees (due to the baby boom period) with higher educational qualifications entered the labor market some years later (Whelan, 2010; Honohan and Walsh, 2002).

1 Foreign direct investment (FDI): Capital export by an economic unit of one country to another country with the aim of acquiring property, setting up factories or subsidiaries, acquiring foreign companies or participating in them with a share (Hardes et al., 2002).

Since January 1, 1973, Ireland has been a member of the EEC, which was later completely absorbed by the EU. With the accession to the EEC, a steady convergence in living standards occurred which finally reached those of other European economies. The economic situation was enhanced by the employment of people with higher educational qualifications in the nonagricultural, export-driven production which raised the average income per capita. What is more, higher incomes in the agricultural sector were expected, because of high EEC support prices. Besides, more women participated in the labor market (Honohan and Walsh, 2002). However, as the figure below shows, Ireland's economic growth was never noticeably above the EU growth average during the decades from Ireland's accession to the time of the Celtic Tiger phenomenon (Honohan and Walsh, 2002).

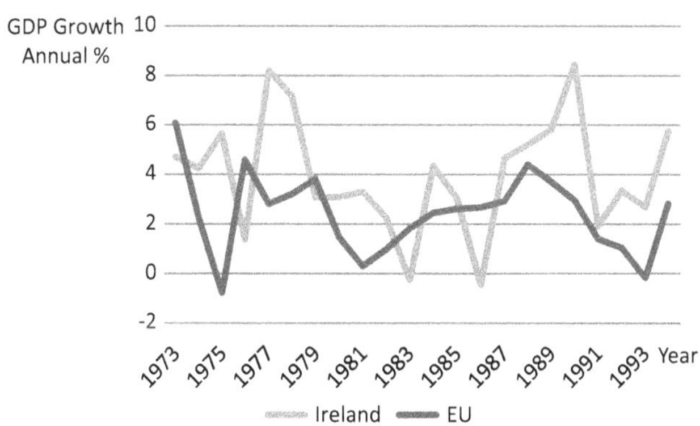

Figure 23: GDP Growth (Annual Percentage) Ireland and EU 1973–1994 (World Bank Group, 2017e)

There was the convergence theory on the one hand and other promising aspects enabling economic growth on the other hand. To name a few, the EEC membership, focusing on industrial policies, attracting FDI encouraged by grant incentives, a profits tax exemption, low corporate tax rates, the increased rate of investment in education, the good location being in the vicinity of Europe, and the English language. Moreover, the historically grown linkage to the United States due to mass-immigration of Irish people in the time of the Great Famine was in turn a key provider of FDI. However, Ireland's economic upturn did not last (Whelan, 2010; Honohan and Walsh, 2002).

Ireland suffered from the oil crisis in 1973. The subsequent inappropriate fiscal and monetary political decisions impeded Ireland's possibilities for economic growth (Honohan and Walsh, 2002; Whelan, 2010; Whelan, 2013). The second oil crisis in 1979/ 1980 also hit Ireland hard. Inappropriate fiscal and monetary political decisions continued and subsequently, the spiraling debt, high tax rates, and high interest rates of the early 1980s further slowed down economic growth (Honohan and Walsh, 2002; Whelan, 2010; Whelan, 2013). An example of the inappropriate political decisions is the failure of building a stable fiscal environment and a wage formation process that would keep Irish labor competitive. This was furthered by an aggressive fiscal policy including growing debt, high tax rates, and high interest rates which were meant to help quickly overcome the consequences of the oil crises. However, high taxes, for example, put pressure on the supply price of labor. A substantial decrease in demand followed. Cross border trafficking from Northern Ireland to the Republic became extensive because of the high taxes on, for instance, alcohol, tobacco, and other consumer durables. Last but not least, the unemployment rate did not respond in the way expected to the expansionary fiscal policy. Although jobs were created, too many of them were dependent either directly on government spending or indirectly on deficit financing and, therefore, were not sustainable (Honohan and Walsh, 2002). Consequently, from 1980 until the beginning of the 1990s, the Irish economy was marked by stagnant real GDP growth rates which even became negative with -0.2 in 1983 and -0.4 in 1986, as the table 'GDP Growth (Annual Percentage) Ireland and EU 1973–1994' above shows (Honohan and Walsh, 2002; Whelan, 2013; World Bank Group, 2017e). In addition to this, the government debt to GDP increased in the highly indebted country in 1987 to over 109%.

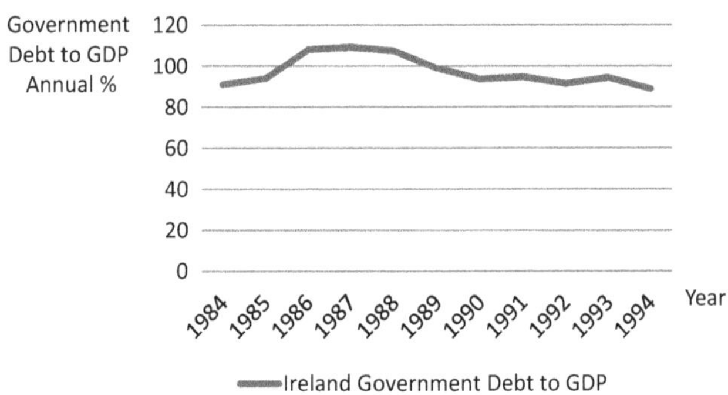

Figure 24: Ireland Government Debt to GDP 1984–1994 (Fedec and Sousa, 2012)

The unemployment rate was significantly higher compared to Ireland's European neighbors, such as the United Kingdom, France, Germany, and Italy.

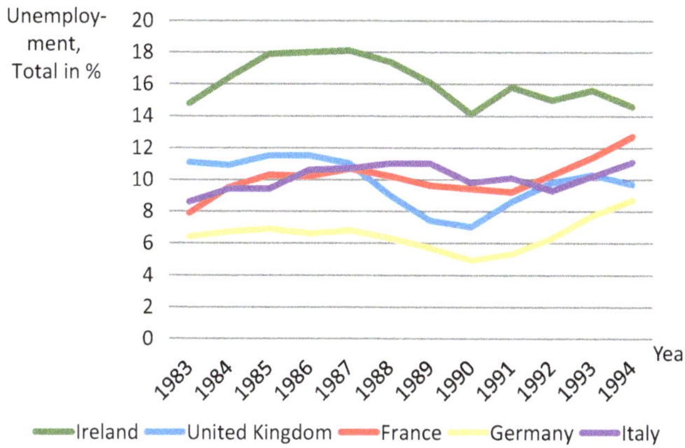

Figure 25: Unemployment, Total in Percent in Ireland, United Kingdom, France, Germany, and Italy between 1983 and 1994 (World Bank Group, 2017f)

The rate reached an all-time high of 18.01% in 1987.

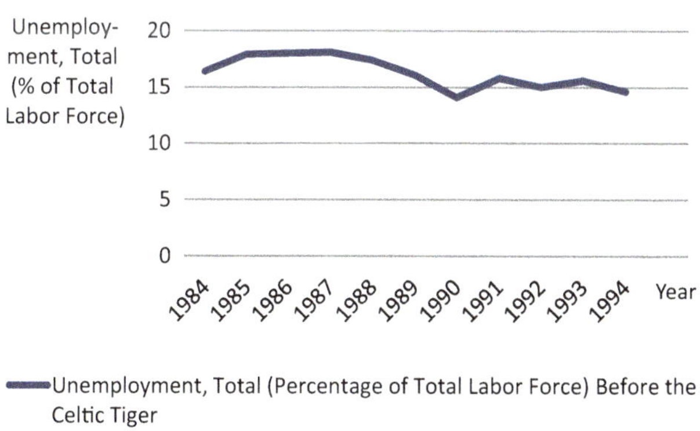

Figure 26: Unemployment, Total (Percentage of Total Labor Force) 1984–1994 (World Bank Group, 2017g)

In addition to the unfavorable economic situation which was accompanied by a falling standard of living, 200,000 inhabitants left the country between 1981 and 1990 (Buti, 2008).

Ireland's membership in the EU allowed it to benefit from EU structural funds that invest in the economic development of poorer member states, such as Ireland. Further, the membership led to an economic upturn because restrictions on trade were eliminated and new trading partners within the EU were acquired. In the 1990s, the establishment of a stable monetary policy cleared the way for the participation in the Euro currency giving traders within the Eurozone exchange rate certainty (Whelan, 2010).

3.2 The Celtic Tiger 1994–2007

Until the 1990s, Ireland was an economically underdeveloped and underperforming country lagging behind other EU member states and one of the poorest countries within the EU. However, the economic landscape changed and Ireland's economy eventually gained the lead over its European neighbors. The Celtic Tiger was born (Honohan and Walsh, 2002).

3.2.1 Evaluation of Ireland's Economic Growth

One of the contributing factors to Ireland's economic growth was the larger population because with more workers available output rises (Haughton, 1998). In 1989, only one third of the Irish population was employed, this being the lowest rate within the Euro zone (O'Connor, 2007a). As mentioned before, Ireland had high birthrates from the 1970s to the 1980s, and as a result, in the 1980s, a large portion of the population was under the working age. In addition to this, by the mid-1990s, when the Irish economy started to grow, many Irish who had emigrated because of bad economic conditions returned home and took up jobs in Ireland (Honohan and Walsh, 2002; Whelan, 2010). A second factor generating growth of real GDP was the higher share of the population at work. During the 1960s and 1970s, the female labor force increased in the European neighbor countries, such as the UK, but not in Ireland. However, in the early 1980s, Irish women caught up and began to participate in the labor market (Whelan, 2010). These conditions enabled an employment growth of about one million when comparing the years 1983 to 2007. The third contributing factor was higher productivity. Irish economic growth is also a result of the shift from low productivity agriculture to high productivity industry and services. This was enabled by universal free secondary education, as mentioned before, and expanded higher education. These developments reflect a strong improvement regarding competitiveness. As a consequence, the productivity of the labor force was improved and the average income rose (Haughton, 1998; Whelan, 2010; Honohan and Walsh, 2002).

Rapid economic growth allowed the Irish government to lower taxes, increase spending, and substantially reduce the debt GDP ratio (Whelan, 2010).

3.2.2 *Comparison of the Celtic Tiger with the Asian Tigers*

The economy of Ireland grew rapidly within a decade beginning in the 1990s. From 1990 to 1999, the real GDP growth averaging 7% significantly exceeded the default value for convergence processes of 2% and was clearly above the EU average (World Bank Group, 2017h; Barro, Sala-i-Martin, 1992; Dauderstädt, 2001). The country's economy experienced a boom which is reflected in its highest real GDP growth rates between 1995 and 2000 with around 10% per year (World Bank Group, 2017i; Honohan and Walsh, 2002). Government debt to GDP decreased continuously from 78.5% in 1995 to 23.6% in 2006, and the rate of unemployment also decreased from 12% in 1995 to 4.3% in 2000 (Fedec and Sousa, 2012; World Bank Group, 2017j).

Referring to its rapid economic growth, a British economist in 1994 labeled Ireland the 'Celtic Tiger'. Why a connection can be made between the Irish and the word 'Celtic' is already explained in Chapter Three, Section 1.1 and Section 2.3. The expression 'Tiger' was used in analogy to the fast developing Asian economies of South Korea, Taiwan, Singapore, and Hong Kong. These are often called 'dragon economies' or 'tiger economies' derived from the East Asian symbols of wealth and power. Ireland was seen as a country that within half a decade transformed itself from one of the most underdeveloped and poorest regions of Europe into what was often referred to as a model country of the EU (Haas and Neumair, 2013; Gardiner, 1994).

However, according to Honohan and Walsh (2002), there was no economic miracle in Ireland and the comparison to the East Asian Tigers, such as Southern Korea, Taiwan, Singapore, and Hong Kong, therefore lags (Honohan and Walsh, 2002). Although these Asian countries are very different with regard to natural resources, population, culture, and economic policy, they had rapid, sustained growth with highly equal income distributions between 1970 and 1990 in common (Page, 1994).

Table 2: Annual Real GDP Growth in Percent (1970–1999): Ireland, Three Selected Asian Tiger Economies, and the EU (World Bank Group, 2017k)

	Ireland	**Republic of Korea**	**Singapore**	**Hong Kong**	**EU**
1970–1979	4.9 (1970 n/a)	10.5	9.5	9	3.6
1980–1989	3.1	8.6	7.8	7.4	2.3
1990–1999	7.1	6.7	7.3	3.6	2.2

Taking into account that an economic crisis began in Asia in 1997, GDP growth rates up to 1997 are even higher for the examined Asian countries (Dieter, 2002).

Table 3: Average Real GDP Growth in Percent (1990–1997): Republic of Korea, Singapore, and Hong Kong (World Bank Group, 2017k)

	Republic of Korea	Singapore	Hong Kong
1990–1997	7.7	8.6	5

During the 1990s, Ireland seemed to be an economic tiger similar to the Asian ones. However, the Asian countries reached high GDP growth rates from the 1970s onward and up to the millennium, whereas Ireland only reached such GDP growth rates within a 5 year timespan in the 1990s. It was therefore not Ireland's similarity to East Asia that earned it the title of a 'tiger,' instead it was the fact that Irish economic growth was exceptional compared to the rest of the EU. Essentially, Ireland's economic performance cannot be compared with the Asian countries (O'Hearn, 1998). Also, if the Irish economy grows again after the heavy impacts of the worldwide financial crisis of 2008, this cannot be considered as a return of the Celtic Tiger because the factors which led to the growth mentioned before and other reasons which will be explained in the following, cannot be repeated (Whelan, 2010).

3.3 The Irish Housing Boom

A number of economic aspects reflected the country's poor past, for instance, roads and public transport were underdeveloped by international standards. However, in 2000, Ireland's GDP caught up with the EU average, the unemployment rate was extremely low by international standards, and the income of Irish people was much higher than during the 1980s.

At this point, two aspects contributed to the housing boom. First, Ireland had a relatively small housing stock (Whelan, 2010). According to Somerville (2007), it was the smallest stock per capita in the EU. The housing market can usually be explained in terms of demand and supply. Factors that affect housing demand are, for instance, current and expected future house prices, income per household, mortgage rates, demographics, and credit availability. Factors that are likely to influence housing supply without regard to house prices are, for instance, the available land for development, planning and zoning restrictions, and the cost of building, which include the costs of raw materials and labor. Consequently, a change in any of these influences will have an effect either on the supply or demand curve of housing which leads to a potential variation in prices (McQuinn and O'Reilly, 2006). With a growing population and growing incomes, housing demand rises, too.

Second, the Economic and Monetary Union (EMU) allowed Irish financial institutions to provide access to mortgage financing at historically low rates (Whelan, 2013). In the mid-1990s, lower interest rates in combination with higher incomes and lower unemployment rates led to higher private investment in housing (Honohan and Walsh, 2002).

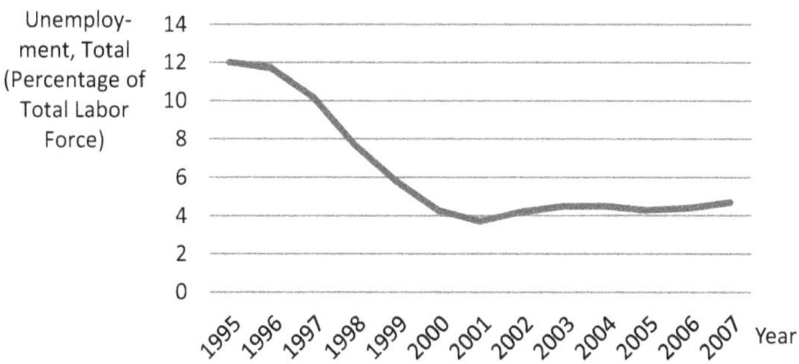

Figure 27: Decline of Unemployment in the Celtic Tiger Years 1994–2007 (World Bank Group, 2017l)

These conditions were jointly responsible for an extraordinary construction boom (Whelan, 2010). For instance, house completions rose from 19,000 in 1990 to 50,000 in 2000, and further increased to 93,000 in 2006.

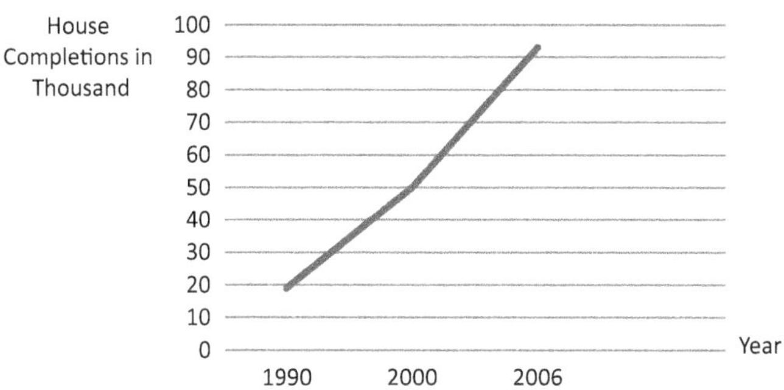

Figure 28: House Completions in Thousand in Ireland Between 1990 and 2006 (Whelan, 2010)

The total stock of dwellings increased from 1.2 million homes in 1991 to 1.4 million homes in 2000, and finally rose to 1.9 million homes in 2008.

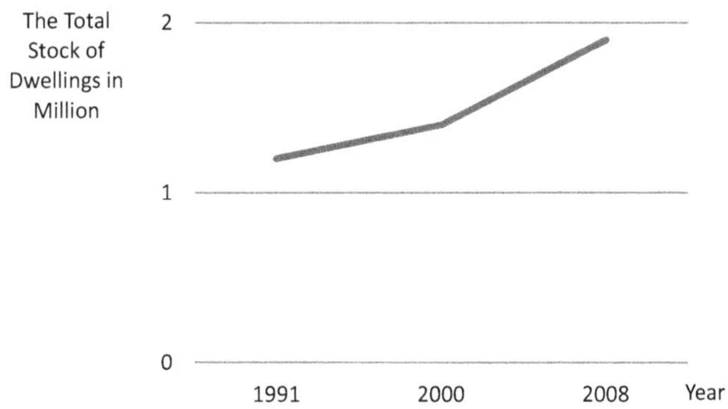

Figure 29: The Total Stock of Dwellings in Ireland between 1991 and 2008 (Whelan, 2010)

As house completions nearly quintupled between 1990 and 2006, construction became a dominant factor in the Irish economy. The demand for housing was additionally raised by the labor force employed during the construction boom which came from the EU member states in Eastern Europe, and other emigrants, such as homecomers looking for better working conditions. In 2007, 13.3% of all employees were accounted for by the construction sector. In contrast, in the UK and the US, the share of employment accounted for by construction was below 8% (Whelan, 2010).

The enormous increase in new housing did not lead to a stabilization or decrease in housing prices because the supply was not able to cover the growing demand. The demand was supported by the growing ability of people to finance owner-occupied dwellings. This was possible due to income tax cuts, low interest rates, and tax incentives, such as the abolition of the stamp duty tax[2] on house purchases (Theurer, 2010; McQuinn and O'Reilly, 2006; Whelan, 2010; Whelan, 2013). Consequently, the economy became highly dependent on the construction sector (Whelan, 2010).

2 Stamp duty is a tax on the value of residential, and other property at point of sale. The purchaser has to pay stamp duty on residential property. The rate of duty increases with the sale price, up to a maximum rate (Somerville, 2007).

McQuinn and O'Reilly (2006) state that between 1995 and 2005, prices for new Irish houses rose by almost 260%. They draw attention to various sources, such as the IMF (McQuinn and O'Reilly, 2006). The tasks of the IMF are to identify global economic trends, rate the performance of its 188 member countries, and alert a member country when problems arise. Further, it provides know-how to governments on how to overcome economic difficulties. The staff of the IMF publishes the *World Economic Outlook* (WEO), a report analyzing and forecasting economic developments and risks at a global level. It is usually prepared twice a year as documentation for meetings of the IMF Committee and forms the main instrument of the IMF's global surveillance activities (IMF, 2014). In their country report no. 03/242 from 2003, the IMF argues that some analysts felt that house prices were not out of line with fundamentals, such as real income and real interest rates. This means that with rising incomes demand also rises, in this case for housing, and low interest rates lead to an increase in the investment rate because it is cheap to borrow money. Experts expected house price inflation to moderate considerably without a significant risk of a crash. In contrast, the IMF also quotes other experts who warned that a bubble was likely. These experts identified the possible existence of a house price bubble due to speculative activity by investors which led to an overvaluation of house prices. The estimates of an overvaluation of house prices were likely to burst and they forecast price declines of 30% or more (IMF, 2003; Kennedy, Girouard, André and van den Noord, 2005). Morgan Kelly, professor of economics, considered the situation to be even worse. He warned against massive and prolonged falls in real house prices in the range of 40–50% (Kelly, 2006). In addition to this, the IMF quotes official authorities conceding that they were concerned about risks but reassuring that there were adequate cushions to absorb the effects of potential shocks without systemic distress (IMF, 2003; Kennedy et al., 2005). Despite the warnings that prices for real estate were significantly over-valued, they continued to rise (IMF, 2003; McQuinn and O'Reilly, 2006; Kennedy et al., 2005).

Whelan (2010) states that any reasonable analysis of the economic circumstances in early 2007 would have suggested that a substantial economic decline was about to happen. Reasons for this are first, that since 2000, labor force participation rates had reached effective full employment with the measured unemployment rate reaching 4.3% so that further growth was unlikely. Second, the aforementioned demographic factors were no longer working in favor of economic growth because the share of the population that was of working age had peaked. Third, the population growth, caused by immigration and since then a key factor for housing demand and economic growth, was not appropriate to guarantee sustainable high growth rates. Fourth, the economic dependence on the construction sector, which was predicted to shrink due to the very potential decline of house prices which consequently, would lead to a decline of profitability in the construction business (Whelan, 2010). An economy heavily dependent on the construction sector then had to be restructured.

3.4 Busting of the Property Bubble – The Property Market Crisis

The Irish government in charge at that time placed much of the guilt for Ireland's economic downturn on the international financial crisis. However, Ireland had been heading in the direction of an economic downturn even before the international recession arrived. Still, the international financial crisis made things even worse (Whelan, 2013).

Despite experts' publication of over-valuation of Irish real estate prices and the warnings against economic dependence on the construction sector by various sources, such as Kelly and the IMF, the official bodies, such as the Irish government or the Central Bank of Ireland (CB) did not intervene to cool the property market over the Celtic Tiger period (Kelly, 2006; Whelan, 2013). There was governmental consensus that there would be a 'soft landing' of the Irish housing market. Kelly argued that house prices had risen 30% faster than income. Additionally, rents had fallen compared with income since 2000. If the housing boom had been due to rising incomes and more people that needed homes, rents would also have risen. However, rents had fallen and this shows that the Irish housing boom had become a speculative bubble. Kelly predicted that if prices for real estate were expected to decrease, potential buyers would not buy. Reasons for this were the loss in value of real estate on the one hand and on the other hand the fact that waiting for prices to stabilize on a lower level would enable people to buy houses for less money. In addition to this, the owners of empty real estate could not expect further capital gains, and Kelly predicted the sale of this real estate so that the owners would not have to pay mortgage rates any longer. The more owners wanted to sell their real estate, the faster prices would decrease. Rents compared to mortgages were extremely low so that people would rather decide to rent a house in a residential area with good infrastructure than pay the same amount of money as mortgage rate in a more uncomfortable area with poor infrastructure, such as medical care, shopping facilities, or educational institutions. As a result, prices for real estate would further decline. Kelly further expected that when house prices declined, they would overshoot and end up undervalued. Therefore, he reckoned in 2006 that prices could fall, relative to income, by as much as 50% (Kelly, 2006).

Indeed, after the property bubble burst more people rented a home than during any time since the early 1980s (O'Brien, 2015).

By late 2007, Irish house prices had begun to fall from the peak levels. As house prices fell, the demand for new houses collapsed. House prices fell by about 50% from their peak values, as Kelly had predicted a year earlier (Kelly, 2006; Whelan, 2013). The collapse of the construction sector soon followed. The decline in the construction sector's employment rate directly accounted for the rise of the Irish unemployment rate (Whelan, 2013). Between 2006 and 2010, for instance, the number of employed bricklayers fell by approximately 82%, employment of plasterers fell by almost 71%, and architects by 61% (Department of Housing, Planning, Community and Local Government, 2014).

3.5 Fiscal Crisis

Fiscal policy is a part of financial policy. Whereas financial policies include all measures that affect public revenue and expenditure, the fiscal policy of a state signifies, among others, its ability to reduce or raise taxes and spend money to stabilize economic growth (Samuelson and Nordhaus, 2010).

Shortly before the recent financial crisis, the general view was that debtors and creditors had learned from their mistakes, and that financial crises would not occur in the long term, at least in emerging and developed economies, because of better informed macroeconomic policies and more selective lending practices (Reinhart and Rogoff, 2009).

The global financial crisis which began in the United States in 2007 and peaked in 2008 was probably the worst financial crisis since the severe worldwide economic downturn of the 1930s (United States, 2011). The crisis originated in the U.S. home loans market. From there, the crisis spread rapidly to other markets, sectors, and countries – including Ireland. The beginning of the crisis is marked by August 9, 2007, when the Fed and the European Central Bank (ECB) first intervened in response to the collapse of the interbank market (Dewatripont et al., 2010).

In 2007, Ireland's public finances were in a good fiscal condition. However, they turned out to be heavily dependent on the construction sector because this was the substantial source of government revenue. The rapidly rising unemployment led to a significant loss of income tax revenues from employees in the construction sector as well as significant losses of income tax revenues from construction activities, such as the tax revenues from stamps and capital gains. Further, the significant rise in unemployment led to a vast increase in social welfare payments. As a consequence, the Irish government significantly cut back public sector pay and non-welfare spending, raised income taxes and VAT rates, and cut back on investments.

Ireland's economic downturn provoked by the collapse of the construction sector, the resulting increase in unemployment, and the associated budgetary deficit would have been bad enough. Despite budget surpluses in the Celtic Tiger years, Ireland was abruptly confronted with a fiscal gap. At the beginning of 2008, things changed dramatically for Ireland. The country fell into a severe recession and entered an economic depression. In 2009, it became clear that without fiscal adjustments, Ireland was heading for significant annual deficits. The real GDP experienced a radical break-in and fell from 3.8% in 2007 to -4.4% in 2008 and -4.6% in 2009 (World Bank Group, 2017m). Government debt to GDP increased from 23.6% in 2006 to 120.1% in 2012 (Fedec and Sousa, 2012). The rate of unemployment also jumped from 4.7% in 2007 to 14.7% in 2012 (Alderman, 2010). Eventually, the Irish banking crisis furthered the recession. The subsequent political decisions ultimately led the country into bankruptcy (Whelan, 2010; Whelan, 2013).

3.6 Banking Crisis

Since the late 1960s, the Bank of Ireland (BOI) and the Allied Irish Banks (AIB) virtually formed a duopoly. The size of the two big banks made it difficult for other banks to coexist until the foreign banks entered the market in the 1990s (Ross, 2009). The Anglo Irish Bank (Anglo) was established in 1964 and achieved significant growth from the mid-1990s onward due to the acquisition of several other banks. These three banks were Ireland's largest banks before the crash (Donovan and Murphy, 2014; Theurer, 2010).

Since 2002, the housing industry had largely been financed by Irish banks. The Irish banks rapidly expanded their mortgage lending and granted loans on huge property development projects to businessmen. The majority of these loans were used for investments that could only be served if real estate prices had further risen. First and foremost, Anglo focused on property-related loans but AIB also copied the business model and they multiplied the value of their assets between 2003 and 2007. Until 2003, these banks had operated in a traditional manner meaning that mortgages were financed domestically through the deposits of financial institutions with loans being approximately equal to deposits. Since 2003, they changed the funding model to a more speculative form of financing (Whelan, 2013; Donovan and Murphy, 2014). A decisive factor here was external competition. The economic growth encouraged foreign institutions, for instance the Bank of Scotland, to enter the Irish financial market.

These new actors introduced new models of financing, such as 100% mortgage (a loan covering the total value of the lender's property which at the same time serves as security). This is called speculative financing. These models made it significantly easier for buyers of real estate to acquire funding. Domestic banks did not want to be at a competitive disadvantage to the newcomers and offered similar financing models. As a result, the demand for real estate increased because of the ease of financing property. Consequently, property prices continued to rise (Donovan and Murphy, 2014).

Although the CB had the task of regulating the banks, it did not intervene. Moreover, none of the other organizations, such as the IMF or European Commission expressed any concerns (Whelan, 2013; Nyberg, 2011). The IMF merely pointed out the fact that rapid credit growth led to vulnerabilities. Bank lending to construction and real estate corporations amounted to 47% of GDP. The household debt piled up until it reached 160% of household disposable income. The IMF noted that with adjustable-rate mortgages rising interest rates would increase the households' debt burdens. However, the IMF emphasized the economic strength and the well-performing banking system, factors that lead to a well-capitalized, profitable, and liquid banking system. Further, the IMF argued that stress tests carried out by the CB indicated that the major lenders had suitable buffers at their disposal to cover a range of shocks. They predicted that even a jump in the unemployment rate and a fall in house prices would not exhaust any major lender's stock of liquid assets (IMF, 2007).

Whelan (2010) argues that, in contrast to the housing bubble in the United States, subprime lending was insignificant in Ireland. Loose mortgage criteria may have played an important role in fueling the boom in house prices. However, losses on mortgage defaults were not the problem that caused the crash of the Irish banks. These losses would have been significant but the Irish banks were almost certainly well enough capitalized to have been able to deal with these losses. A major factor that contributed to the collapse of the Irish banks resulted from their loans to property developers. For instance, Anglo granted some of the largest property developers billion-euro loans for their growing projects. Other financial institutions did not want to lag behind and doubled their balance sheets by 2008 by implementing the same lending practices (Theurer, 2010). The value of Irish houses declined significantly from their highest level. The value of much of the speculative development land bought near its highest value became virtually worthless (Whelan, 2010).

3.7 The Guarantee Decision

In the course of the collapse of the construction sector in 2008, international investors raised concerns about the potential risks of the existing property investment loans of Irish banks. As a result, the Irish banks faced increasing difficulties in raising funds on bond markets. For instance, Anglo was losing funds and running out of eligible collateral to be used to borrow from the ECB and defaulting on its liabilities was a likely risk. Other banks feared the negative impact on their operations if such a default was to occur. The senior management of the largest Irish banks asked for help from the government (Whelan, 2013).

After a radio news program reported about a lack of confidence in the banking system, people began to withdraw their money from the banks. Concerns among politicians arose that this might lead to a run on the banks (Whelan, 2013; Corcoran, 2008).

As a result, on September 30, 2008, the government introduced a blanket guarantee of bank liabilities for a period of 2 years for almost all of the existing and future liabilities of the domestic Irish banks (Whelan, 2013; NTMA, 2012). The decision of the government to provide a blanket guarantee can only be explained by the fact that the government must have believed the assurances of the CB that the banks were fundamentally sound and were merely suffering from a short-term liquidity problem. The government must have been convinced that the guarantee would not have an impact on the state finances on a grand scale. The advantage of a blanket guarantee was that it sent a signal to the financial markets that the Irish banks were sound and this, in turn, allayed the fears of international and private investors which stabilized the market as planned (Whelan, 2013; Donovan and Murphy, 2014).

However, the property market broke down gradually and investors did not invest in equity in Irish banks. Consequently, the significance of bailing out bank creditors for taxpayers slowly became evident. In December 2008, the government assumed a state capital of €2 billion each to BoI and AIB and €1.5 billion to Anglo to avert bankruptcy. In January 2009, scandalous mismanagement of Anglo became public and as a consequence, the government nationalized Anglo and replaced its senior management (Schulz, 2010; Whelan, 2013). Six banks, namely AIB, BoI, Anglo, Irish Life and Permanent, Irish Nationwide Building Society, and the Educational Building Society were covered by the blanket guarantee (FTD, 2008). All of them were eventually nationalized with the exception of BoI which was not fully nationalized. In February 2009, the government had to adapt capital assistance for BoI and AIB amounting to

€3.5 billion each. In May 2009, Anglo admitted that they had lost €4 billion capital and predicted a further €4 billion in losses. In September 2010, the Irish government estimated that Anglo would cost them approximately €30 billion which was almost €7,500 per person living in the state (Frisell, 2015). The Irish government realized that the final bill for recapitalizing the Irish banks would be massive. In spite of the huge capital buffers of the Irish government, the international markets became increasingly alarmed by these developments and concerns arose that the banking sector would destroy the creditworthiness of the Irish state (European Commission, 2011; Whelan, 2013).

When the guarantee expired on September 29, 2010, it was succeeded by the Eligible Liabilities Guarantee (ELG) Scheme. The ELG provides for certain liabilities of a number of Irish credit institutions to be guaranteed by the Minister for Finance. The ELG Scheme was amended with effect from midnight on March 28, 2013, so that new deposits made on or after that date would no longer be guaranteed under the Scheme, which was intended as a step toward the normalization of banking activity (NTMA, 2013).

3.8 Bailout and EU – IMF Program

The economist Frisell (2015) states that the bailout decision will go down in Irish history as a very costly mistake. He further reasons that Anglo should never have been included in the blanket guarantee and argues that the costs in terms of credit losses outweigh the short-term benefits of a general guarantee (Frisell, 2015).

On November 21, 2010 the costs were so high that the Irish government sought help from the ECB and the IMF (Frisell, 2015). Actually, the Irish government had little choice other than to ask for help from the EU and the IMF. Failing to find improvement in the banking situation, the ECB made its continued support for the Irish banking system dependent on Ireland applying to the EU and the IMF for a lending program (Whelan, 2013). Hudson (2014) states that the Irish banks were too big to be saved by the Irish government alone without driving the country into bankruptcy. In late November 2010, the Irish government agreed to a multi-year funding deal with the EU and the IMF. A program of €85 billion financial assistance was agreed on with the European Commission, the IMF, and ECB. The ECB along with the European Commission and the IMF were involved to supervise Ireland's compliance with EU stability and growth pact rules (European Commission, 2011).

In return for this funding, the program contained obligations to restructure the banking sector in order to restore financial market confidence in the Irish economy's banking sector, to implement further fiscal adjustment to restore fiscal sustainability, and to introduce various reforms, such as a structural reform package to strengthen growth (Whelan, 2013; European Commission, 2011). Moreover, the Irish government introduced a reformed tax on assets, reduced the minimum wage, canceled 20,000 jobs in the public service sector, and also cut salaries in the public service sector (Irwin, 2013; Endres, 2013; Alioth, 2009). In January 2012, the government raised VAT by 2% to 23% total in addition to raising certain excise duties and reducing social expenditures (Endres, 2013).

Ireland is often called a bright example, for instance by the German government, of how well austerity works. However, with investments virtually shutting down, government and private investment in Ireland nearly collapsed and are very low until today in comparison with Europe. In the long term, there will be negative impacts on the infrastructure and the economic growth. The Irish government is more focused on spending cuts than on tax increases (Collins and Volmer, 2015). Companies based in Ireland pay only 12.5% corporate taxes on their profits. In contrast, in Germany, corporate profits are taxed with nearly 30% and in the U.S. State of New York with 40% (Bundesministerium der Finanzen, 2016). The low taxes were considered a recipe for success by the Irish government because they attracted international corporations and, as a result, new jobs were created. Since the financial support of the other European states was accepted, Ireland's government is under massive pressure to raise corporate taxes. However, the Irish government has stated several times that they are not considering touching the tax (Endres, 2013). These imbalances were responsible for the fact that poorer households suffered more from the consequences of the crisis. In addition to this, the public sector was underfinanced. This affected, for instance, the health system and social housing. For a while the system was able to achieve these savings but now more and more serious problems are arising in all areas of public services. When it comes down to austerity, if taxes are continually increased and spending is cut, the economy will inevitably stall. Consequently, some economists argue that Ireland was only able to recover after the austerity measures had been ended (Collins and Volmer, 2015).

Chapter 5: A Layered Perspective on the Social Ecology of Ireland

Lejano and Stokols (2013) define ecology as referring to the various fields of study of the relationships between organisms and their respective environments. McDonnell and Pickett (1990) explain human ecology as "the discipline that inquires into the patterns and process of interaction of humans with their environments" (McDonnell and Pickett, 1990, p. 1233). Young (1974) describes the research area of human ecology as a 'fragmented field' without structure. He refers to a movement in the discipline of human ecology that investigates out of the laboratory with its controlled experiments on human behavior and into the field of direct observation of behavior in an unconditioned environment. He argues that structure is needed because it provides the means for subsistence and reproduction (Young, 1974). This chapter shows how to integrate field observations by means of a structure and thus offers the possibility of reproduction but it also provides an example of how this structure can be applied to other research questions.

The social ecological framework based on Bronfenbrenner, brings up the revision of relationships between the individuals and their environment and emphasizes that individuals are connected to their physical and social surroundings as explained in Chapter Two, Section 3. It is a concept of social ecological contexts as nested environments and layers with different levels of proximity to the individual. The social ecological framework, based on Bronfenbrenner, (please see figure 30) illustrates the influences of environments, such as social and cultural contexts, on human behavior. Figure 30 shows some examples of influences on the individual in each layer. For instance, the microsystem is the layer closest to the individual and contains the structures with which the individual has direct contact, such as the family, peers, workplace, religious affiliation, or neighborhood. The mesosystem encompasses the interrelations between two, three, or more important settings that contain the individual during a specific period of time in his or her life. The arrows between family and peers, etc. in the mesosystem illustrate that the mesosystem is an 'in-between level' because an individual participates in more than one microsystem during a certain period of time (Ting-Toomey, 2011). There are relations between the microsystems in which an individual is involved and the arrows represent the overlaps and communication between the settings and show that there is information in each setting about the other ones. An example for this is the connection between an individual's church and his or her neighborhood, such as an Irish Catholic living in a Protestant neighborhood. The exosystem, such as the economic system or the political system, is an extension of the mesosystem and includes other social structures that do not themselves contain the individual but have an effect upon or encompass the direct environment of the individual and therefore influence what happens there (Bronfenbrenner, 1977). An example for a force within the larger social system in which the individual is embedded is the unemployment rate which has an effect on economic stability (McLeroy, Bibeau, Steckler and Glanz, 1988). The macrosystem refers to the all-encompassing patterns of a culture or a social group, such as values and beliefs, of which the different systems or layers are tangible manifestations and therefore characterize a culture (Bronfenbrenner, 1979). The chronosystem refers to how the individual and the environments change over time. This means that the chronosystem encompasses change or consistency over time, not only in the characteristics of the person but also of the environment in which that person lives. There are, for instance, external changes, such as changes in the employment status. To move to another city, for instance, and to find a new job affects contexts at all other levels, such as a new neighborhood (Bronfenbrenner, 1994).

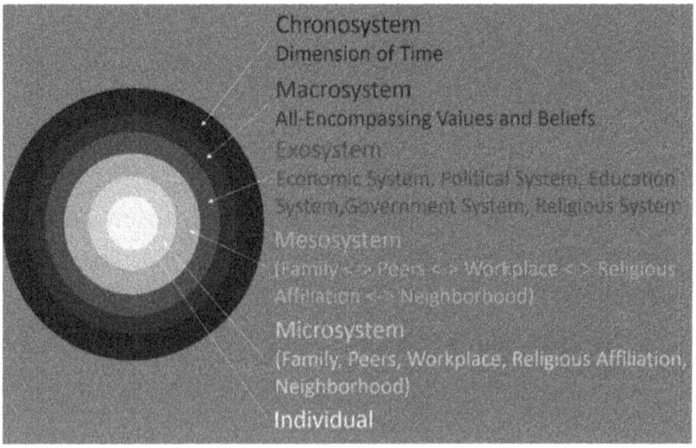

Figure 30: A Layered Perspective Based on Bronfenbrenner's Ecological System Theory (Tregaskis, 2015)

Building on this knowledge, the following concept of the analysis focuses less on Bronfenbrenner's macro-, exo-, meso-, and microsystem, but instead involves simultaneous, not separate, examination of behavior at two or more layers (Oetzel, 2009). Therefore, the approach of the following analysis is divided into bottom-up effects, which examine how lower levels, such as individuals, affect higher levels, such as politics, institutions, and even culture. The top-down effects examine how higher levels, such as culture, politics, and institutions, affect lower levels, such as interpersonal relationships and individuals. These effects assume a cumulative effect passing up or down from one level to the next in a systematic manner. However, by definition, the layered perspective is not a linear one. It takes into account multiple issues and all layers are interconnected through loops and links (Oetzel, 2009). Thus, interactive effects assume a simultaneous process which is a conglomeration of multiple dimensions of social phenomena that produces outcomes and can be observed in society (Zhang and Ting-Toomey, 2014; Lejano and Stokols, 2013). These interactive effects are illustrated in the following analysis of this Chapter, Sections 1.4, 2.4, 3.3, 4.3, 5.3, 6.3, and Chapter Six, Sections 1.3, 2.3, 3.3, 4.4, 5.3, 6.3.

In this section, the ecological approach is translated into the Irish perspective. The analysis first examines the influences of the individual on the layers by which he or she is surrounded. Then the influences on the individual from the outer layers are illustrated by specific cases. The interactive effects, which are present in both cases, are explained subsequently. There is no sharp distinction between the different layers because mutual influences permeate all layers.

1 A Layered Perspective on Personal Identity and Irish Legislation

Identity is made up of various layers, as explained in Chapter One, Section 3. Together these layers make up an individual's identity which is the combination of the unique qualities of an individual. The multiple identities that an individual holds are composed (besides social and cultural aspects) of personal aspects (Oetzel, 2009). Such personal aspects are also influenced by an individual's physical characteristics, such as gender, age, physical ability, and many others. Some biologists assume that sexual preferences are also determined by the cooperation of several genes and can even be inherited. Thus, according to this line of reasoning, sexual identity is not consciously chosen and an individual's sexual preference is a physical characteristic, such as skin color (Kehse and Witte, 2015; Berger, 2015; Lüpke, 2014).

In some situations, the layers of identity may be consistent with one another. In other situations, they may be contrary or inconsistent. The individual layer as a component of identity influences the other layers and vice versa. Individual identities can also have very different effects on the shared social identities. In some circumstances, individuals inherit an identity that is not consistent with the collective's perspective. Culture changes because individuals challenge traditions with their unique identities and when a significant number of people share the same perspective, culture will change (Oetzel, 2009). The Netherlands was the first country to legally allow marriage for same sex couples in 2001, Ireland followed in 2015, and Germany in 2017. Today, the legal situation for homosexuals is similar within Europe (Nier, 2017). Thus, it seems as though the European countries are conform concerning their views and subsequently also their jurisdiction concerning this issue. In contrast, in Sudan, Saudi Arabia, Yemen, Iran, Iraq, in some regions of Somalia and northern Nigeria, as well as in some regions of Syria homosexuals face the threat of death penalty (Nier, 2017).

1.1 Value of Family in Irish Society

The value of the family is firmly anchored in Irish society. The results of the large survey on the Irish conducted by the EVS highlight the importance of the family for the Irish. The figure from 2008 shows that 99% of the participants in Ireland agreed that family is 'very important' or 'quite important' in their lives. This is the same result as in 1999. As Figure 31 below shows, Ireland ranks among the European countries in which family is valued the greatest. In contrast, the survey shows that in Germany only 95% of the participants agreed that family is very or quite important in their lives (Atlas of European Values, 2011a).

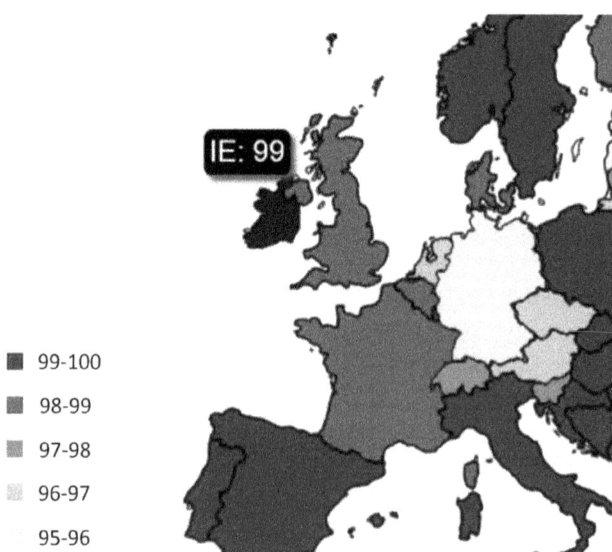

Figure 31: Percentage of Irish People Who Say Family is 'Very Important' or 'Quite Important' in Their Lives in 2008 (Atlas of European Values, 2011a)

It is notable that there is a higher percentage of Catholics in Ireland which ranges around 90%. In contrast, in Germany just one-third of the population is Catholic (Statistische Ämter des Bundes und der Länder, 2012; Dalton and Cavan, 2014). The influence of religious affiliation is discussed in detail in the following Section 1.2.

The Irish Constitution, in its version of 2009, determines that a family is founded by marriage (Department of the Taoiseach, 2010). Marriage, in turn, is considered as a union between a man and a woman (High Court, 2006). Consequently, family is quite important to the Irish, however, legally, it only comes into existence through marriage in the form of a union between a man and a woman.

The EVS data show that Irish society is increasingly tolerant regarding the acceptance of homosexuality. For instance, the survey asked the participants whether they thought homosexuality could be acceptable with the score 0 meaning 'never' and the score 100 meaning 'always'. The result was score 19 in 1981, 36 in 1999, and 47 in 2008 (Atlas of European Values, 2011b).

Therefore, the question arises how the Irish society copes with the issue of same-sex couples in the context of family. This was clarified by a referendum held on May 22, 2015 in which a narrow majority voted for legislation of same-sex marriage. Thus, the Constitution was changed in order to extend civil marriage rights to same-sex couples – a referendum being the only way to change the Constitution in Ireland.

1.2 Bottom-Up Effects

In 2006, the High Court Case of Katherine Zappone and Ann Louise Gilligan was one of the first major public events in the debate on the recognition of same-sex marriage in Ireland. The plaintiffs Katherine Zappone and Ann Louise Gilligan unsuccessfully fought before the Irish High Court for recognition of their legal Canadian marriage in Ireland. They demanded that the state and also society, by means of legalization, should accept them as the persons they are. They also argued that the denial of recognition of their marriage had far-reaching consequences, such as the obstacles in leaving property to the other, and the taxes which had to be paid because they were not married under Irish law. The judge argued that the common understanding of marriage is that it is a union between a man and a woman and eventually, their Canadian marriage was revoked by Irish court ruling (High Court, 2006). Although Zappone and Gilligan lost their lawsuit, bringing their case against the state to court attracted considerable attention – both from the public and the media. As a result, more and more people became aware of the discrimination in the legislation (Dwyer, 2008).

Another example of how individuals can influence society is the homemade video, posted on the video-sharing website 'YouTube' shortly before the marriage referendum in 2015, by the elderly married couple Brighid and Paddy Whyte. In the video, the couple is sitting at home on their sofa and urges the audience to vote for 'yes' in the same-sex marriage referendum. They explain that their son Pádraic is gay and that for them the importance of family is a traditional Catholic value. In their opinion, full acceptance of gay marriage can support an entire family. The homemade video not only received attention within the internet community. The story was published on the front page of a local newspaper, as well as in the nationwide *Irish Independent*, and even the *New York Times* reported on the YouTube video (Irish Independent, 2015; Ingber, 2015).

Individuals create, negotiate, and reflect their identity through interaction with other people (Oetzel, 2009; Orbe and Harris, 2015). Thus, one can assume that these individuals gave impulse to the subsequently held referendum.

1.3 Top-Down Effects

The Irish laws against homosexuality dated from the Victorian era and were effective for more than 140 years. The 'Offences Against the Persons Act' from August 6, 1861, chapter III, No. 61 made 'unnatural offences,' such as intimate relationships between same-sex partners, an offence punishable by penal servitude (Government of Ireland, 1861). In June 1993, Ireland finally passed a bill which decriminalized homosexuality and removed the Victorian-era rulings from the Irish legislation (Sheils McNamee, 2015).

Nevertheless, the Irish Constitution reflects the minds of the founding fathers that created it and thus also reflects the mind of that time. It idealizes the family, as article 41 signifies "[t]he state recognises the Family as the natural primary and fundamental unit group of Society" (Department of the Taoiseach, 2010, art. 41, section 1, No. 1). Although marriage is not defined by the Constitution, the further sections of article 41 imply that marriage is a union between a man and a woman. An indicator for this is the reference to the special protection of the woman as mother. "In particular, the State recognises that by her life within the home, woman gives to the State a support without which the common good cannot be achieved" (Department of the Taoiseach, 2010, Article 41, Section 2, No. 1).

According to Hofstede's model of 'The Stabilizing of Culture Patterns,' societal norms lead to the development and pattern maintenance of institutions in a society with particular structures and ways of functioning, in this case legislation. The Constitution is, by definition, the written principles about the form and structure of a state and determines its own rights and obligations and that of its citizens. Thus, the Irish Constitution reinforces the societal norms, as well as the ecological conditions that led to their creation (please see Chapter One, Section 2.3) (Hofstede, 2003).

Indeed, the Constitution does not refer to marriage as being between a man and a woman. However, in 1937, there was merely one point of view, namely that marriage was entered between heterosexual partners, since homosexuality was prohibited by law. The High Court affirmed in 2006 in the case of Katherine Zappone and Ann Louise Gilligan that the framers of the Constitution in 1937, in referring to marriage and the family, were thinking in the context of a union between man and woman (High Court, 2006).

In 2010, 'the Civil Partnership Act' was passed and gave gay couples more rights than they had previously been afforded. The passing of the Civil Partnership Act was considered an important milestone (Sheils McNamee, 2015). Eventually, in 2015, the decision was made to hold a referendum over legislation. Some scholars speculate that this decision may have arisen due to the latest developments regarding granting rights to homosexuals. Politicians probably feared repercussions if a marriage equality law were struck down by the Supreme Court and then would have to go to referendum anyway. Thus, the government decided for a precautionary referendum (Elkink, Farrell, Reidy and Suiter, 2016).

1.4 Interactive Effects

Voting behavior should not be considered in isolation, but rather within the broader setting of its institutional, cultural, and social context. The 'Yes campaign' was managed with broad civil society involvement and with the support of all political parties represented in the Dáil. Thus, Elkink, Farrell, Reidy, and Suiter (2016) argue that voters who were unhappy with the government were more likely to vote against the same-sex marriage. The 'Yes campaign' was highly organized and concentrated its message on the argument that the referendum was about equality for all people.

The 'No campaign,' including conservative Catholic groups and the Catholic Church itself, focused on traditional family values with messages, such as 'Children need a Mother and a Father'. Consequently, one can argue that a voter, who disagreed with the church in any way, was more likely to vote for 'yes' (Elkink et al., 2016).

1.4.1 Media Influences

In general, referendum campaigns in Ireland are commonly focused on national television, local and national radio and opinion pieces in the local and national media. However, in the case of the marriage referendum, campaign management and organization intensively used social media. For instance, Twitter and Facebook were used to remind voters to vote on polling day, recorded their vote after polling, and called for carpooling to help voters get to the polls. Twitter released a global heat map of the activity.

Irish emigrants have no right to vote from abroad, but many did not let that fact stop them from casting a ballot in the marriage referendum. Mainly young voters from all over the world returned to Ireland to cast their votes. 72,000 tweets using the hashtag #HomeToVote had been posted on the social media site, as people traveled back to Ireland to vote from as far away as Canada, Australia, Africa, and Asia shared photos and messages (Kenny, 2015; Elkink et al., 2016).

1.4.2 Social Influences

On May 22, 2015, the majority of the Irish voted for the legislation approving same sex marriage. Representatives of the 'No campaign,' such as the Vatican, considered the result of the Irish referendum a 'defeat for humanity' as *The Irish Times* reported (Agnew, 2015). Other statements of representatives of the Catholic Church labeled the result 'bereavement' (McMahon, 2015). Since the mid-1990s, the Catholic Church's reputation has been gradually eroding. Irish political classes have lost their respect for the Catholic Church. The Taoiseach (the Irish prime minister) of that time, Enda Kenny, criticized the Vatican for its attitude concerning the outcome of the referendum. This public criticism was appreciated by the press as a significant milestone on Ireland's journey away from being a mono-Catholic state into a 21st century European republic (Stanley, 2015).

However, one can argue that the outcome of the referendum could also have been influenced by the overwhelming revelation in the media of sexual abuse scandals in Ireland and the rest of the world in which the Catholic Church was involved. The scandals became public in the mid-1990s and reached a climax regarding public attention in 2009 when the extensive *Ryan Report*, which investigated the extent and effects of abuse on children from 1936 onward was published on May 20 of that year. The report consists of five sections with a total of about 2,500 pages (Department of Health and Children, 2009). It provides comprehensive evidence of the misconduct of representatives of the Catholic Church and reveals the state's failure of properly performing its supervisory role. The press did not classify this as the mere failure of a few but rather held responsible a 'dysfunctional system'. The revelations about the true extent of this dysfunctional system resulted in a breach of trust toward the institutions church and state (Bunting, 2009). Therefore, it can be assumed that the church in its function of a moral model and the state whose legislation is based on the moral guidelines of the church, lost their credibility and assertiveness. This shows the interactive effects between the institutions and society.

The *Murphy Report*, was published in November 2009. It investigates the handling of a representative sample of sexual abuse cases by Church and State authorities against clerics operating under the aegis of the Archdiocese of Dublin in the period from 1975 to 2004. Although it was not the intention of the *Murphy Report* to reveal whether the crimes actually took place, but rather to record the manner in which complaints were dealt with by Church and State authorities, the report received strong public attention (Department of Justice and Equality, 2009; Government of Ireland, 2002). Breen and Healy (2016) conclude that this scandal played a significant role in the profound change in the Irish Catholic landscape by examining data based on the European Social Survey (ESS) (Breen and Healy, 2016).

1.4.3 Economic Influences

In addition to this, economic circumstances may have influenced the outcome of the referendum. Ireland was one of the poorest states in the EU during the 1980s. However, in the 1990s, Ireland's economy began to grow rapidly with growing continuing until 2007 (O'Hearn, 1998; Honohan and Walsh, 2002; Whelan, 2010). The case of Katherine Zappone and Ann Louise Gilligan occurred in this period of economic height. Hardiman and Whelan (1998) state that the economic development led to various changes, for instance, changes in social interaction which led to a weakening of traditional norms and values. The religious worldview, typical of traditional societies, loses its importance and is replaced by secularized religious and moral values. This leads to a heightened autonomy of individuals regarding the development of their own values and norms (Hardiman and Whelan, 1998). Consequently, economic development can also give rise to a process of cultural development.

2 A Layered Perspective on Religious Affiliation

Religion is probably the most powerful and pervasive force leading human beings to act (Kimball, 2008). It is a common human interest to find meaning and make sense of human existence. "For the vast majority of people worldwide, their religious tradition – like family, tribe, or nation – anchors them in the world. Religious traditions provide structure, discipline, and social participation in a community" (Kimball, 2008, p. 209). Religious individuals find adequate answers to certain issues, including moral, social, family, life, and spiritual issues in their religion (Breen and Reynolds, 2011). Religion unites people in a community based on shared beliefs and values. Through engagement in collective rituals and practices, the community develops a shared way of understanding the world. People within the same community develop a common sense of what they consider to be right or wrong, good or bad. People strive for protection of the community and their shared beliefs and values. The sense of community is strengthened through practices and symbols. Anything that threatens or undermines the sense of community also threatens and undermines the sense of self (Inglis, 2005). Samovar et al. (2013) state that religion, perception, and behavior are intrinsically interwoven. The behavioral dimension of religion is widespread, relevant, and sometimes volatile.

2.1 Religion as a Part of Identity

"Religious categorization cannot be easily fitted into classifications of countries and civilizations" (Sen, 2007b, p. 60). Viewing individuals in terms of their religious affiliation has become quite common in cultural analysis. However, it neglects seeing human beings in terms of alternative affiliations other than, for example, religion. In many contexts, such a classification can be rather helpful. Yet taking it as the overarching basis for social, political, and cultural analysis in general would result in overlooking all the other associations and loyalties an individual has and that could be significant for the person's behavior, identity, and self-understanding (Sen, 2007b).

In the case of Ireland, there is obviously an exceptional relationship regarding religion. But even here, it is shown that religion is only one part of Irish identity. The relationship between the Irish people and the Catholic Church which represents the faith of the vast majority in Ireland is discussed below.

2.2 Bottom-Up Effects

The bottom-up effects examine how individuals influence religious organizations. The individual is able to reinforce and recreate cultural norms, such as religion, through his or her behavior. If the individual accepts cultural norms, he or she will follow them and sanction others who do not. However, if the individual does not accept cultural norms he or she will resist them and also encourage others to resist them either subtly or directly. Also, if the majority of people have the inclination to adjust to new attitudes and redefines overarching beliefs and values, it is possible to bypass firmly established religious doctrines (Oetzel, 2009).

Fogarty, Ryan, and Lee (1984) state in their book *Irish Values and Attitudes* that "[t]he first, and correct, impression when religious beliefs and practices in Ireland are compared with those in Britain or Europe as a whole [...] is that Ireland remains an outstanding religious country" (Fogarty et al., 1984, p. 8). They drew their conclusions from interpreting the results of the first EVS which was conducted in 1981. Until the present day, Ireland remains religiously homogenous. The majority of the Irish citizens identify themselves as Catholic (Quinn, 2010). As the census of 2011 shows, the vast majority of the Irish, with nearly 90%, are Catholic. An overview of the past 150 years shows, that other religions play no significant role – see figure below (Keating and Martin, 2007).

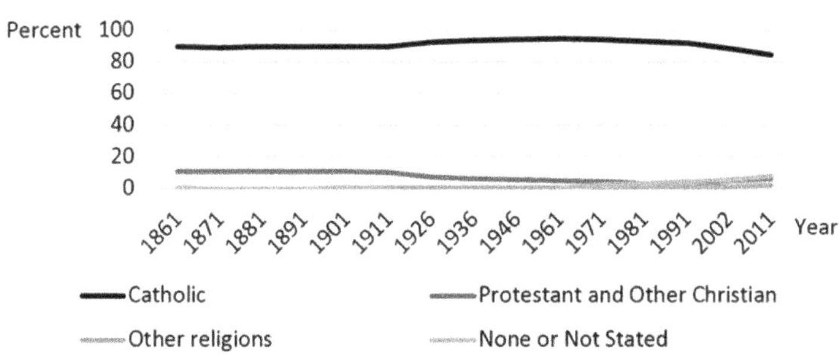

Figure 32: Religious Affiliation of the Irish 1861–2011 in Percent of People interviewed (Dalton and Cavan, 2014)

Taylor, professor of anthropology, emphasizes the relationship between Catholicism and nationalism in Ireland with a focus on the 19th century. The Catholic Church gradually managed to achieve power and wealth. Taylor points out that the church took a stand as the confederate of the oppressed and impoverished peasantry and presented itself as a representative of Irish culture and identity. However, especially since the middle of the 19th century, the Catholic Church had an increasingly reluctant attitude toward actual peasant culture. Instead, it surrendered more to the doctrines of the Roman Pope than ever before and made every effort to eliminate distinctively Irish religious practices in favor of the holy rites of the Roman Catholic Church (Taylor, 1993).

Until the middle of the 19th century, the Irish Church was an independent, informal institution with 'irregular' practices from the viewpoint of the Catholic Church. However, there were significant changes in the Irish church service when the Archbishop of Armagh and Dublin Paul Cullen, who was a faithful supporter of the Pope, introduced significant modifications to make practicing Catholics of the Irish people. This period marked the foundation of the modern Irish Catholic Church and is known as the 'devotional revolution' which took place from 1850 to 1875 (Larkin, 1984). The Archbishop of Armagh organized and restructured the Church. One of the central topics was that sacraments were to be administered more often and only in church. Previously, the Irish had not been strictly observant Catholics. Confession, mass, and even marriage ceremonies were held at home. These and other 'irregularities' were forbidden and bishops were told to encourage people to attend church. In Cullen's opinion, probably influenced by his residence in Rome, interference in political matters was a church obligation (McCaffrey, 2006). Thus, a single man had a lasting effect on Irish Catholicism.

2.3 Top-Down Effects

The top-down effects reveal how religious organizations influence the individual. Even with its influence fading recently, the Catholic Church has the power to influence Irish politics, school, and the life of individuals until today. Larkin (1984), professor of Irish history, states that the devotional revolution "...provided the Irish with a substitute symbolic language and offered them a new cultural heritage with which they could identify and be identified and through which they could identify with one another" (Larkin, 1984, p. 83). Catholicism became a universal cultural statement of ethnic identity in Ireland. The disestablishment of the Church of Ireland in 1869 cleared the way for the Catholic Church to become the powerful institution which assumed to interfere with

Irish politics. This institution continues to be closely involved in the provision of education, health and welfare services, as explained in the subsequent Sections 2.4.2 and 3.

However, much of this involvement is being renegotiated as the Catholic Church redefines its mission in the light of decreasing memberships and the demand for a more multifaceted and equal society in the 21st century (Keating and Martin, 2007; Larkin, 1984).

2.4 Interactive Effects

Minkov (2011) states that some cultural traits change faster than others. He considers religiousness as the most resistant cultural value. Even if religion is not entirely immune to change, it is significantly more resistant to external influences than other values (Minkov, 2011).

The scope of this dissertation cannot illustrate the extensive and changing historical relations between Catholicism and Irish nationalism in detail. However, a brief overview, in order to make sense of the particular circumstances in the mid-19th century, will shed light on the dynamics.

2.4.1 Emergence of a Catholic Irish Identity

In the beginning, from the 5th to 12th century, there was the period of the Celtic Church during which Catholicism was represented by various local monastic groups. Irish nationalism played no role and religion was the only distinction between the Irish and the Vikings. Later, in the 12th century, the Norman invaders, who were connected to the Roman Catholic Church, brought a new aspect to the relation of Catholicism and Irish identity. Ethnic conflicts between the ultramontane Normans (clerical political idea within the Catholic Church that places high importance on the prerogatives and powers of the Pope) and the native Irish arose. In the 16th century, the newly Protestant England led the Irish clergy into an alliance with the Catholic Church's authority. The Protestant conquest of Ireland in the 17th century strengthened Irish ties to Rome. Irish local clergy were persecuted as adversaries by the Protestant invaders. Thus, Catholic clergy became emblematic of local religious and folk culture (Taylor, 1993). At the beginning of the 18th century, most of the land in Ireland was owned by the Protestant English and Scottish settlers who had come because of the policy of plantation (please see Chapter Three, Section 1.2). Native landowners became Protestant in order to keep their estates. The newcomers inevitably quickly acquired sole control over the economy next to dominating the social, cultural, religious, and political life. The Protestant

Church was the state church and Catholics were prohibited to vote or become members of parliament. However, in the three southern provinces, the great majority of the population remained Catholic (Coakley, 1998). Catholicism became the decisive factor which distinguished the Irish from their suppressors. The devotional revolution was aided by the reduction of population due to the Great Famine (please see Chapter Three, Section 1.4). The psychological effects of the Great Famine also helped to secure the position of the Catholic Church which took on a key role in establishing Catholicism as an essential part of Irish national identity (McCaffrey, 2006; Larkin, 1984). At the end of the 18th century and the beginning of the 19th century, the Catholic Church became more organized. However, the Church became authoritarian and ultramontane devotionally with the appointment of Paul Cullen in 1850 (Taylor, 1993). In the late 19th and early 20th century, the Protestants, a religious minority whose privileges were fading, gradually lost more and more of their influence and finally also lost their control over the government (please see Chapter Three, Sections 1.5, 1.6) (Coakley, 1998).

2.4.2 Religious Affiliation in the Present

Although today most of the Irish are still Catholic and a two-third majority states that religion is important in their lives, the percentage of the Irish who attend religious services at least once a week apart from weddings, funerals, and christenings decreased by half from 83% in 1981 to 41% in 2008. So there are more people stating that religion is important to them than people attending church on a regular basis (Atlas of European Values, 2011c). Even with these declines, Ireland can still claim to be one of the most Catholic countries in the western world and the Catholic Church is still a pervasive force in Irish life, even though the Catholic approach to questions, such as family and morality, has changed and traditional Catholic certainties in this area have faded. New patterns of behavior have spread quite easily without undermining religious affiliation among Catholics even though they are nominally in conflict with Catholic teaching. Consequently, for the majority of Irish people, changes in issues, such as family and morality, in recent decades has not meant that they have abandoned Catholicism altogether, but rather that they have redefined what this means in their personal lives (Fahey, 1998). Economic development, and in particular the Celtic Tiger years, have contributed to this change (Hardiman and Whelan, 1998).

The emerging liberal attitude polarized Irish society and public policy was confronted with the question of how to manage issues based on the values of the Catholic Church, such as same-sex marriage, divorce, and abortion. A pervasive anxiety of conservative parties about declining family stability provided the material for political mobilization regarding moral issues and shaped national politics which has led to a number of highly effective conservative political campaigns on moral key issues (Fahey, 1998). In addition to this, there are immediate causes of declining credibility. In particular, the series of clerical sexual abuse scandals of the mid-1990s. These incidents can fit into a broader discussion of secularization. However, such scandals undermine the credibility of the church regarding its expertise on certain matters, such as morality (Breen and Reynolds, 2011).

3 A Layered Perspective on Health Care Contexts

The social ecological framework emphasizes a shared responsibility for public health. The individual is responsible for choosing a healthy lifestyle. Health care organizations are responsible for providing effective, appropriate, and coordinated care. Finally, the government is responsible for developing effective health policies and passing the respective laws (Oetzel, 2009).

The middle of the 20th century was a time of significant change for the Irish healthcare system. In the post-war years, politicians improved the healthcare system, for instance, by increasing hospital facilities, radiological examinations, and offering free examinations for people suffering from tuberculosis, a widespread disease among poor people at that time. However, the Catholic Church interfered with politics. For instance, advanced plans for medical care, including free ante and post-natal care for mothers and extending free healthcare to all children under the age of 16 without requiring a means test to overcome the high levels of child mortality – known as 'Mother and Child Scheme ' – were undermined, foremost by the Catholic Church. This resulted in a remarkable controversy in Irish society, subsequently known as the 'Mother and Child Scheme'.

3.1 Bottom-Up Effects

The bottom-up effects take account of individual cases or individual organization of, for example events, walks, or protests, for change. Individuals become pioneers for health issues. They heighten public awareness and attention by their energy and dedication in addressing health issues and encourage others to tag along. In this way, the individual health issue becomes a public health issue. Thus, they give impetus, for instance, to social or political changes regarding health issues. Some pioneers are able to make a significant difference on particular health issues (Oetzel, 2009).

Noël Browne was the Minister for Health from 1948 to 1951. He had personal reasons to reform healthcare service. Due to tuberculosis he lost his parents and two of his siblings. As his family was of lower socioeconomic status, they could not afford adequate medical care (Murdoch, 1997). This personal experience may have influenced his decision to study medicine. He was educated at Trinity College in Dublin. After passing his exams, he became a medical practitioner but decided in the mid-1940s to enter politics. Influenced again by his personal experiences, he judged public health to be Ireland's most urgent need and consequently made this his foremost political objective. He advocated an anti-tuberculosis program and became Minister of Health in 1948. Further, he started various reforms, such as setting up the first Irish national blood transfusion service and introducing successful actions to combat the spread of tuberculosis. What is more, he was the one who suggested the 'Mother and Child Scheme' (Murdoch, 1997; Dwyer, 2011; Houses of the Oireachtas, 2016). However, his scheme was rejected by various parties. As a consequence of the quarrels, Browne was forced to resign in April 1951 (Murdoch, 1997; Kinealy, 2004; Houses of the Oireachtas, 2016; O'Regan, 2016).

3.2 Top-Down Effects

There are various factors related to the organization of the health care system which influence health care contexts with regard to the individual. The health care system can prevent health-seeking behavior based on socioeconomic status (Oetzel, 2009). For instance, the funding and accessibility of the health care system influences the degree to which individuals use health care. As mentioned above, tuberculosis was a widespread disease among poor people who had no access to medical care. Additionally, there are various factors related to the society which influence health care contexts with regard to the individual, such as larger societal, historical, and legal factors. The nature of the health care system has its basis in the culture in which the system operates (Oetzel, 2009).

There were several parties that opposed the reform proposals of the 'Mother and Child Scheme'. First, some wealthy lobbies blocked the free medical service because they feared that the socialization of medicine would have a negative impact on their privileged position within the Irish society. Second, the reform envisaged state-paid medical officers. Therefore, the medical profession, such as private practice doctors, feared a negative impact of free healthcare on their income. Third, and most important, the representatives of the Catholic

Church considered this demand an outrageous request and used its power and influence to interfere with the ongoing legislation process. The Catholic Church blocked free medical service for a variety of reasons. One aspect was the fear of the Catholic Church that the 'Mother and Child Scheme' would pave the way for liberal family planning and birth control (Murdoch, 1997). Representatives claimed that the scheme was in direct opposition to the rights of the family and of the individual because it discussed issues like family planning, including instructions with regard to sex relations, chastity, and marriage. However, the church felt these topics belonged to the remit of the church and from its point of view, the state was not qualified to interfere. The Catholic Church also rejected the increasing role of the state in the life of the individual. Finally, another reason for blocking the scheme was the rejection of Noël Browne as a person, because even though he was Catholic, he had been educated at Trinity College in Dublin (Dwyer, 2011).

It must be noted that Trinity College was founded by the Anglican Queen Elizabeth I in 1592. Many universities were founded at that time across Western Europe to give prestige to the state in which they were located. The idea of a university college for Ireland emerged when the English state was strengthening its control over Ireland, and its founders considered the establishment of a university an essential step in bringing the Protestant Reformation to the country (Robinson-Hammerstein, 2005). Therefore, Catholic representatives opposed people educated at Trinity College and rejected the treatment of Catholics by these health professionals even if they themselves were Catholics. At that time, the Archbishop of Dublin banned Catholics from entering Trinity College without the prior permission of the church, under pain of effective excommunication (Dwyer, 2011). This power of the Catholic Church was based on a decree passed in 1929 stating that no Catholic person could attend a non-Catholic educational establishment without special permission, a policy that also applied to Trinity College in Dublin (Kissane, 2003). Browne received no cabinet support when he tried to push through his reform opposing the resistance of the bishops. Eventually, Browne was forced to resign (Dwyer, 2011).

3.3 Interactive Effects

The ability to provide this form of universal health coverage was prevented by historically, politically, and culturally established elements. Further historical and traditional reasons explain why the Catholic Church has such great influence in Ireland. This case showed the power of the church in a new light and was intensely discussed by the public (Dwyer, 2011).

After his forced resignation, Browne turned to the media. He appeared on Radio Éireann to defend the scheme. Further, he passed on the correspondence between the opposing parties to the editor of one of the biggest newspapers in Ireland, *The Irish Times*. *The Irish Times* published this correspondence which revealed the influence of non-political parties on Irish politics (Dwyer, 2011). The public often becomes aware of social problems when they are focused on by the media which is called media advocacy. In this case, it involved the strategic use of mass media for the purpose of advancing health policy. The media were used to promote the health agenda of a particular group, here free health care for mothers and children. The media are able to move the masses and this ultimately has great influence on legislative decisions because politicians want to be reelected (Oetzel, 2009).

The subsequent controversy remains a noteworthy event in the history of Irish healthcare. The debate that emerged turned out to be a great church-state crisis. The 'Mother and Child Scheme' demonstrates how much of the early social policy reflected the close relationship of the state to the Catholic Church and serves as an example for the power of the church while at the same time revealing the weakness of the Irish government in the 1950s (Kinealy, 2004; Murdoch, 1997; Houses of the Oireachtas, 2016). This issue shaped the development of healthcare services in the future years (Houses of the Oireachtas, 2016). Keating and Martin (2007) speculate that the agricultural heritage of Ireland in combination with the majoritarian Catholic tradition ensured the maintenance of a fundamentally conservative base within politics. Indeed, the image of an Irish Catholic State remained strong for many decades. It was only with the economic developments that real changes occurred, that is, when the agrarian country transformed itself and within a few years was catapulted to an equal economic footing with its European neighbor countries (Keating and Martin, 2007).

4 A Layered Perspective on Attributions and Attitudes

Attributions are the explanations of others' or of a person's own behavior. Everyone who observes, or is engaged in interaction with one another, tries to make sense of the other person's behavior. These attributions influence the assessment of other people's behavior. The attributions are related to a person's attitudes, his or her predisposition toward an object or person. The attitudes include a person's likes and dislikes (Oetzel, 2009). Negative attitudes toward other people, or other cultural groups, are expressed through stereotyping, ethnocentrism, prejudices, and racism, which are explained in Chapter One, Section 3.3.

Attributions and attitudes can be treated as individual phenomena, meaning that these aspects of social cognition are viewed as the responsibility of individual people. Individuals can make improvements by being more mindful. However, this point of view neglects the sources, for instance, of stereotyping and prejudice. Thus, the layered perspective helps to explain these aspects of social cognition (Oetzel, 2009).

4.1 Bottom-Up Effects

The bottom-up effects examine how individual biases influence society. For example, people who express prejudice may influence others. Whether individuals have a lasting and deep impact on others seems to depend on the power these individuals possess. In general, people only have power when others choose to give it to them. However, in some situations persons are limited in their choices, for instance, when the other individual is above them in a fixed hierarchy, such as superiors at the workplace or government officials. But there are also people who have this power because they have control over what others see and do, such as an editor of a magazine or newspaper. The individual biases of an editor have influence on other people because he or she can determine which pictures and stories are shown and told. The presentation of information in the media is often biased in a particular direction because of the entertainment functions of the media. Individual executives have the power to influence the way in which certain cultural groups are presented (Oetzel, 2009).

During the 19th century, an anti-Irish attitude was common in the British press as illustrated by stereotypical images of vilified Irish people (Hickman, 2005). For instance, the British satirical newspaper *PUNCH* frequently published cartoons with Irishmen depicted as apelike creatures, implying that they were below the level of human beings. This is a racist viewpoint. The editors of *PUNCH* had the power to shape people's opinion in a particular direction.

The stereotypical Irishman was featured as 'feckless, stupid, drunken, combative, and relentlessly talkative'. The Irish people were despised by the British, and Irish society was attacked at all levels (McCaffrey, 2006).

The editor of *PUNCH* changed his mind in the late 19th century and even demonstrated his support to Irish Home Rule (Cathcart, 1994). He "...showed a genuine sympathy for what he considered genuine Irish sentiment and suffering..." (Spielmann, 1895, p. 106). However, a pronounced negative stereotype of the Irish people remained strong within the British society.

Figure 33: 'The British Lion and the Irish Monkey,' April 8, 1848 (Lemon, 1848)

Figure 34: 'The Irish Frankenstein. "The baneful and blood-stained Monster *** yet was it not my Master to the very extent that it was my Creature? *** Had I not breathed into it my own spirit?",' May 20, 1882 (Burnand, 1882)

4.2 Top-Down Effects

The top-down effects reveal how societal and organizational institutions have an impact on the individual's attributions and attitudes. One example is the institutionalized discrimination of a cultural group, for instance, by differential access to goods, such as the grocery distribution during the Great Famine, or services, such as education and health care. These are regularly organized actions that maintain the dominance of one group over another. There are different types of institutions which can influence an individuals' attribution and attitudes. In the following, the media and public policies are discussed.

Negative stereotyping of Irish is first recorded in the 12th century with the Norman chronicler Giraldus Cambrensis who used them to support Henry II's claims to Ireland and justify the Norman invasion of Ireland (Cambrensis, 1982; Kostick, 2005). Since the invasion of the Normans, the Irish were denounced again and again by their invaders who, in this way, sought to justify, for instance, seizing land from the Irish people leaving them to starve and also treating them badly, arguing that they were not human and therefore did not have the same rights as they did. This helped the Normans to maintain dominance over the Irish people.

In the case of the British media, it can be argued that not only the editors' opinion influenced the public, but also that the editors of *PUNCH* presented images of what they thought people wanted to see because the publishing company wanted to sell their press products. The British media used stereotyping for a simple representation of the Irish as a cultural group. However, these images helped create and reinforce the stereotype of the Irish for many British readers. Therefore, the media has an important functional role in shaping the attributions and attitudes of people (Oetzel, 2009).

Public policy also influences an individual's attitudes and attributions. The vast majority of people in a society comply with the laws, however, laws can negatively influence people's attitudes (Oetzel, 2009). During the period of the Great Famine in Ireland, there were smaller famines in Belgium and Russia. The governments of Belgium and Russia imported food for relief purposes and closed their ports for the export of food, in contrast to the British government (Kinealy, 2006). "With the public attitude in Britain increasingly against further Irish assistance, the government felt no compulsion to act or to make any further attempt to relieve the distress of the starving Irish" (McCaffrey, 2006, p. 170). The negative attitude of the British public influenced the attitude of the government decision-makers and in turn, the refusal of the British government to help the Irish strengthened the negative attitude of the public because they were confirmed in their view that the Irish were not worthy of help. Consequently, the Great Famine also became a political issue.

4.3 Interactive Effects

Since the invasion of the Normans, when the country came under the rule of the British crown, the Irish suffered from negative attribution and attitude by the English (please see Chapter Three, Sections 1.2 to 1.6). Already in the 12th century, the Norman churchman Giraldus Cambrensis or Gerald of Wales, who visited Ireland in 1183, described the Irish as untrustworthy and "filthy people, wallowing in vice" in his book *The History and Topography of Ireland* (Cambrensis, 1982, p. 106). He was a member of one of the leading Norman families and therefore, a very influential character of his time. With his book, he shaped a negative stereotype and fueled prejudices and racism against the Irish depicting them as underdeveloped people living in a primitive country.

Thus, cultural prejudice, stereotyping, and racism played a role in the treatment of the Irish by the British government. Among the influences that had an effect on the British government's treatment of Irish economic problems, cultural alienation was significant (Sen, 2007b). The Great Famine generated a struggle for the distribution of food (please see Chapter Three, Section 1.4). As Tajfel and Turner point out, conflicts between group interests heighten identification together with a positive attachment to the in-group (Tajfel and Turner, 1986). While poverty in Britain was associated with economic change and fluctuations, poverty in Ireland was widely viewed by the British as being caused by laziness, indifference, and ineptitude. Therefore, the British did not see it as their duty to relieve Irish distress (Sen, 2007b). The negative attitude of the British did not seem to change throughout the centuries. Even though Ireland became a full-fledged part of the United Kingdom by the Act of Union, it was not perceived as such by the English.

5 A Layered Perspective on Media

Media are layered in various aspects. Printed or broadcasted messages are created with a certain ideology in mind, but in turn, that ideology is produced for an audience. Thus, all media have top-down effects but it is also important to consider the bottom-up components. Individuals play an important role in influencing the media, for instance, through ownership or creation of media, or by the way in which an individual consumes media (Oetzel, 2009). For instance, historically the Irish have often been portrayed as a hard-drinking and therefore, the connection of Irish and heavy drinking has become a common stereotype (Mullen, Williams and Hunt, 1996; Helmreich, 1982).

5.1 Bottom-Up Effects

Media consumption considers a key component of bottom-up effects which is that audiences are active consumers of media. The creators of media encode mediated messages consistent with an ideology in their products. The audiences decode the messages transmitted by media and choose how to interpret them. There are different strategies of how people can cope with the transmitted messages. First, people can reject media consumption entirely and thus, completely reject the messages, for instance, by not buying newspapers, not switching on the television or radio. Second, people can consume media but ignore components of the messages by, for example, rejecting the stereotypes presented there (Oetzel, 2009). David Mandelbaum (1965), professor of anthropology, states that alcohol is the most important drink from a cultural perspective. It was historically the most widespread in use, the most valued as a ritual and societal artifact, and the most deeply embedded in diverse cultures (Mandelbaum, 1965). "Alcohol is a cultural artifact" (Mandelbaum, 1965, p. 281). Alcoholic beverages, such as wine, play an important role in Christian belief, for example, when receiving the Christian Communion by the consumption of the consecrated bread and wine. As Mullen, Williams, and Hunt (1996) state, the important effect of religion on alcohol use needs to be taken into account (Mullen et al., 1996). Thus, an audience may ignore the stereotype of Irish heavy drinkers because they interpret the drinking of alcohol as part of Christian culture. Third, an audience can also accept the messages and ideologies transmitted by the media (Oetzel, 2009). For instance, abroad, especially among Irish Americans, the consumption of alcohol was symbolic of Irish immigrants in America and their identity in the 19th century. It became a means of rediscovering and asserting their ethnic identity and heritage because Irish immigrants consumed alcohol for the reason of acculturation or reassertion of cultural identity in which "[a]cculturation is the dual process of cultural and psychological change that takes place as a result of contact between two or more cultural groups and their individual members." (Berry, 2005, p. 698; Mullen et al., 1996). With this experience, media audience may agree with the stereotype of Irish who excessively consume alcohol. Fourth, people can become advocates, by the attempt to contact the one in charge for the report and prompt him or her to differentiate the point of view in the presentation (Oetzel, 2009). According to WHO statistics, the consumption of alcoholic beverages in Ireland does not significantly deviate from other European countries, such as the United Kingdom or Germany (Anderson, Møller and Galea, 2012). Thus, if the media portray the Irish as outstanding heavy drinkers, people can appeal for a more differentiated presentation.

Finally, an individual can choose to create his or her own media product. Although the majority of the people are not likely to have the resources for producing a newspaper or a TV spot, a single person has the power to share his or her opinion via the internet due to online social networks, such as Facebook, video channels, such as YouTube, blogs, and other forms. In this way, an individual is able to reach a huge amount of people to share his or her opinion with them (Oetzel, 2009).

5.2 Top-Down Effects

The top-down effects of media focus on the fact that media is produced for audiences. The degree of an audience's reception of certain media messages determines the strength of the effect of the message on an individual's beliefs, attitudes, and behaviors. Oetzel emphasizes that studies found out that stereotypical presentations of people in the media affect the interpretations of the audience and can reinforce those stereotypes (Oetzel, 2009).

5.2.1 Reinforcement of Irish Stereotypes by Irish Companies

Irish companies strive to transmit a positive image of Ireland and the Irish and therefore, use synergy effects on Irish products to emphasize the sublime and honorable Irish characteristics. For instance, the Irish whisky company Tullamore Dew released a print campaign in 2014 in which the Irish are portrayed as charismatic, poetical, and riotous.

Figure 35: 'Irish True' Advertising Campaign of Tullamore Dew in 2011 (Charles, 2011)

'Campaign,' which calls itself the world's leading business media brand serving the marketing, advertising and media communities, reported on the new global advertisement campaign of the whisky company Tullamore Dew. The author describes the advertisement campaign as 'fresh' with striking images and charismatic characters that evoke the spirit of the Irish. The slogan of the campaign is 'Irish True'. The global brand director of Tullamore Dew states that it was their intention to establish a different definition of 'Irishness,' one that the people can relate to all over the world and that is rooted in the spirit of the people (Charles, 2011). Tullamore Dew uses social media platforms, such as Twitter.

5.2.2 Reinforcement of Irish Stereotypes by the Irish Government

Another example for a top-down effect that shows how media forms and reinforces stereotypes is that the Irish government promoted its own matters. The 'Dairy Produce Marketing Act, 1961,' determines in section 4, no. 3 that the board 'An Bord Bainne' is formed to endeavor and to improve and develop the marketing of milk products outside the state (Government of Ireland, 1961). The board was renamed to Ornua on June 1, 2015. The word *Ornua* is derived from the Irish language with *or* meaning 'gold' and *nua* meaning 'new'. Thus, the new label of the board headquartered in Dublin means 'new gold'. According to the corporate homepage, it is responsible for approximately 60% of Ireland's dairy exports to more than 100 countries with annual sales amounting to over €2 billion. Brands merchandised by Ornua are Kerrygold products, such as butter, cheese, yoghurt, and cream liqueur, Pilgrims Choice, Dubliner cheese, MU cheese, and BEO, a milk powder sold in Africa (Ornua Co-operative Limited, 2017a; Ornua Co-operative Limited, 2017b; Ornua Co-operative Limited, 2017c).

Thus, one can assume that the marketing campaigns of Ornua, present in more than 100 countries, have an enormous influence on people's perception of Ireland and significantly contribute to forming the image of a pure Irish green landscape and the stereotypical image of friendly people living in harmony with nature. Ornua also uses social media, such as Twitter and YouTube.

5.3 Interactive Effects

While in the middle of the 19th century, the Irish were very poor, dependent on British rule and suffered from the Great Famine (please see Chapter Three, Section 1.4), the independent Republic of Ireland of the 21st century experienced an economic upturn. Political incentives, such as low taxes, attracted especially

American high-tech giants, such as Google, Facebook, and others to set up their European headquarters in Dublin (Hudson, 2014). This gave the Irish a successful and urbane image, in contrast to the poverty-stricken, rural people of the 19th century. In addition to this, these large American companies were important employers for the small country, as they employed very many people.

The change in the portrayal of the Irish people can certainly be explained by the economic situation. The multimillion dollar investment of Tullamore Dew has been driven by the brand's rapid growth through a large increase in consumer demand for Irish whisky (Charles, 2011). A recent study reveals that there are causal connections between income and alcohol consumption. The study shows that the more income a household had per year, the more likely it was that alcohol was consumed on a regular basis in this household. Even though the people with higher income consumed alcohol more regularly, they were less likely to be excessive drinkers (Ascarelli, 2016). Thus, the study indicates that an economic upturn with lower unemployment rates and higher income would lead to more alcohol consumption. As a result, it can be assumed that the economic situation in Ireland led to the higher sales figures of Tullamore Dew. In turn, Tullamore was able to realize a multimillion dollar investment in a marketing campaign which formed an affirmative stereotype, not only of a company, but also of a whole country.

In the case of Ornua, Ireland's economic development also played a significant role. Joining the EEC in 1973, which enabled access to European markets, paved the way for Ornua's success. Its presence in more than 100 countries allows its advertising campaigns, showing Ireland's pure nature and building an image of friendly people living in harmony with nature, as mentioned above, to reach a huge amount of people.

6 A Layered Perspective on History

The layered aspects of history are multifaceted. History is the retelling of past events and represents the collective memory of a society. Consequently, it shapes cultural identity, social relations, and structures. History is part of collective memory and cultural identity. Negative events, so called historical trauma, are an intergenerational topic. History permeates and has an impact on all layers from culture to the individual, the so-called top-down effects. However, individuals also have the power to create, recreate, revise, and tell history, and shape a new future. Consequently, strong bottom-up effects exist, too (Oetzel, 2009).

6.1 Bottom-Up Effects

The bottom-up effects examine how individuals make and shape history. They change the course of history, such as Brian Boru, Charles Stewart Parnell and Éamon de Valera and are sometimes considered superhuman figures, as introduced in Chapter One, Section 2.2.2 and Chapter Three, Section 3.2. These people had a significant impact on Irish history and inspired and influenced many people. However, everyday people also rewrite history and can change the future (Oetzel, 2009).

In the previous Section 1 of this chapter, Katherine Zappone, Ann Louise Gilligan, and Brighid and Paddy Whyte are examples for ordinary people with no great political power and of no extraordinary wealth or stardom (High Court, 2006). The same is true for the politician Noël Browne who fought for better living conditions, especially for the Irish poor (Dwyer, 2008). All of them fought against the perceived injustices by going public and drawing attention to these injustices and in this way influenced other people. These are the many people who then followed their inspirers. Even though these people may be hidden in history, they have had a great impact on the future of Irish society.

Individuals help to capture hidden histories. Although the Great Famine is a well-known and unforgotten event in Irish history, it was blended out for a long period of time because of the deep wounds it left behind in Irish memory and a lack of responsibility of the British government. It was not until 150 years after the Great Famine that Tony Blair, the British Prime Minister of that time, first mentioned the lack of responsibility shown for the Irish people at that time and issued an apology in 1997 for British governmental behavior during the Great Famine in Ireland. This was appreciated by Irish politicians. The Irish Prime Minister was cited in the British *Independent* saying that British Prime Minister Blair's way of dealing honestly with the past would allow wounds to heal in the future (Marks, 1997). Kinealy (2006) argues that because the world seems no closer to preventing such disasters, studying the Great Famine in Ireland continues to have a relevance that goes far beyond a mere understanding of a decisive period of change in Irish history. She raises the question of how a developed world, with access to wealth and vast resources, is able to coexist alongside deprivation and famine. Further, the Great Famine is worth addressing within the context of social justice and human rights because famine still exists in the world today. For instance, political instability and obstruction of the economy is associated with hunger (Kinealy, 2006).

6.2 Top-Down Effects

Top-down effects are that history is the collective memory of a culture and shapes the cultural identity of members of that cultural group. Individuals have their own personal interpretation of this history and identity, however, past events influence that interpretation (Oetzel, 2009).

Further, history shapes public policy and the ensuing impact on organizational and individual behavior. For instance, immigration policy is influenced by history. In much of its history, Ireland was a country of emigration. Within 60 years, from 1841 to 1901, the population halved, mainly due to emigration and fatalities resulting from the Great Famine, and the population still continued to decrease. The majority of the emigrants leaving Ireland in the 19th and 20th century immigrated to North America. However, with the beginning of the Great Depression in the United States in the 1930s, these emigration flows broke off abruptly. Since then, most Irish who left Ireland immigrated to the United Kingdom, especially during World War II and its immediate aftermath, because many of them found work in the British war industry and the post-war reconstruction phase. Thus, for a long time, Ireland was characterized by a decreasing population and high emigration rates. However, the situation changed significantly in the time of the Celtic Tiger. Rapid economic growth brought considerably more immigrants into the country. Initially, immigration flows consisted mainly of Irish returnees but from 2000 onwards, a huge number of non-EU citizens came into the country, mainly looking for work but also refugees seeking asylum. Before 2003, the Irish work permit system was dominated by the employers with almost no state intervention. The extent of this development posed major challenges for policy makers and some quick political decisions were poorly conceived. Until today, Irish immigration policy is largely based on government decisions rather than on laws. However, due to the economic collapse in 2007, immigration has declined significantly and Ireland could soon record more emigrants than immigrants again. The future will show whether migrant workers return to their home countries, but it is probable that some will stay. Experts argue that the rapid change in the composition of the population has not yet led to serious integration problems. However, the poorly developed integration policy should be pushed forward and refined now in order to prevent social tensions within the population regarding the struggle for jobs in the future (Quinn, 2010).

6.3 Interactive Effects

History is part of the collective memory and shapes cultural identity (Oetzel, 2009). However, economic success provides the prerequisite for cultural identity to unfold in its entire splendor. Economic success, for example, enabled investments with which the Irish language and art could be promoted. Contrary to the years of oppression and poverty, Irish culture became something to be proud of. Experts argue that Ireland created a new image of itself as a modern, liberal, progressive, and multicultural country. Yet, it does not deal with the negative events of its past, such as the psychological legacy of colonialism, nor with its problems in the present, such as social injustice. The urbane center of Dublin is used as the common visual style for the whole country and shows a successful and 'more marketable' image of Irishness (Kirby, Gibbons and Cronin, 2002).

The Celtic Tiger posed major challenges for the Irish society. The economic success captured an important moment in Irish history, in which economic, social, and cultural structures were undergoing a fundamental transformation. This period of major transformation has provoked much discussion about the impact of the changes on values, culture, and psychological patterns (Moane, 2002). For instance, a decline in the power of the Catholic Church is also associated with the rise of the Celtic Tiger (please see Chapter Five, Section 2) (Kinealy, 2006; Hardiman and Whelan, 1998).

Chapter 6: A Layered Perspective on the Economic Ecology of Ireland

The recent worldwide economic crisis was a historical event, which had a deep impact on the Irish economy and Irish society. Although the Irish economy was hit hard by the worldwide financial crisis, Ireland would have had serious economic challenges even without it (Whelan, 2010; Whelan, 2013). The scars left by the economic crisis in Ireland are still evident throughout Irish society. Debates about the causes and effects of the events, along with questions regarding the responsibility of those involved, attracted public attention for a long time. New information on many aspects of the crisis and its consequences emerged little by little (Donovan and Murphy, 2014).

The multilayered model takes into account the influences of environments. In the following, the ecological approach is applied to the economic development of Ireland, in particular, with a focus on the Celtic Tiger period. The approach reveals the interrelations of politics, financial institutions, control mechanisms, and the media that together influenced human behavior. As a result, this approach can help to gain an understanding of the environmental influences that led to the fall of the Celtic Tiger.

The following analysis is focused less on Bronfenbrenner's macro-, exo-, meso-, and microsystem, but involves a simultaneous – instead of separate – examination at two or more layers (Oetzel, 2009). The approach is divided into bottom-up effects that examine how lower levels affect higher levels and top-down effects that examine how higher levels affect lower levels. The interactive effects assume a simultaneous process, meaning a conglomeration of multiple dimensions of different phenomena, which produces observable outcomes (Zhang and Ting-Toomey, 2014; Lejano and Stokols, 2013).

1 A Layered Perspective on Housing Acquisition

The Irish had always been preferential home owners. An increase in owner occupation is documented from 1946 onward to 1991, the year when owner occupation reached its peak. In this year, the proportion of owners of private dwellings nearly reached 80%. This proportion remained stable until 2002. From 2002 to 2006, homeownership declined by 9.5% and in 2012 came close to the lower European average of owner occupation. Due to the crisis, the percentage of people below the age of 25 and living with their parents increased in the years 2006 to 2011. These changes can be related with a rising unemployment rate in this age group provoked by the crisis. After 2007, credit was less available and due to falling market prices for homes, there was little motivation to purchase (NESC, 2014). The bursting of the property bubble led to more people renting than at any time since the early 1980s (O'Brien, 2015).

1.1 Bottom-Up Effects

Oetzel points out that a layered approach helps to identify how certain contexts support or inhibit behavior (Oetzel, 2009). Lejano and Stokols (2013) state that a layered perspective prompts a critical reevaluation of certain assumptions made about the nature of the value of goods. They argue that a common statement is that value is simply and completely determined by the intersection of supply and demand curves (Lejano and Stokols, 2013). However, people never act entirely rationally. Shiller (2000) argues that "…there are patterns of human behavior that suggest anchors for the market that would not be expected if markets worked entirely rationally" (Shiller, 2000, p. 136). Donovan and Murphy assert that bubbles imply irrational behavior (Donovan and Murphy, 2014).

1.1.1 Responsibility of Irish Households with Regard to their Balance Sheet

After the period of the Celtic Tiger had ended, Irish households were blamed to be partially responsible for the economic breakdown because of their excessively high number of housing purchases.

Lejano and Stokols (2013) argue that there were social, moral, rational, and financial indications alerting to the bubble but that these were ignored. They mention moral and rational considerations which should have led households with increasing levels of indebtedness to exercise greater caution regarding financial obligations (Lejano and Stokols, 2013). In contrast, Whelan (2010) states that the accusations against Irish households of them behaving carelessly and thereby contributing to the economic breakdown are untenable. He argues in line with the CB, that it is misleading to concentrate only on statistics for household debt, without looking at the other side of the balance sheet, such as household assets. Although Irish household debt rose substantially during the boom period, there was also an increase in assets (Whelan, 2010; Kelly, Cussen and Phelan, 2007). The force which drove changes in household net worth between 2001 and 2006 were increases in the value of households' housing assets. It was not until 2007, in the environment of decreasing house prices and accordingly decreased investment in housing assets, that household net worth also declined (Cussen, Kelly and Phelan, 2008). Thus, the changing economic environment influenced the composition of assets and liabilities of Irish households over the years after the bursting of the bubble. Therefore, the CB advises measuring household wealth in terms of both financial and real estate assets. The CB acknowledges that summative balance sheets provide useful information about the financial position of the household sector as a whole but also state that it gives no indication of how assets and liabilities are distributed across the sector (Kelly et al. 2007).

Further, the CB argues that the rate at which households incurred liabilities, such as mortgage rates to purchase property, grew at a pace similar to the acquisition of total household assets. By this, the households ensured a relatively stable saving rate over the Celtic Tiger period from 2002 to 2006 (Cussen et al. 2008). Whelan claims that instead of behaving irresponsibly, Irish households continued to save. Thus, despite the increased levels of debt, their net worth also increased significantly (Whelan, 2010).

1.1.2 Responsibility of Irish Households with Regard to Herd Behavior

The economist Robert Shiller (2008) identifies an epidemic irrational public enthusiasm for real estate investments as the core of the crisis. He states that the latest speculative housing bubble promoted the belief of the public that the prices for real estate would increase significantly because of the combination of the growth of population, economic growth, and the limited building areas in big cities and capitals (Shiller, 2008). "Investors are said to be euphoric or frenzied during booms or panic-stricken during market crashes. In both booms and crashes, investors are described as blindly following the herd like so many sheep, with no minds of their own" (Shiller, 2000, p. 135). Indeed, people do not act entirely rationally. The 'herd effect' is a decision-making behavior connected to investments and is an often discussed phenomenon influencing human behavior (please cp. Csipek, 2007).

Lejano and Stokols (2013) also interpret the households' behavior as a 'buying frenzy'. They argue that buying property is subject to individual income constraints. Thus, households misinterpreted, disregarded, or were mindless – as a consequence of herd behavior – of the difference between income expectations derived from long-run and sustainable sources, such as employment, and the mainly speculative expectations of income from subjective values within the real estate market. This circumstance psychologically kept households from exercising greater caution in times of increasing levels of indebtedness. Lejano and Stokols (2013) point out that paying a high price for a piece of real estate based on the expectation of an extensive price increase is a self-referential autonomous system which is dissociated from the actual material basis of the household and the actual value of the property (Lejano and Stokols, 2013).

One aspect in favor of the herd behavior theory regarding the imprudent purchase of real estate is that the Irish bought real estate over their needs. People with an average income owned three and more homes (Theurer, 2010). "Excessive focus on promoting owner occupation by means of general subsidies and tax incentives encourages owners to acquire accommodation in excess of their needs, tending to create a combination of 'over housing' at one end of the system…" (Memery 2000, p. vii).

In contrast, it is disputable, whether the savings and investment decisions of Irish households really were reckless, irresponsible, or based on herd behavior and group thinking. For despite the warnings, there was also reassuring reasoning of a 'soft landing' by credible sources, such as the media, banks, politicians, and financial regulators, such as the CB. Thus, it can be assumed that households tried to make the best decisions they could with the information available (Whelan, 2010).

1.2 Top-Down Effects

Somerville (2007) mentions economic considerations, such as tax incentives, which were in favor of house purchases. In 1982, the Commission on Taxation published in their report that "[the] tax and other advantages attached to owner-occupation have encouraged people to acquire their own houses and have resulted in a very high proportion of owner-occupied houses in Ireland by international standards" (Hederman O'Brien et al., 1982, p. 138). Further, the commission stated that they considered owner-occupation as a desirable social goal which should be encouraged by setting up incentives. However, they admitted that, because of the incentives, the demand for housing increased above real needs leading to an increase of prices of existing houses. This, in turn, made it more difficult for buyers to acquire their own homes (Hederman O'Brien et al., 1982).

In addition to this, the Irish government pursued a policy of low interest rates. Low interest rates imply low revenues but in return it becomes very cheap to borrow money. As a consequence, prices for real estate rose fast.

1.3 Interactive Effects

The economist Somerville (2007) states that the high occurrence of owner occupation in Ireland has various reasons. He claims that a possible explanation for this can be found in Irish history. "Historical factors relating to land tenure and to landlord and tenant legislation are a further part of the explanation of the level of owner occupation" (Somerville, 2007, p. 129).

1.3.1 Historically Determined Pursuit of Property

Lee (2008) argues that for hundreds of years, Catholics were forced to watch their Protestant counterparts who made up the social upper class and dominated the more prestigious professions, particularly in church, law, medicine, and trade. Thus, social imbalances may have led to a certain degree of envy (Lee, 2008). In the 19th century, "Irish Catholicism displayed an obsession with the materialistic…" (Lee, 2008, p. 16). However, this envy seemed to fade since the 1990s and made way for the insight that it was possible for everyone to achieve prosperity because the economic change had occurred so quickly that it was visible for everyone – this was the birth of the Celtic Tiger. The perception of Ireland as an economically undeveloped country was transformed into the image of a rising country with an affluent and dynamic society (Haughton, 1998).

The Irish people had already been driven from their land by the Normans and experienced a similar situation through the policy of plantation at the beginning of the 17th century. An eviction was a demonstration of the power of wealth and property over the right of a family (Siggins, 2014). Pádraic Kenna, an expert in the field of housing law, states that the Irish have deeply historically rooted sentiments regarding evictions (Kenna, 2011). The land issue was still a central topic in Irish politics of the 19th century. Irish landlords represented more than just land or property owners. They represented a world view and lifestyle because land ownership implied social status and reputation, as well as economic and political power. They lived a very privileged life and constituted the social elite of the 19th century. Their power derived from their land ownership (Kinealy, 2004). Next to being important for social acceptance, land also became an essential issue during the potato blight. As the Irish population grew, it was common to subdivide properties to increase the rents. This led to smaller farms. The potato had an enormous yield compared to other crops. When the potato blight hit Ireland, the cultivation area of single farms had become too little for the Irish farmers to survive through the yield of wheat crops (McCaffrey, 2006). As a result, striving for land tenure and property ownership could be seen as an important issue for the collective memory of the Irish.

Furthermore, Somerville refers to the series of 'Land Acts' which were passed by the Parliament of the United Kingdom to bring about land reform. British legislation established owner occupation as the basis of land tenure in rural Ireland. Despite the new law rural poverty could not be eliminated for the time being. Later, landlords were gradually bought out and tenant farmers became owner occupiers. In 1914, two-thirds of the former Irish tenants owned their own farm (Somerville, 2007; Kinealy, 2004). Thus, it can be assumed that owner occupation for the Irish is considered as regaining power and social status.

Even 150 years later, the owner occupation was still an ongoing topic. In 1997, an article in *The Irish Times* questioned why so many Irish were seeking ownership of their homes and for this purpose accepted huge mortgages for the subsequent 20 or 30 years. The article argued that elsewhere in Europe, there was no 'obsession' with home ownership but instead it was common to rent. The article concluded that therefore other Europeans often enjoyed a better lifestyle. In the article, the Irish desire for home ownership was identified as a crucial factor in the process of driving up house prices to an alarming degree. Ruairi Quinn, the Minister for Finance in Ireland from 1994 to 1997, expressed his concerns about increasing house prices. *The Irish Times* states that he worried that the surge in house prices would fuel inflation (Irish Times, 1997).

1.3.2 Social Identity and Ownership

According to the social identity theory, the long suppression by the British and the deep impact of the Great Famine on Irish self-esteem could be triggers for the Irish belief that the nature and structure of the relations between themselves and others is characterized by marked stratification, making it impossible or very difficult for them to get rid of the perceived image of an underprivileged nation. The economic and social realities of a society may be such that the impossibility of an autonomous escape becomes an everyday reality that determines intergroup social behavior. The major characteristic of social behavior related to this belief is that the Irish households did not act as individuals on the basis of their individual characteristics but instead joined the majority with regard to their purchasing decisions (Tajfel and Turner, 1986).

2 A Layered Perspective on Irish Politics

Keating and Martin (2007) describe Irish politics as centralized and monopolistic within the context of a personalist political structure. Further, they argue that this environment has led to a culture of nepotism and cronyism between government ministers, senior administrators, and organized representative groups, which is supported by the Irish electoral system (Keating and Martin, 2007). Their view is supported by a tribunal in Ireland which also concluded that corruption had come to affect every level of Irish political life. The investigative body, known formally as the *Tribunal of Inquiry into Certain Planning Matters and Payments* and informally as the *Mahon Tribunal*, investigated accusations that politicians sought bribes from property developers in return for favorable decisions on land rezoning. The report painted a devastating picture of Ireland's political culture and caused great consternation throughout Irish society (Dalby, 2012; Flood and Mahon, 2013). Following the publication in 2012, the Irish party Fianna Fáil intended to expel the members that were found to have received corrupt payments. However, various politicians resigned from the party before they could be expelled (RTÉ, 2012). Other politicians and officials received prison sentences for tax evasion and for non-cooperation (Reilly, 2012; McDonald, 2016).

2.1 Bottom-Up Effects

Economists, such as Kelly, pointed out the threat to the Irish economy by concentrating on construction activity. However, government representatives did not take action to cool the property market. There was a strong national consensus, not only among the public, but especially among politicians, that there would be a 'soft landing' (Whelan, 2013; Kelly, 2006; Kelly, 2007; Theurer, 2010). Various individuals in the political landscape contributed to the economic situation (Nyberg, 2011). In the following, the actions of important decision-makers which influenced the political environment are discussed.

The economist and government advisor Peter Bacon issued the so-called *Bacon Reports* in association with the architect Fergal MacCabe and the economist Anthony Murphy. These are economic reviews and assessments of the housing market in Ireland, published in 1998, 1999, and 2000. In the report of 1999, he states that since 1998, the housing market had been characterized by runaway inflation and widespread panic buying of new houses. He indicates that the government took action to cool down the housing prices and that the recommendations in his reports were implemented by the government which helped stabilize housing prices. He resumes that "[t]here is considerable and growing statistical evidence of a slowdown in the rate of increase in new house prices" (Bacon, MacCabe and Murphy, 1999, p. 47). He then continues that "[t]here is widespread consensus that Government actions have played a key role in achieving this slow-down" (Bacon et al., 1999, p. 47). However, in 2001, the government reversed some of the measures, such as the cutting of stamp duty to investors, without consulting him. Bacon was later a respondent in the banking inquiry. He admitted that the measures he had recommended regarding the housing market were reversed too early by the government, which ultimately led to increases in property prices (Lynch et al., 2015a; Gleeson, 2015a).

Mary Harney, the Tánaiste (deputy prime minister), stated in 2000 that the government had created an attractive economy. She emphasized that companies from the United States would find a country in Ireland which believed in the incentive power of low taxation, economic liberalization, and regulation but not overregulation, in contrast to other European countries (McDermott, 2010). The Irish government pursued a strategy of low taxation and in their opinion this would stimulate growth – in the same way in which high taxes lead to low growth and high unemployment (Dunne, 2001). Whelan points out that the decisions made about the balance of public spending and taxation were political decisions. These remarks of Harney sparked off debates in Ireland about the socio-economic model that Ireland had chosen because major U.S. companies benefited from low taxation whereas social spending was cut. Ireland had a situation with an increase in public spending and falling tax rates. However, the government did not intervene to stop these undesirable developments (Whelan, 2010).

Bertie Ahern, the former Prime Minister of Ireland, admitted in an article, published in the *Financial Times*, that his decision in 2001 to create a new financial regulator, was one of the main reasons for the collapse of the Irish banking sector. The newly created regulator – namely the Irish Financial Services Regulatory Authority (IFSRA) or in short Financial Regulator (FR) – was established in 2003 as an autonomous body within the CB, under which the supervision of all financial institutions operating in Ireland was consolidated (Government of Ireland, 2003; Central Bank of Ireland, 2003). After the establishment of the new regulator, Ahern admitted that there was no exchange of information between him and the new regulator. As a result, he was unaware of the actual situation of the banks (Murray Brown, 2009). Further, Ahern accused the banks of having behaved irresponsibly. He blamed the CB and the FR for never really having controlled the banks or taken legal measures against them (Egan, 2009). Further, he did not allow criticism of the government for the economic crisis (Breadun, 2009).

Charlie McCreevy, the Minister for Finance from 1997 to 2004, was warned repeatedly by EU officials that Ireland's property market was overheating. Yet, he did not take the warnings seriously (McDermott, 2010). Instead, the minister defended his policy (Sheehy, 2015; Irish Times, 2015). Even after the property bubble had busted and the Irish government had started an official investigation into the reasons, he stated that in his opinion, the government had done a "very, very respectable job" (Lynch et al., 2015b, section 1672).

Alan Ahearne, professor of economics, warned the Minister for Finance Brian Lenihan, in office from 2008 to 2011, of the banks' actual financial status before the blanket guarantee was enacted. He stated that he had the impression that the minister may not have had an accurate picture of the banking system when he met with him to talk about the crisis. Ahearne advised the minister to obtain a precise and accurate picture of the banks' situation, and pointed out the importance of knowing what their loan books really looked like. During the inquiry, Ahearne stated that the minister thanked him for this piece of advice and admitted it to be valuable (Lynch et al., 2015c; Gleeson, 2015b). The Irish Banking Inquiry Commission concluded in their so-called *Nyberg Report* that the lack of suspicion and the absence of appropriate information regarding the underlying quality of the banks' economic situation were likely to have had a significant impact on the alternatives considered reasonable on September 29, 2008. Further, the *Nyberg Report* claimed it to be decisive that decisions for the management of a crisis be based on proper information representing reality. However, decisions were made on the false assumption that all banks were – and would remain – solvent. There is no other way to understand the decision of the government to provide a broad guarantee (Nyberg, 2011).

Taking into account the findings of the *Mahon Tribunal* at the beginning of Section 2, which documents the existence of various references to the fact that many politicians and officials received corrupt payments, it can be concluded that there was not just a lack of understanding of the actual financial situation, but that the decision-makers did not intend to deal with the actual financial situation because of their involvement.

2.2 Top-Down Effects

Karl Whelan, professor of economics, accused the Irish government that in 2007, when a substantial slowdown became apparent, warnings were ignored in the implementation of economic policy. He admitted that Ireland was a small and open economy, and therefore, it certainly would have slithered into a recession no matter what actions would have been taken by the government. However, he held the Irish government responsible for overheating the Irish economy. In particular, he criticized a failing housing policy which bloated the public sector. The public sector provides services on behalf of the government, such as defense, health services, infrastructure, and housing policy. Thus, Whelan considered the Irish government a main guilty party for the economic crisis and its social consequences for Ireland (Barro and Grilli, 1996; Whelan, 2010; NESC, 2014). He blamed the Irish politicians for their over-optimism regarding economic growth in the period of the Celtic Tiger. In his opinion, this over-optimism led to a number of serious political errors (Whelan, 2010).

Although tax revenues had continued to rise throughout the boom, the composition of these revenues had basically changed. In particular, income tax rates were frequently cut. The substantial increases in income meant that the income tax revenue still rose every year but income taxes as a share of GNP fell by approximately 7% compared to the 1980s. In addition to this, there were money grants to first-time buyers between 1977 and 2002. For instance, buyers of new houses were eligible for relief of stamp duty (Whelan, 2010). Moreover, the rates of stamp duty applicable to residential property decreased constantly (Whelan, 2010; National Stamp Duty Office, 2016). This tax reduction enabled even more real estate transactions (Theurer, 2010). Thus, the government created incentives to buy property.

Then again, the government received enormous tax revenues generated by the construction sector during the boom, for instance, in form of stamp duty, capital gains taxes, and VAT. With tax revenues being heavily dependent on the construction sector, after the bursting of the bubble, state revenues decreased all the more, leading to an even higher increase in budgetary deficit (Whelan, 2010; Theurer, 2010).

Whelan speculates that the government did not expect the housing market, and therefore the rest of the economy, to be affected to a noticeable degree in the case of an economic downturn (Whelan, 2010; Kelly, 2006). In fact, there was actually cross-party agreement that the Irish economy could continue to grow (Whelan, 2010).

2.3 Interactive Effects

Whelan (2010) argued that a sharp economic slowdown was going to follow any decline in house prices and this event preceded the global crisis. The over-optimism that pervaded economic policymaking in Ireland in the years up to 2007 left the economy in a very dangerous position (Whelan, 2010).

However, Donovan and Murphy (2014) counter that politicians not just influenced but also reflected the predominant way of thinking at that time. Politicians are only able to execute their mandate effectively if their policies are accepted by the majority of their respective voters. The general election campaigns confirmed that the expansionary budgetary policies received approval by an overwhelming majority in 2007. In 2002, the main party of the opposition indicated overruns in government spending and in turn suffered its worst electoral defeat ever. In 2007, no concerns about extensive government spending were addressed in their campaign. Instead, all parties in the 2007 election promised to continue to lower the taxes and increase expenditure. Topics, such as the sustainability of the property boom, the state of the banking system, or the effects of wage increases in the public and private sector on competitiveness, were never a central theme in the 2007 election campaign or before. Donovan and Murphy conclude that the mindset of the key officials, and their policy actions or inactions, did not evolve in a vacuum. For instance, they were influenced by the general public perception and in the case of political parties, dependence on votes (Donovan and Murphy, 2014).

Politicians relied on the stability mechanisms, which obviously failed. Various institutions, such as the CB in their Financial Stability Report (FSR) of 2006 and the Economic and Social Research Institute (which claims to provide independent research to support economic policymaking in Ireland) in their report of spring 2007, predicted growth. The FSR of 2006 states "that the economy will continue to grow quite strongly" in 2007 and further predicts, even if slightly weaker, growth for 2008 (CBFSAI, 2007a, p. 14). The Economic and Social Research Institute states "[f]or 2007, we expect another strong year of growth" (Barrett, Kearney and O'Brien, 2007, p. 1).

After the 2007 election, the former chief economist of the CB and board member of the IMF Michael Casey predicted that a forthcoming economic downturn would lead to punishment of the new government by voters not being able to understand why the times of the Celtic Tiger were over. However, he admitted that it was unlikely that any government would be able to do anything to prevent a recession at this point. Further, he speculated that the new government which had to preside over such an economy was likely to suffer electoral damage for a very long time to come. The prize to be won at the 2007 election could turn out to be a heavy burden in his opinion. Further, he resumed that lost confidence of producers, consumers, and investors would impact the medium-term prospects of the economy (Casey, 2007).

Patrick Honohan and his colleagues (2010) also blame political decision-makers for significantly contributing to the economic overheating and in this context mention the unsustainable dependence on the construction sector which was encouraged by the incentives. This also contributed to creating a climate of public opinion of an ongoing and never-ending upswing (Honohan et al., 2010).

3 A Layered Perspective on the Irish Banks

The banking inquiry report did not and could not assess the actions or inactions of single individuals within organizations. The commission of the banking inquiry report regarded it neither appropriate nor fair to do so because larger developments within banks tend to take place as a consequence of complex interactions between many people. In their opinion, it was not generally possible to infer how a certain unit in the bank functioned and how its members operated individually. They concluded that any reference to a bank, its board, or any of its committees or functions was not intended as a reference to any individual (Nyberg, 2011).

However, Ross and Whelan accuse all bankers of being reckless crooks. Ross (2009) states that there definitely were crooks among the bankers in Ireland and that conspiracies between regulators and bankers were nothing new. Bankers, in his opinion, always worked to create a culture pursuing quick profits. In 2010, it became public that the BoI overcharged borrowers. As a result, some of their customers lost their homes because of too high interest rates imposed by the bank. The scandal triggered enormous public disapproval (Murray, 2016; Reddan, 2016). However, Ross mentions that there had been bailouts before 2008. Small groups had regularly grabbed control of banks at the expense of taxpayers. Thus, Ross calls the Irish banking history 'shameful' because of its recurring banking scandals. As evidence for this, he cites the recurring rise and collapse of smaller banks caused by mismanagement and also specifically the rescue of AIB, one of Ireland's biggest banks, by the state in 1985 because AIB was too big for the state to accept a collapse. However, in his opinion, the activities of the larger banks suggest that banking skullduggery was prevalent (Ross, 2009). Whelan (2010) argues that reckless banks enabled the credit-fueled spending binge of Irish people and blames the control mechanisms, such as the FR, of doing nothing against this undesirable development. These reasons led to the housing bubble (Whelan, 2010).

3.1 Bottom-Up Effects

The economist Raghuram Rajan (2005) states that the competition between managers can lead to superior performance but can also lead to misconduct of the managers. As an example for perverse behavior of managers, he mentions that a manager herds with his peers on investment choices. This behavior gives the manager the psychological security and comfort of not underperforming compared to his peers. Rajan states that herd behavior can lead to over- or undervaluation of assets (Rajan, 2005). The *Nyberg Report* identifies the willingness of bank managers to accept higher risks by providing more and extraordinary larger loans as an important reason for the gradual increase in financial fragility in Ireland (Nyberg, 2011). Honohan et al. also argue that banking practices played a significant role in contributing to the crisis. They state that there is evidence for a comprehensive failure of bank management (Honohan et al., 2010).

In addition to this, there were significant mistakes in the forecasts made by the bank experts. For instance, in April 2007, at the beginning of the property collapse, Ulster Bank's internal analysts predicted a worst-case scenario fall in house prices of 20% (Murtagh, 2016). Donovan and Murphy see possible reasons for such misinterpretations of the data in the fact that training programs for junior staff were cut for cost-saving reasons. At the same time, the banks encouraged their more experienced managers, versed in risk management, to retire and replaced them by junior staff with no knowledge of the credit cycle. The junior staff was incentivized by sales-based bonuses. Besides, the boards of the banks determined goals that could only be achieved by constantly increasing lending. Bank employees were also encouraged to borrow from their own employer which led to a number of banking executives holding a huge amount of real estate. Donovan and Murphy further specify that this change in banking culture was evident at the top levels and point out that at the height of the bubble, there was no specialist in risk management on the board of AIB (Donovan and Murphy, 2014).

Although the *Nyberg Report* questions the possibility of assigning the blame to individual participants, it is striking how some involved decision-makers have behaved, even if they were not solely responsible for the crisis.

3.1.1 Revelations of the Irish Independent

Evidence emerged which should challenge the honesty of the bankers. On June 24, 2013, the *Irish Independent* provoked a media, political, and public storm and rocked Ireland's financial establishment by publishing telephone records. The audio recordings that were leaked to the *Irish Independent* are from the bank's own internal telephone system and were recorded at a time when the crisis was reaching its climax, beginning on September 18, 2008 and continuing in the following months. The revelations with the headline 'Inside Anglo: the secret recordings' display a reckless attitude of decision-makers at the bank during the financial breakdown (Williams, 2013a; Feehan, 2013). Involved persons on the records are decision-makers in high positions at Anglo, such as John Bowe the Head of Capital Markets at Anglo at the time, Senior Manager

Peter Fitzgerald, Director of Retail Banking at Anglo at the time, and David Drumm, Chief Executive Officer of Anglo at the time (Feehan, 2013). Bowe, who had been involved in negotiations with the CB, tells Fitzgerald how Anglo was luring the state into giving it billions of euros (Williams, 2013a; Theurer and Plickert, 2013). The two bankers talk about the need to disguise the real extent of Anglo's problems in order to get the Irish government to use taxpayers' money to save the bank (Theurer and Plickert, 2013). Further, Bowe admits to his colleague Fitzgerald that Anglo had reported the need for a bridging loan of 7 billion euros to the CB in order to avert bankruptcy but that he knew in fact much more money was needed. Bowe states that the sum is fictitious (O'Carroll, 2013). He explains his strategy this way: he wants to pull the CB in, get them to write a big check so that they have to stick with their strategy in order to not lose their money (Harrison, 2013). Thereupon, Fitzgerald suggests that the CB would then be involved too deeply to give up their support (Feehan, 2013). Further, Bowe states that they will never pay back the bridging loan, although they promised the CB to pay it back as soon as possible (La Roche, 2013; Murphy, 2013). Michael Noonan, Minister for Finance from 2011 until the present, recalls Brian Lenihan, his predecessor as Minister for Finance until 2011, saying that Anglo requested 7 billion euros to avert bankruptcy. Then, a couple of weeks later, Anglo demanded more money and finally, another couple of weeks later, there was again a demand for further support (Murphy, 2013). The managers in question later issued statements denying they were part of a strategy to mislead the CB and stated that they knew of no such effort (Harrison, 2013). Kelly, who had correctly predicted the meltdown of the housing boom and the construction sector, was heavily attacked by the Anglo bankers, which was revealed in further records. They denounced Kelly's research quality to the point of accusing him of doing no research and that he was just making empty claims. In addition to this, they accused him of using the media to destroy the confidence in the banking sector, blamed him of sabotage, and even uttered threats (Quinlan, 2014). Drumm, stated that they were abusing the bank guarantee and warned his executives not to be caught abusing it (Williams, 2013b).

These revelations clearly show that the bankers were well informed about the actual financial situation and, in particular that their actions were carried out with full intent.

3.1.2 International Reactions

The revelations also triggered strong criticism of the managers of Anglo on an international level. The German Chancellor Angela Merkel strongly condemned the Irish bank's executives for mocking Germany because deposits from Germany had flown into Anglo as a result of the bank guarantee. She stated that the behavior of the managers damages democracy, the social market economy, and the trust in the Irish as a partner. The Irish Taoiseach, Enda Kenny, also admitted that the furor had damaged the country's standing (Williams, 2013b; Traynor, 2013).

3.2 Top-Down Effects

As explained in Chapter Four, Section 3.6, since 2001, the financial system was based on a more speculative form of financing. The growth of the Irish economy encouraged foreign institutions to enter the Irish financial market and herd behavior became common among Irish banks in an attempt to protect and grow their market share. Anglo was the first to introduce the risky business model. However, rather than assessing prudently the risky nature of the model, AIB and BoI also adopted the model in an attempt to aggressively compete with Anglo for market shares (Donovan and Murphy, 2014). Therefore, in 2006, the sustained significant growth in domestic lending and the imprudent behavior on the part of the banks should have given reason for serious concern among the authorities. The FR had full access to any banking information it called for. Regulated banks were required to report, for instance, on their largest borrowers, growth in lending, the sector distribution of lending, and how lending was funded. This information was also available to the CB (Nyberg, 2011). However, neither the FR nor the CB expressed concerns or exerted pressure regarding the Irish developments and institutions. This behavior of non-intervention gave the banks additional confirmation in assuming that there was nothing to worry about (Ross, 2009).

In 2013, the *Frankfurter Allgemeine Zeitung (FAZ)* reported that the bankruptcy of the banks had cost more than 30 billion euros in the end. The extremely high sums for the small country in the attempt to save Anglo and two other bankrupt banks were the main reason why the Irish state itself was on the edge of insolvency. At the end of 2010, Ireland applied for financial support from the European Rescue Package and was granted a multi-billion euros aid program from other members of the Eurozone and the IMF (Theurer and Plickert, 2013; Whelan, 2013). The aid program covered a total of 85 billion euros to meet the debt and to compensate the succession costs. 17.5 billion euros are contributed by Ireland itself. The rest is granted to Ireland in form of loans from European member states and the IMF between 2010 and 2013. The total credit grants of 85 billion euros have been fully paid to Ireland. The aid program was terminated as planned in December 2013 (Bundesministerium der Finanzen, 2016).

3.3 Interactive Effects

Economists consider the Celtic Tiger period in two parts. In the first part of the period, from 1994 to 2000, there was an exceptionally high overall economic growth: Real income rose significantly, there was immigration from EU neighbors, the unemployment rate was exceptionally low, and the labor force increased because of demographic factors, as mentioned before. Consequently, more people were able to acquire a house for themselves. As a result, the increase in house prices was linked closely to economic fundamentals. The lending practice was based on the traditional model, as explained in Chapter Four, Section 3.6 (Whelan, 2013; Donovan and Murphy, 2014). In 2001, property prices cooled down. Events outside Ireland had a significant impact on the Irish economy, such as the busting of the dot.com bubble, which began in March 2000, and the destruction of the World Trade Center in New York on September 11, 2001 (Fehr, 2008). Consequently, there was an abrupt decline of investments from U.S. companies (Frentz, 2003; Donovan and Murphy, 2014). However, instead of taking actions, such as stabilizing the construction sector at a sustainable level, the Irish property market was resuscitated by introducing a wide range of fiscal incentives for property buyers. At the same time, banks changed their financing models. Indeed, there were whistleblowers, however, they were numerically inferior. The *Nyberg Report* speculates that expressing contrary views could have led to sanctions for the whistleblower. Moreover, the boom times caused sceptics to doubt rooting against the prevailing and apparently validated consensus of an outperforming economy (Nyberg, 2011). From then on, the Celtic Tiger phenomenon changed and the property market became a bubble that ended up poisoning all sectors of the economy (Whelan, 2013; Donovan and Murphy, 2014).

Journalist and author Simon Carswell also expressed his views before the banking inquiry commission about the connection between state authorities, local authorities, banking institutions, and the property sector in the run-up to the banking crisis. He stated that the relationships between banks, politicians, builders and regulators were very close at the highest levels. He revealed developers donating money to the leading political party Fianna Fáil, senior politicians mixing with prominent builders at quasi social events, and former politicians working as lobbyists for construction and financial industry groups.

Therefore, no group could really express concerns without blaming another. He argued that for the parties involved it was comfortable and self-serving to stay in the crowd and stick with the consensus, particularly because so many people made so much money (Kelly, 2015a; Lynch et al., 2015d).

4 A Layered Perspective on the Irish Financial Services Regulatory Authority of Ireland (IFSRA)

Financial supervision of credit institutions had previously been undertaken by a dedicated department within the CB (Donovan and Murphy, 2014). However, in 1998, the Irish government decided to establish a single regulatory authority for the financial services sector because the existent system of sanctions and penalties for financial institutions were considered ineffective. The only option for the CB seeking to punish a bank was to withdraw its license, but this was an extreme move and would lead to mutually assured destruction. As a consequence, it was very unlikely that anyone would ever take this step. Thus, it was the government's intention to create a system of regulation which was efficient, accountable, and reduced the probability of regulatory failure. David Llewellyn, professor in the field of money and banking, argued in an interview in 1999 that there were pros and cons on either side – establishing an independent regulator or appointing the CB as the single regulatory body. Both options had to be finely balanced and he added that there was no single right answer to the question (Kelleher, 1999; Donovan and Murphy, 2014). Thus, the government decided to establish an 'Implementation Advisory Group' chaired by Michael McDowell, the Attorney General of that time. This group was set up to advise the government on the role and functions of the single financial regulatory authority, such as prudential supervision and consumer protection and also on the range of financial service providers to be overseen by the authority including, among others, banks, finance companies, and moneylenders (McDowell, 1999; Murray Brown, 2009). Yet, the issue itself, as to whether there ought to be a single regulatory authority, was never a matter of consideration for the 'Implementation Advisory Group' (Kelleher, 1999). Nevertheless, in 1999, the *McDowell Report* recommended the creation of a new regulatory authority and the removal of any direct supervisory responsibilities from the CB (McDowell, 1999; Donovan and Murphy, 2014). The CB disagreed strongly with the main recommendation of the report. It argued that there were no reasons for transferring existing regulatory functions elsewhere and referred to high risks, such as a loss of regulatory expertise (Central Bank of Ireland, 1999). In addition, the

CB warned that removing its regulatory functions would involve risks for the international reputation of the Republic (Kelleher, 1999).

Finally, it was agreed that a separate FR would be set up within an overall new structure called the Central Bank and Financial Services Authority of Ireland, abbreviated as CBFSAI.

4.1 Structure of the CBFSAI

The CBFSAI is comprised of two divisions, the FR and the CB. The FR became responsible for the micro-prudential supervision, i.e. the development and implementation of the regulatory framework at the level of individual banks and other financial service providers (Barwell, 2017; Donovan and Murphy, 2014). This is the traditional form of banking supervision which primarily monitors compliance with qualitative (e.g. risk management) and quantitative (e.g. equity ratio, minimum capital ratio) guidelines at the individual institution level (Barwell, 2017; Trautmann and Mäkelä, 2017a; Nyberg, 2011). Whereas the CB was in charge of systemic financial stability matters, i.e. the analysis of the micro-prudential where appropriate and the macro-prudential functioning of the financial sector (Honohan et al., 2010). Macro-prudential supervision of the entire financial system includes the functions of those supervisory authorities in charge of identifying, evaluating, and easing risks for the financial system as a whole. Macro-prudential supervision has the task of maintaining the soundness and stability of the entire financial system. Macro-prudential supervisory authorities can issue warnings about undesirable developments and recommend measures for hazard prevention (Trautmann and Mäkelä, 2017b; Barwell, 2017).

Both authorities, the CBFSAI and the FR, were governed by independently appointed boards. However, a majority of the board members of the FR also sat on the CBFSAI board. The two institutions shared overhead resources, such as human resources. Thus, the actual independence of the two boards is questionable (Donovan and Murphy, 2014).

4.2 Bottom-Up Effects

The following shows how both wings of the CBFSAI failed and the roles of some key decision-makers of the FR and the CB are examined.

4.2.1 The Financial Regulator

On the one hand, there was the FR. According to Donovan and Murphy (2014), the FR reassuringly reported to the Minister for Finance Brian Lenihan in September 2008, that there was no cause for significant concern regarding the state of the Irish banking system. The former Chief Executive Officer (CEO) of the FR, installed since February 2006, was also invited by the commission of the *Nyberg Report.* He argued in favor of a blanket bank guarantee on September 29, 2008 stating that this would provide more certainty to the markets (Ross, 2009). Explaining his recommendation, he said that there were initially two options considered. The first was a nationalization of Anglo combined with a guarantee for the five remaining banks. The second was a guarantee for all the banks. However, he had had concerns about confusion in the market regarding nationalized banks and guaranteed banks. Questions about the strength of the nationalized bank in comparison with the guaranteed bank would have arisen. This confusion would not have led to desirable inflow of liquidity but would have strengthened the undesirable outflow of deposits (Hancock, 2015). In that case, all banks would have risked being adversely affected. Consequently, he advised the guarantee decision extending it to cover the depositors in all banks concerned in the same manner (Hancock and Minihan, 2015). He argued that the banks merely suffered from a liquidity problem, a shortage of money to fund day-to-day operations, but that there was no issue of possible bank insolvency which called for consideration. However, it was in fact a solvency crisis in the financial system. The Irish banks did not have enough resources to cover losses on loans in case of an economic decline (Honohan et al., 2010; Carswell, 2010; Donovan and Murphy, 2014).

He declared that the common opinion was that there would be a 'soft landing' of the Irish property market and that the analysis of the CB gave the FR comfort. He relied on the banks for the analyses of risk management. Consequently, no action through the regulator was necessary because each individual bank was in compliance with its regulatory requirements. He admitted that the regulatory system, in which he worked at the time, had failed and expressed his regrets (Hancock, 2015). Further, during the questioning, he stated that he was 'deeply sorry' for deficiencies in the regulatory system. He conceded that the regulatory authority had had the power to set ratios and, from a contemporary point of view, an intervention would have been necessary and the regulator could have found a way (Lynch et al., 2015e; Hancock and Minihan, 2015). However, in his opinion, the primary responsibility for the crisis was to be found within the banks themselves. He stated that the boards and directors of the banks had deserted their customers (Hancock, 2015).

4.2.2 *The Central Bank of Ireland*

On the other hand, there was the CB. The main instrument for fulfilling the task of its macro-prudential supervision was the FSR, published once a year from 2004 to 2007. Officially, the FSR was published by the CBFSAI, however, the report was prepared by a small group of economists working within the CB (Donovan and Murphy, 2014). The CB had the power to contribute to overall financial stability because it had the right to issue an order on the activities of the FRs and it also had the power to advise the government. Yet, there are no records of such advice or even of efforts aimed in this direction. The macroeconomic developments between 2005 and 2006 should reasonably have raised concerns on the part of the CB (Donovan and Murphy, 2014; Nyberg, 2011). The risks were addressed, for instance, by the FSR in 2007:

> In the Financial Stability Report 2006 the overall assessment was that financial stability risks had increased since the previous year's Report was published. However, the overall conclusion was that the Irish financial system continued to be in a good state of health" (CBFSAI, 2007a, p. 25).

Thus, the risks were judged to be insufficiently alarming to take major restraining policy measures. Among all these authorities, only a very limited number of individuals, in boards or among staff, assessed the risks as weighty enough. Additionally, these few people failed to convince the persons in charge to take stronger measures. However, the *Nyberg Report* concludes that this cannot explain the lack of clear confidential warnings and therefore speculates about a 'state of denial' within the CB (Nyberg, 2011). In 2005, the economist Thomas O'Connell, who holds the position as Assistant Director General and Chief Economist of the CB's economics division bore witness to the commission of the *Nyberg Report*. He was, among others, responsible for economic analysis, research and publications, monetary policy and financial stability. He said that in 2001, he realized that things had run out of the rudder and that a massive property bubble had developed. However, the FSR remained reassuring, stating that this did not correlate with their data. He argued that opposing views within the CB were not well received and that concerns had been blocked from reaching a higher level in the bank due to political and property interests on the top management level (Gleeson, 2015c). Further, O'Connell stated that principally three seniors in the bank had had the 'final say' in amending the stability report before it was sent to the board, one of them was the former CB Director

General Liam Barron. He stated that Barron decided to exclude warnings about the overvaluation of property from a 2007 financial stability report (Kelly, 2015b). O'Connell claimed that the senior managers within the bank simply did not wish to know about the problems or that they did not wish to do anything about them (Carolan, 2016).

4.3 Top-Down Effects

In 2000, Ireland participated in the Financial Sector Assessment Program (FSAP). FSAP was launched in 1999 and is a cooperation of the IMF and the World Bank. The goal of the program is to support countries in reducing the possibility of financial sector crises. The FSAP provides a framework through which assessors and authorities are able to identify financial system vulnerabilities and helps to develop appropriate policy responses in the case of risks. The program evaluates a country's financial sector by investigating the soundness of the financial system versus its vulnerabilities and risks that increase the possibility of financial sector crises. It also evaluates a country's developmental needs, respectively its infrastructure, institutions, and markets. And finally, it looks at a country's compliance with nominated financial sector standards (Mekhova, 1999; IMF, 2006a).

4.3.1 The IMF Country Reports

The IMF Country Report No. 06/292 of August 2006 stated in its executive summary that the Irish financial sector had continued to perform soundly since its participation in the FSAP. Further, the IMF pointed out that the Irish financial institution's profitability and capitalization were at that time very strong, with Irish banking sector profits among the highest in Western Europe. The IMF highlighted the good performance of the major Irish banks which received upper medium-grade to high-grade ratings from the international rating agencies. In addition to this, according to the financial stability policy framework, the IMF complimented the creation of an organizational structure and a consistent corporate culture that were expected to enhance financial stability while responding to the challenges imposed by EU legislation. The centralization of common functions and harmonization of processes and procedures contributed to the reduction of regulation costs. The exchange of information and expertise between different areas of supervision was facilitated and a consistent method for prioritizing supervisory resources across institutions was developed. The report did also point to some of the risks existing in the Irish economy. In particular, it mentioned the dependence on an overheated property market and the reliance on wholesale funding (IMF, 2006a). It stated that the "private sector credit has increased very rapidly since 2000. Credit has grown fastest for personal and commercial real estate finance, so that banks' balance sheets have become increasingly concentrated in property-related lending" (IMF, 2006a, p. 14). In comparison with the rest of Western Europe, Irish institutions' lending was more concentrated in this area. Consequently, the report predicted that Irish financial institutions were exposed to any general downturn in world property prices that might occur (IMF, 2006a). However, the general conclusions of the IMF were reassuring. In its report 'Ireland: 2006 Article IV Consultation—Staff Report; Staff Supplement; and Public Information Notice on the Executive Board Discussion,' the IMF stated that Ireland's economic performance remained strong because economic policies were in line with fund policy advice. "In addition, even a substantial withdrawal of private sector deposits would not exhaust the stock of liquid assets at any major lender, given banks' ample liquidity" (IMF, 2006b, p. 10). Finally, the conclusion of the IMF report indicated that the "…banking system is resilient to a range of shocks" (IMF, 2006a, p. 19).

According to the economists Reinhart and Rogoff, international institutions, such as the IMF, can play an important role in risk mitigation, for instance, by promoting transparency in data reporting. In this way, lack of transparency can be prevented which is the main cause of crises (Reinhart and Rogoff, 2009). However, internal investigations into the IMF indicate a widespread lack of understanding and lack of clear communication of the mounting risks. There were incentives to comply with prevailing views, even if a proper analysis would have identified growing risks (Nyberg, 2011). Honohan and his colleagues assessed the reassuring report of the IMF as followed: "In hindsight such an unwarrantedly favourable report by an authoritative international body was clearly unhelpful" (Honohan et al., 2010, p. 92).

4.3.2 The Role of the ECB

The ECB is the central bank for the euro, Europe's single currency. Since the beginning of 1999, the ECB is responsible for monetary policy to maintain price stability in the euro area (European Central Bank, 2011; European Union, 2012, article 127, section 1). The ECB has succeeded in achieving relative price stability.

> In 2003, in the context of the evaluation of the monetary policy strategy, the Governing Council confirmed the quantitative definition of price stability and clarified that,

in pursuing price stability, it will aim to keep the euro area inflation rate at below, but close to, 2% over the medium term (European Central Bank, 2011, p. 9).

The required low interest rate policy was based on average inflation throughout the EU which essentially reflected developments in the largest countries, such as Germany. Germany spoke up for low interest rates in favor of strengthening its economy against the background of the German reunification at the beginning of the 1990s. However, this policy was not suitable for the Irish economy because in 2000, Irish inflation was higher than the European average. Together with low interest rates, these developments encouraged more borrowing and lending and fueled the property bubble. However, neither Irish politicians nor financial leaders raised concerns, complained that ECB interest rates were too low, or urged that they be raised (Donovan and Murphy, 2014).

Further, Donovan and Murphy (2014) point out the weak architecture of the Maastricht Treaty. In the design phase of the contract, there was considerable national opposition to any strong role being given to the ECB in financial supervisory matters which affected the content of the treaty. Consequently, the tasks of the ECB do not include any reference to financial supervision, although the Maastricht Treaty provides the possible involvement of the ECB in Article 105, Section 5 and Section 6 (European Union, 1992). However, there is no reference that the application of this article was ever seriously practiced. Besides, unanimous assent is required by all members of the Council of Ministers and this is extremely unlikely under consideration of the overall opposition to giving the ECB a strong role in financial supervisory matters. As a consequence, financial supervision was effectively understood as a national responsibility to execute (Donovan and Murphy, 2014). After the crisis, there were demands to strengthen centralized European involvement in supervision. For instance, the *De Larosière Report*, published in 2009, states that the world's monetary authorities and its regulatory and supervisory financial authorities can and must do much better in the future to reduce the risks of economic crisis. The report considers the suggestion that the ECB could play a major role in a new European supervisory system. While the *De Larosière Report* supports an extended role for the ECB in macro-prudential oversight, it does not support any role for the ECB regarding micro-prudential supervision. In contrast, Whelan (2009) argues in favor of such a solution (De Larosière, 2009; Whelan, 2009). Thus, experts disagree on some key issues and only the future will show how things turn out.

The *Financial Stability Reviews* from December 2006 and June 2007, published by the ECB, raised concerns about vulnerabilities and associated risks. The reviews pointed out the appearance of an increasing abrupt and unexpected loss of market liquidity of the financial system which could pose significant challenges. However, the reviews also stated that the financial system in the euro zone was generally in healthy condition and still predicted a favorable economic outlook. The reviews argued that the most likely prospect was that financial system stability would be maintained in the next period (European Central Bank, 2006; European Central Bank, 2007). Thus, the ECB also failed to recognize the forthcoming crisis. Whelan (2010) argues that because the already volatile situation was not recognized as such, the procedures were presumably inadequate.

4.4 Interactive Effects

The Irish culture of strong relationships contributed to the crisis. Michael Casey, a retired economist at the CB and board member of the IMF, argues that regulation must become tougher by imposing more sanctions and penalties. Close relationships between regulators and banks, which are difficult to avoid in a small country, have to end. He suggests that the enduring practice of former governors and senior regulators joining the boards of banks on their retirement has to be stopped (Casey, 2008; Ross, 2009). As Casey states, at the end of the day, the most crucial aspect of banking and finance is personal integrity (Casey, 2008). Keating and Martin (2007) also address strong relationships within the Irish political and institutional environment.

Although the FR and the CBFSAI were governed by independently appointed boards, a majority of the board members of the FR, such as the chairman, also sat on the board of the CBFSAI, which was chaired by the governor. The two institutions also operated under the same roof and shared overhead resources, such as human resources (Donovan and Murphy, 2014).

The Irish politician and author Shane Ross denounces the CEO of the FR as a failure as a regulator, however, he admits that the CEO was also a victim of the system. The Central Bank of Ireland and the Irish commercial banks were conjoined from their beginnings through cross-directorships, which led to a culture of common purpose. In his opinion, a regulation based on principles rather than on rules ensured these, ultimately destructive, relationships. Because of these relationships, the banks did not fear intervention or any other consequences through the FR and therefore exploited the opportunities given to their advantage and used to full capacity the possibility of excessive lending (Ross, 2009). As Donovan and Murphy (2014) state, when the development of a crisis became clear, the FR had little substantial information on the extent and nature of the true bank exposures.

Honohan and his colleagues document the approaches adopted in the reports of two important sets of representative bank inspections carried out by the FR. Honohan et al. (2010) state that they "give a flavour of the interaction between inspectors and the banks being inspected" (Honohan et al., 2010, p. 69). The first set of reports gives a picture of significant deficiencies of three large banks from 2005 to 2007 regarding their commercial property lending activities. However, as Honohan et al. note, overall supervision was focused on procedural aspects, for instance, on how the bankers worked. It did not seek to verify the business models of the banks, for instance, by asking for additional provisioning or capital buffers against increasingly risky loans. Indeed, there were findings which gave cause to concern and they were reported by the commercial property Lending inspection of April-May 2006. The reactions of the inspected banks were mixed but it seems to be symptomatic that one of the inspected banks rejected the findings classified as risky. The management of the bank argued against each point at the concluding meeting of the inspection (Honohan et al., 2010).

The CEO of the FR was accused in the *Nyberg Report* that he had 'extremely cozy' relationships with the banks. He answered that he really did not know what that meant. He described the relationship as having an exchange of ideas and he would go no further than that (Hancock and Minihan, 2015).

This could have supported the unwillingness to consider the real risk of an imminent problem which then led to the failure of taking adequate action to steer against it. In addition to this, public opinion plays a significant role in this context. Honohan et al. (2010) state that "'Rocking the boat' and swimming against the tide of public opinion would have required a particularly strong sense of the independent role of a central bank in being prepared to 'spoil the party' and withstand possible strong adverse public reaction" (Honohan et al., 2010, p. 16).

In conclusion, the *Nyberg Report* points out that the desire to assign responsibility for the crisis can be a useful precondition in the prevention of similar events in the future. However, it is more important to identify the causes for failures, rather than assigning individual blame or responsibility. Furthermore, the nature of systemic banking crises hardly ever allows responsibility to be fairly allocated. There are always several circumstances that contribute to a systemic banking crisis. All of these circumstances need to occur together to cause a systemic crisis. Considering only some contributors would not result in a balanced picture. However, people in decision-making positions are ultimately responsible for their decisions. The higher and consequently more influential their position, the greater their responsibility is for their choices and actions.

The *Nyberg Report* points out that the FR was in charge of micro supervision and the CB was in charge of the oversight of financial stability in the economy (Nyberg, 2011). Thus, the FR and the CB are considered profoundly responsible for the Irish banking crisis. Yet, faults in the design and implementation of the construction of the euro zone together with the passive attitude of European authorities also contributed to a lack of sound domestic financial regulation (Donovan and Murphy, 2014).

5 A Layered Perspective on External Control Mechanisms

In the following, it will be examined, whether some external control mechanisms, such as rating agencies or auditors, commented in their reports, or other communication, on objectionable developments regarding the banks' changed business models, strategies, and lending practices.

Rating agencies are private companies which assess the creditworthiness of companies of all economic sectors including financial instruments, financial products, as well as states and their subordinate authorities, by rating. The results are opinions, for instance, about the future ability to meet obligations completely and in time (Hückmann, 2003).

External auditors provide services, such as assurance including financial audit, tax, consulting and advisory services (Davies, 2015; EY, 2017). The auditors of the three biggest Irish domestic banks were Ernst and Young (EY) for Anglo, KMPG for AIB, and PricewaterhouseCoopers (PwC) for BoI (Donovan and Murphy, 2014).

5.1 Bottom-Up Effects

A report by the American rating agency Fitch Ratings, published in September 2006, revealed that Ireland was rated with high risk in suffering a banking crisis due to excessive lending growth. However, the report also reassured that strengthening in a number of banking systems had reduced overall bank systemic risk (a system-wide crisis) even if continued pace of credit growth in some countries could lead to worsening (Fitch Ratings, 2006; Schwab, 2010).

One of Ireland's oldest financial institutions, the Irish Nationwide Building Society (INBS), developed a unique business model. It was different from those of any of the other covered banks as it concentrated primarily on speculative site finance, which was very profitable in a rising property market. However, INBS neglected to build up solid risk management frameworks. The *Nyberg Report* revealed that there was no evidence of even basic analysis or reporting of fundamentals, such as concentration risk[3] and the adequacy of security (Deutsche Bundesbank, 2006). The absence of such fundamentals should have raised concern on the part of the rating agencies. Anglo, in particular, was extensively admired domestically and abroad and hailed, among others, by rating agencies as a role model for other Irish banks to emulate. In general, rating agencies gave the Irish banks strong credit rating (Nyberg, 2011).

5.1.1 The Role of the Rating Agencies

William Harrington, a former senior president at Moody's – one of the three big rating agencies alongside with Standard & Poor's (S&P) and Fitch Ratings – stated that rating agencies suffer from a conflict of interest because they are paid by the banks which they pretend to rate objectively. Harrington revealed that Moody's uses a long-standing culture of intimidation and harassment to influence its analysts to ensure that the ratings are in line with what the company's clients want. Further, he accused Moody's of actively harassing analysts whose ratings reflected their private conclusions instead of the higher ratings that issuer clients want. He specified that the management rewarded lenient voting because the management's aim was to mold analysts into pliable corporate citizens who cast their committee votes in line with the irrevocable corporate view of maximizing earnings of the largely captive franchise (Neate, 2011; Blodget, 2011). Because the agencies gave good ratings to products, banks bought risky debts that they would in general have stayed away from (Luyendijk, 2012; Neate, 2011; Blodget, 2011; United States, 2011).

There is also evidence that other rating agencies worked in the same fashion. S&P gave good ratings to toxic securities. Email references from S&P employees show that they were not duped by the securities' issuers. Comments, in which they express their hope of being wealthy and retired by the time the fraud would bust, are evidence for the fact that they knew exactly what they were doing. Consequently, their objectivity can be doubted because it shows that they gave false ratings on poor-quality, high-risk mortgage bonds and thereby ignored that people were counting on them to give an independent view regarding the safety of investments (Zamansky, 2013).

---

3 Concentration risk is a banking term generally referring to the level of risk in a bank's portfolio due to an unbalanced distribution of e.g. business partners, sectors, or countries which can generate losses to such an extent that the solvency of the institution in question can be endangered (Deutsche Bundesbank, 2006).

5.1.2 The Role of Other External Control Mechanisms

Besides the suspected deliberate deception by the rating agencies, the external auditors did not identify or report the risks due to the changes in lending practices of the banks (Donovan and Murphy, 2014). Consequently, whether the bank audit specialists at the different auditing firms recognized the covered banks' growing vulnerabilities or not also seemed to be a question of interest. PwC – normally the auditor of BOI – was instructed by the FR to examine Anglo regarding its financial and capital position. PwC's report, *Project Atlas – Anglo Irish Bank Corporation plc Summary Report Extracts*, was issued in February 2009 and is a summary of three reports on Anglo, encompassing 294 pages, prepared by PwC and dated September 27, November 27, and December 17, 2008 (PwC, 2009). PwC concluded that the bank had no solvency problem, even though property prices had fallen by more than 30% from the peak by then (PwC, 2009; Frisell, 2015; Whelan, 2013).

Nevertheless, the consulting firm Oliver Wyman highlighted Anglo's business performance. It announced Anglo the winner of 170 best performing companies and bestowed Anglo with the title world's best bank in 2006 on their corporate site (Cotterill, 2011; Frisell, 2015).

The *Nyberg Report* states that bank auditors should display a certain amount of professional skepticism and raise concerns when they observe an increase in property and financing risks on the market. The auditor should have taken notice and consequently questioned the sustainability of the business model of the banks. Further, the report argues that one would expect to find a formal note of this in the annual audit plans, reports of audit findings, or management letters. However, no such auditor comments are contained in the unqualified audit reports on the covered banks prior to, or immediately after, the guarantee. What is more, the auditors confirmed that there was no evidence of non-compliance with accounting standards. The report concludes that rating agencies, auditors, analysts, and investors remained calm and optimistic until the crisis in fact broke out (Nyberg, 2011).

5.2 Top-Down Effects

The rating agencies claim that they only submit opinions. "Ratings, including Rating Watches and Outlooks, assigned by Fitch are opinions…". "Ratings are not facts, and therefore cannot be described as being 'accurate' or 'inaccurate'" (Fitch Ratings, 2014, p. 4).

S&P argues in a similar way that "[t]he analyses, […] are statements of opinion as of the date they are expressed and not statements of fact or recommendations to purchase, hold, or sell any securities or make any investment decisions" and that "[u]sers of ratings or other analyses should not rely on them in making any investment decision. S&P Global Ratings' opinions and analyses do not address the suitability of any security" (Standard & Poor's, 2016, corporate site).

The Financial Crisis Inquiry Commission – which was created to examine the causes of the financial and economic crisis in the United States – concludes that the rating agencies awarded assessments that were too good and let investors believe that their investments were relatively safe. Further, the rating agencies betrayed the investors who trusted and relied on them without further questioning their analyses (United States, 2011).

The external audit has a decisive role at the heart of the financial reporting system. Registered external audits are required by law. The auditors were required to report a true and fair view, which means looking at compliance with applicable accounting standards and applicable laws and regulations of the respective banks' financial statements and giving reassurance regarding the financial health of the banks, such as BoI, AIB, and Anglo (Nyberg, 2011; MacCann, Courtney and Daly, 2008). Lejano and Stokols (2013) state that accounting practices should result in greater credit risk ratings for increasing borrowed capital (Lejano and Stokols, 2013). Donovan and Murphy (2014) argue that auditors did not recognize or notify the risks inherent in the banks' change in lending practices. However, the *Nyberg Report* states that professional skepticism should have alarmed the auditors about growing property and funding exposures and should have caused them to raise questions about the sustainability of a bank's business model. It is open to discussion, why the banks in question actually required state support in 2008, although all of them had received unqualified audit reports that gave reassurance regarding the financial health of the banks from various auditing firms shortly before the guarantee (Nyberg, 2011).

5.3 Interactive Effects

Keating and Martin (2007) argue that there is evidence for the fact that violation rather than observance of rules and laws was honored. They refer to several recent tribunals which investigated political and financial scandals in Ireland (Keating and Martin, 2007). An example for this is the publication of telephone recordings between Anglo bankers by the *Irish Independent* and the subsequent investigation (Williams, 2013a; Williams, 2013b; Theurer and Plickert, 2013; Feehan, 2013; O'Carroll, 2013; Harrison, 2013; La Roche, 2013; Murphy, 2013). The outcome of the investigation supports the view that a culture of non-compliance to rules existed with respect to business behavior. Thus, a culture of bending or breaking rules emerged which revealed a certain attitude toward taking risks. This creates the impression that decision-makers were proud of their ability to evade and avoid responsibilities – something which was perceived to be fine as long as he or she got away with it (Keating and Martin, 2007).

For instance, the former CEO of Anglo, was cited in the *Irish Independent* with regard to abusing the bank guarantee and warning his executives not to be caught (Williams, 2013b). Further, he was cited in an article in the *Irish Mirror* saying that he did not know what morality was (Ferry, 2014). There are currently 33 charges against him under two separate bills concerning alleged offences committed at the now defunct Anglo. He has to testify before court in two trials taking place in 2017 and 2018 which will judge on his involvement (Gallagher, 2016; Hayes, 2016). While he is still awaiting his trials, two former Anglo chiefs were found guilty by a jury of criminally conspiring to mislead investors although they both denied trying to mislead investors until the end (Maher, 2016; Keena, 2016).

6 A Layered Perspective on Media

In January 1988, *The Economist*, a weekly news magazine with focus on economic topics, published a survey on Ireland with the title 'The poorest of the rich'. Less than 10 years later, the magazine portrayed Ireland as 'Europe's shining light' (Peet, 2004; Donovan and Murphy, 2014; O'Connor, 2007a). "The role of the media has received relatively little attention in the outpouring of public commentary debate as to the myriad causes of Ireland's crisis" (Donovan and Murphy, 2014, p. 158).

6.1 Bottom-Up Effects

Most Irish people were caught up in the property boom and the associated increase of personal wealth. Many newspaper articles, television and radio programs were the result of a seemingly limitless interest in the housing topic (Donovan and Murphy, 2014). However, some individuals were suspicious about the seemingly never-ending upturn.

6.1.1 Critical Voices in the Media and Reactions

The Irish Times did not hesitate to publish a controversial article by Kelly. He focused on analyzing the Irish property boom after having examined data on house price cycles for all OECD countries since 1970. In this article, he mentions the possible reasons for a rapid freefall of the Irish property sector. His article denies that the house price boom reflected strong fundamentals, such as rising income and rising employment. Kelly (2006) argues if that were the case, the rents would also have risen but this did not happen. Geraldine Kennedy, editor of *The Irish Times* at that time, conceded after her retirement that she received severe criticism from the business community and from political authorities for publishing Kelly's article. She was blamed for damaging the commercial interests of the newspaper and also the national interest (Rafter, 2013).

In the article 'Banking on very shaky foundations,' also written by Kelly in 2007, he questioned the stability of the Irish banking system which had helped to fuel the property boom. This time, Kelly sent his article to the *Irish Independent*. The editor of the *Irish Independent* argued that he would not publish the article because he thought it was offensive. Kelly turned to the editor of *The Sunday Business Post* next who also refused to publish his article. Finally, Kelly went back to *The Irish Times* which published his article in September 2007 (Kelly, 2007; Lewis, 2011; Brown, 2015). Kelly's conclusions were derided by many commentators and were not taken seriously. Kelly states in an interview published in *Vanity Fair* in 2011 that the response to his article was general amusement (Lewis, 2011). Official sides, such as the financial stability report of 2007 argued that Kelly tended to focus on just one factor – the real house prices only – and that his theory did not take into account the fundamental factors typically driving housing markets (CBFSAI, 2007b).

The Irish television broadcasting transmitter RTÉ One, the most popular television channel in Ireland, also broadcast a documentary in 2006 *How we blew the boom* by George Lee, RTÉ economics editor. Lee (2009) states in his documentary that massive mistakes were made. He shows, among other things, the considerable and risky dependence of the Irish economy on the artificial property boom (Lee, 2009; Irish Examiner, 2008).

On the other side, in 2007, Brendan O'Connor, an Irish media personality known from various television shows, published an article in the *Irish Independent*. He stated that although, as he admitted, the Irish housing market was apparently in meltdown, he would buy property even if he had no money arguing that people did not even need money to buy property (O'Connor, 2007b). Although he later conceded that he was wrong, he did not regret the statement he made in the article. He argued that it was a valid position at the time (Sunday Tribune, 2010).

6.1.2 Critical Voices from Politicians and Financial Experts

Besides Kelly, there were other critical voices concerning banking practices, property prices, and political decisions, away from the inebriant boom euphoria. For instance, Shane Ross, the politician and business editor of the *Sunday Independent*, speculated that social status overruled competence in the choice of the vacancy of the Governor of the BoI and among other things criticized that no further candidates had been considered (Ross, 2004).

The teamwork study 'Monetary Policy and House Prices: A Cross-Country Study' was published on the Federal Reserve's website in September 2005 (Ahearne, Ammer, Doyle, Kole and Martin, 2005). It examines developments in the housing market of various countries including Ireland. It shows that periods of prolonged rises followed by protracted falls are an unexpectedly common feature of house prices in advanced countries. The boom can be explained by certain financial conditions, such as low interest rates and financial deregulation combined with other factors, such as demographics and income growth. Ahearne, co-author of the teamwork study, concludes, in line with Kelly, that this unusually high level of house prices relative to rents was mainly supported by large expected increases in house prices and consequently, the property market was pulling itself up (Ahearne et al., 2005; Rafter, 2013).

6.2 Top-Down Effects

The media has an important influence by its choice of events considered to be newsworthy. They are influential organizations in society and consequently have the power to steer the course of public debate (O'Connell, 2014). This situation is an environmental influence, as explained before.

The newspapers derived significant revenue from property developers through their property supplements (Donovan and Murphy, 2014; O'Connell, 2014). As mentioned before, Kennedy, the editor of *The Irish Times* at that time, conceded after her retirement that she was put under pressure from various sides for publishing Kelly's articles (Rafter, 2013). One of the reasons for this behavior of her environment is that the revenue generated through *The Irish Times*' weekly property supplement contributed to a large extent to the newspaper's overall finances. The content of these supplements were also under the newspaper's overall editorial control but according to Donovan and Murphy, quality standards could not be guaranteed, for example, the avoidance of exaggerated descriptions. What is more, the purchase of 'myhome.ie,' an online residential property and lettings website, by *The Irish*

Times for 50 million euros could then have indicated a conflict of interest. The purchase by *The Irish Times* involved an initial payment of 40 million euros and a further 10 million euros once certain business targets were met, that is to say myhome.ie was expected to make a profit of 2.5 million euros in 2006. Consequently, the many people working in media reveled in the new wealth they acquired through the Celtic Tiger by benefiting from higher fees and salaries. As a result, many people had limited motivation – consciously or unconsciously – to reveal concerns regarding the economic situation (McManus, 2006; RTÉ, 2007; Donovan and Murphy, 2014; Rafter, 2013; Browne, 2011).

6.3 Interactive Effects

The Irish Times published an article in 2011 in which it denounced the media as jointly guilty in the 'destruction of Ireland'. The Celtic Tiger was blamed for being unequal and cruel. *The Irish Times* stated that the media gave no warnings because the underlying instability was not recognized by most people working in the media. However, they admitted that the media fueled the property bubble to make millions through property advertisement (Browne, 2011; Rafter, 2013).

Indeed, the media caught up with the all-encompassing boom atmosphere. However, the *Irish Examiner* stated that it was not 'nonsense' that the media was responsible for the loss of consumer confidence that in turn destabilized the economy. The newspaper admitted that the media was guilty of not warning loud and often enough during the boom. However, it argued that only few people would have listened anyway (Irish Examiner, 2008).

Donovan and Murphy interviewed Brendan Keenan, economics editor of the *Irish Independent*. Keenan stated that newspapers were put under pressure by the public, business, and political parties for their independent and objective news coverage when they reported negatively on the economic situation. He concluded that it was not really a question of reporting negatively on the economic situation but that people were instead afraid because they secretly knew that the boom would soon be over (Donovan and Murphy, 2014).

However, as the documentary and various articles show, pressure could be and was successfully withstood (Rafter, 2013). The television documentary by George Lee and the newspaper articles by Kelly are examples for the unprejudiced reporting of, at least, some of the media. It can be argued that the media did not fuel the property bubble and that there was no shortage of warnings of danger. However, a difficulty was that these warnings were contrary to the point of view of financial institutions, such as the CB (Donovan and Murphy, 2014). What is more, even politicians ignored the warnings of the economic risks (Lynch et al., 2015b; Lynch et al., 2015c; Lynch et al., 2015d; Lynch et al., 2015e).

The *Nyberg Report* also concluded that the very limited number of warning voices was largely ignored (Nyberg, 2011).

Chapter 7: A Layered Perspective on Economic Development and Cultural Change of Ireland

Cultural change is a multilayered and multi-contextual phenomenon. However, as Oetzel (2009) states, in a given situation certain factors matter more than others and these factors need to be emphasized. Thus, a study with a layered framework is always limited because it is not based on a linear perspective (Oetzel, 2009).

Minkov (2011) states that culture can be quite steady in the absence of economic development. He claims, however, that a relation between economic development and cultural change exists (Minkov, 2011). In this chapter, the layered perspective is applied to the Irish divorce referendum. The aim is to reveal the interrelations between economic development and cultural change. The divorce referendum provides a context for the application of this model and consequently it is possible to explain a complex social development using the theory of the layered perspective. It also provides an opportunity to demonstrate the practical benefits of a dynamic theory as the layered complexities of the interrelations between economic development and cultural change are shown (Zhang and Ting-Toomey, 2014).

The analysis takes a closer look at the individual rings of the layered perspective model, as illustrated in figure 30. The method of the analysis concentrates on different rings at different times and also compares the same rings of the exo-level and meso-level at different times.

It makes sense to begin with the chronosystem because it explains the importance of the factor 'time' as a prerequisite for the detection of change. The following macro-level analysis explains the development of the environment some years before the referendum which provides the framework for the incident case that is discussed below. It indicates a strong top-down effect.

The exo-level analysis which does not include the individuals, in this case the voters, and the meso-level analysis, which includes the individuals examine a very specific and brief moment in time in 1986 in comparison to 1995. The interactive effects of both layers explain possible factors which could have influenced the behavior and results of the decisions of the voters.

The micro-level analysis and the section about the individual are focused on the time after the referendums and therefore concentrate on the consequences of the new legislation regarding divorce. This is important, since it is the objective of the analysis to reveal changes in behavior, attitude, and values caused by the referendum and the subsequent change in legislation.

With reference to the chronosystem and based on Bronfenbrenner's ecological framework for human development, figure 4 is now adapted to the incident case.

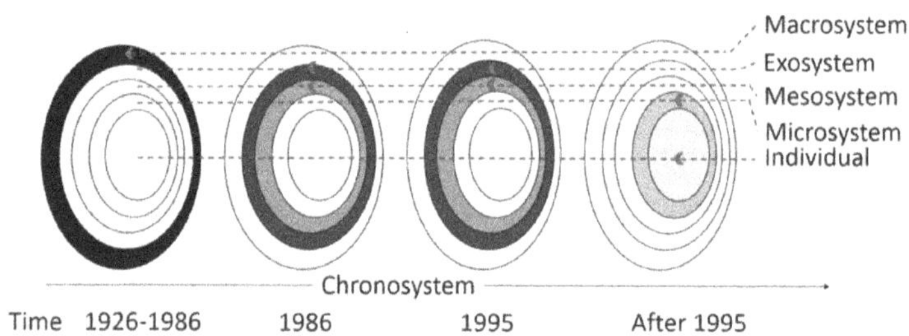

Figure 36: Method of the Analysis of the Decision-Making Process in the Divorce Referendums of 1986 and 1995

1 The Chronosystem

As explained above, the chronosystem refers to how an individual and the surrounding environment change over time. The system 'time' opens up a third dimension for the environment. The system takes into account the chronological age of an individual, but also the surrounding environment and its changes across historical time. Therefore, the chronosystem encompasses change or consistency over time not only in the characteristics of the person but also of the environment in which that person lives (Bronfenbrenner, 1994). Developmental processes are likely to vary in accordance with specific historical events. These historical circumstances affect contexts at all other levels (Bronfenbrenner and Morris, 2006).

In the following Sections 2 to 6, changes in the outcome of the Irish divorce referendum held in the years 1986 and 1995 are examined by applying the social ecological perspective. The first Irish divorce referendum was defeated in 1986, when the majority overwhelmingly voted to keep the nation's ban on divorce by a vote of 935,843 to 538,279 which is a margin of 63% to 36%.

In 1995, a committee which reviewed the constitution, recommended changes in domains in which the influence of Catholic social teaching was most apparent. These elements were, for instance, issues concerning marriage (Constitution Review Group, 1996). Through a historical lens, it is possible to explain why there was no legislative construct which regulated divorce rights. Until 1995, Ireland remained the only member of the EU which had no divorce law (Mayer and Schwepcke, 1995). A second referendum was held in 1995, in which a small majority agreed on the introduction of divorce rights and the approval through legislation followed in June 1996.

2 The Social Ecological Macro-Level Analysis

The macro-level analysis includes the cultural worldview, political ideologies, societal expectancy norms, and the economic system in which the other settings are embedded (Martin and Fabes, 2009). Thus, this analytical level focuses on the 'big picture,' such as the political climate, cultural-level values, and habitual cultural practices that are appreciated or deprecated (Zhang and Ting-Toomey, 2014). Compare figure 36, first onion slice from the left, the outermost macro-level ring. The macro-level ring here covers a time range from 1926 up until 1986 because during this time, the Irish Constitution, among others, the basis for legislation in 1986, was designed and formed.

In this case, the background and political climate on which the Irish Constitution is based is examined. This provides an explanation of how the larger political environment shapes the societal attitudes and the individual's decision-making process. The macrosystem context includes the particular historical time, the place, and the political environment.

When the Free State emerged 95% of the people were Catholic. A conservative Catholic moral established itself and the Catholic Church assumed a dominant role in government policies. The laws of the country reflected the predominantly Catholic belief. Although divorce had been available on a limited basis before independence, in 1926, a law was passed which prohibited divorce within the state. This was not welcomed by all. Irish intellectuals, in particular, argued against this bill.

In 1928, under pressure of the Catholic bishops, a censorship bill was passed. As a consequence, the works of many well-known authors, such as Sigmund Freud, who was a religious critic, and Voltaire, a French Enlightenment writer, who proclaimed freedom of religion in his works and the separation of church and state, were banned. Most Irish authors were banned too, such as George Bernard Shaw and Nobel laureate Samuel Beckett (McCaffrey, 2006; Tögel, 2006). When the Irish Constitution was written in 1937, clerical influence on Irish life had reached its peak. The founders of the new republic made no effort to reduce the significance of the Catholic Church in Irish public life and even went some way toward bringing church and state closer together. What is more, the constitution also reflected the values of the majority of the population. Divorce was not an issue for the majority of the Free State's citizens at that time. Thus, many elements of Catholic social teaching were incorporated into the constitution and in this way, were given practical effect in the Irish courts (Kissane, 2003). The constitution is subject to periodical review. A committee reviewing the constitution concluded that it had stood the test of time well, however, also recommended changes in the constitution in the domains in which the influence of Catholic social teaching was most apparent (Constitution Review Group, 1996). Since the constitution can only be amended by a referendum, different opinions on some articles became a central part of Irish public life in a way that was not envisaged when the constitution was designed. Thus, the constitution became the venue of secularizing and counter-secularizing tendencies in Irish life. The nature of the relationship between the designers of the constitution and the Catholic Church was heavily influenced by the events of the 19th century, e.g. the Great Famine and the humiliation of the Irish by the British people and the British government. The non-Catholic British influence was the most important force that affected the pattern of much of Irish political thought and practice, both in the past and until this day (Chubb, 1982). As a result, a close identification between the Irish nation and the Catholic religion developed, and the politicians defended the prominent role ascribed to the Catholic Church in areas of public policy. For instance, the Constitution of 1937 determined that the President should make a religious declaration when taking up office, which suggests that the state obligations should be evaluated by religious criteria and implicitly identifies the Irish nation with the Catholic religion (Kissane, 2003).

What is more, in the years from 1932 to 1960, in which de Valera dominated Irish politics, the country was economically stagnant. Ireland did not industrialize but remained a rural, agrarian-based economy because de Valera was against change or modernization of any kind. In addition to this, Ireland also lagged behind socially. Access to health care and education were the worst in Europe. As a consequence, 400,000 people left Ireland in the 1950s leaving behind an environment of mass emigration and economic stagnation (McCaffrey, 2006).

With this background context, the interrelations between the macrosystem and its impact on individual behavior become apparent. It explains, among other things, the strong influence of the Catholic Church on Irish politics and, as a result, on legislation. It therefore reveals from the macro-historical level of top-down analysis, how the cultural and political ideologies affected the individuals.

3 The Social Ecological Exo-Level Analysis

The exosystem includes structures that do not themselves contain the individual but have an effect upon or encompass the direct settings of the individual and, therefore, influence what happens (Bronfenbrenner, 1977). Whereas the institutional environment or policies may not directly affect people's behaviors, policies filter through various agencies and then impact people's decisions. These are key institutions, such as church and mass media that belong to this level and they have had enormous impacts. All of them are put in the context of economic development because, for example, unemployment rates affect economic stability (McLeroy et al., 1988). In the following, the exo-level rings of the onion slices of 1986 and 1995 are compared. To visualize the argumentative approach, please see figure 36 which illustrates the comparison of the exo-level ring in 1986 and 1995.

3.1 The Environment of the Divorce Referendum 1986

An example of how strongly the Catholic Church's doctrines permeated the Irish Constitution is that until 1996 divorce was illegal in Ireland. However, according to canon law, an annulment of marriage was possible. When a Catholic married couple separated, they could not be divorced by church law, but they could have their marriage annulled. A church judge examined whether the marriage had actually come into effect. If not, the former spouses were no longer married in the face of the church, or more precisely, they never had been (Wetzel, 2014). The irrefutable attitude of the Irish law to be in line with Catholic teachings is revealed by the fact that the church continued to annul marriages which then regardless of their annulment continued to be valid marriages under Irish law. Thus, remarriage of Catholics who had been granted an annulment were bigamous in the view of the state (Kissane, 2003; Coakley, 1987).

Catholic faith is deeply anchored in Irish life, in the minds, the attitude, laws, and the constitution. Besides the explanation above, further explanations for this are provided by Chapter One, Section 3. Thus, the Catholic Church as an embodiment of the Catholic faith is attributed with great power. Therefore, the power of several anti-divorce campaigns, initiated by the Catholic Church and their representatives, also had a strong impact on people's decision in the referendum.

Another influence on the decision-making process of the Irish in the referendum can be found in the Northern Ireland conflict. In Northern Ireland, Catholics were granted access to education in the 1960s because in 1947, free university education for the entire UK became statutory by the British government. Thus, the people in Northern Ireland could not be excluded from free education because university access was based on academic performance and even Catholics with lowest income had the opportunity to attend university. However, Catholics in general were denied access to employment although they were well-educated (McCaffrey, 2006). In particular the Catholics in Northern Ireland were considered to be nationalists desiring to reunite Ireland. Thus, they were stigmatized as enemies of the state and decent housing was denied to most of them next to other discrimination against Catholicism and Irish nationalism. At the end of the 1960s, Catholic but also Protestant citizens began to demonstrate against the injustices. Initially, these demonstrations were non-violent. The Irish demonstrators were inspired by mass media, such as television, where they had seen the civil rights marches in the United States by black Americans and, in particular, heard the speeches of Dr Martin Luther King Jr (McCaffrey, 2006). However, tension, frustration, and fear grew continuously and paved the way to radical action. Eventually, a violent conflict arose in Northern Ireland in which more than 3,500 people would lose their lives during the next 30 years and which would go down in history as 'The Troubles' (McCaffrey, 2006; Rogers, 2010). Peace was agreed between the parties only through the Good Friday Agreement on April 10, 1998. Such conflicts and turmoil are always detrimental to economic development, as, for example, investments are not to be expected. A sluggish economy then leads, besides other obstacles, to rising unemployment rates.

It is safe to assume that the Northern Ireland conflict, which was an always present topic in the media at this time and which had its origins in the discrimination against Catholics, also had an effect on the decisions made in the referendum. Holding on to Catholic traditions clearly distinguished the Irish from their Protestant neighbors who discriminated against Catholics (please see Chapter One, Sections 3.2.3 and 3.2.4).

In the 1980s, Ireland was in a deep recession, as explained earlier (please see Chapter Four, Section 3.1). As noted, the annual GDP was negative and the unemployment rate was at an all-time high (World Bank Group, 2017e; World Bank Group, 2017f). From the 1960s to the 1980s, per capita income was still around 60% to 70% of the EU average. The state was caught in the debt trap and ranked among the OECD countries with the highest debt (Fink, 2008). By the mid-1980s, Ireland had a public debt-GDP ratio of over 109% and was paying off almost 10% of GDP per year in interest payments on this debt. Tax rates had been raised to excessive levels in an attempt to stabilize the deficit. However, growth had continued to stagnate (Whelan, 2013). The economic situation consequently affected the Irish when during the 1980s many of them emigrated because they had no prospects and they wanted to escape mass unemployment. It can be assumed that many did not see an urgent need in changing divorce rights in light of economic recession and mass emigration.

3.2 The Environment of the Divorce Referendum 1995

During the 1990s, the Catholic Church lost more and more of its power and influence because various scandals became public. As already explained in Chapter Five, Sections 1.4.2 and 2.4.2, the media reported on cases of sexual abuse in Ireland in the mid-1990s and revealed the involvement of the Catholic Church. In addition to this, there were other scandals, for instance, the authority of the Catholic Church was also considerably damaged in 1992 by the revelation that the Bishop of Galway at that time had fathered a child and used church funds to help raise it in America (Kissane, 2003).

Consistent with these events, the EVS shows that the percentage of people who attended religious services apart from weddings, funerals and christenings at least once a week decreased steadily. While in 1981, 83% of the people attended religious services at least once a week, in 1990, it was merely 60% (Atlas of European Values, 2011c). This shows that the Catholic Church as an institution lost its power and influence. Consequently, it is reasonable to assume that people might have felt that the Catholic Church could not give them advice in moral issues concerning the family which also included the divorce issue.

In the 1995 divorce referendum, a Supreme Court decision ruled that the state broadcasting service RTÉ had acted unlawfully through its disproportionate allocation of broadcasting time to the pro-side (Kissane, 2003). A plaintiff won a High Court case in which he made an objection against RTÉ's broadcasting policy during the referendum. He accused RTÉ of allocating uncontested broadcasts only to certain established political parties, with the result that RTÉ was allocating 42.5 minutes uncontested time to the pro-side and only 10 minutes to the contra-side. Therefore, RTÉ did not provide proper coverage of the debate on referendum issues. The judge ruled that RTÉ's failure to allocate an equal amount of time for uncontested broadcasts to the pro-side and contra-side had resulted in inequality which caused unconstitutional unfairness. In return, RTÉ rejected the accusations that they had not been objective (Brennock, 1998).

The rapid economic growth in the 1990s enabled Ireland to rise from the poorest country at the edge of Europe where people emigrated because they had no prospects, to the richest member country of the EU, to which people immigrated to take up employment (Fink, 2008). This enabled the Irish government to reduce taxes and increase spending and in this way to contribute to general prosperity. The Irish government, which induced the referendum in an all-party support for change to legalize divorce, emphasized the changes that had occurred until then, provoked by modernization, urbanization, the overcoming of isolation, and the creation of general wealth. Therefore, the government considered the change in divorce legislation as a step toward bringing Irish law in line with the EU of which Ireland was now not only an appendage but an equal member state due to its economic performance (Christopher, 1997). Since the government contributed to the prosperity of all (through the tax cuts) and all political parties supported the pro-divorce attitude, this may also have influenced voters in their decision to vote for changing divorce rights.

4 The Social Ecological Meso-Level Analysis

The mesosystem encompasses the interrelations between several important settings that contain the individual. These are supportive community actions that have a direct influence on the behavior of the individual. Here, the meso-level context and its interactive effects on people who live in the embedded contexts, in this case the voters, are emphasized (Zhang and Ting-Toomey, 2014). All of them are set in the context of economic development. In the following, the meso-level rings of the onion slices of 1986 and 1995 are compared. To visualize the argumentative approach, please see figure 36 which illustrates the comparison of the meso-level ring in 1986 and 1995.

4.1 The Environment of the Divorce Referendum 1986

In 1986, the governing political parties at that time, Fine Gael and Labour, initiated a divorce referendum and advised the voters to vote for yes. The political parties raised concerns about the failure of the state to deal with the issue of broken marriage. The clause that prohibited divorce by law violated the rights of a small minority of less than 10% of the total population of the Republic, who were not Roman Catholic and whose religious beliefs therefore did not necessarily include the idea of the eternity of marriage. However, the 'national territory' identified in the Constitution referred to the whole island of Ireland. Therefore, it could be interpreted as a potential threat to the civil liberties of the Northern

Irish Protestants, who experienced no comparable restriction and who would thus find the notion of Irish unity particularly abhorrent. What is more, the parties considered a softening of the divorce law as a chance for harmonization concerning political issues with the North. The Prime Minister of that time stated that the amendment was a crucial indicator for the willingness of the predominantly Roman Catholic republic to tolerate the coexistence of different interests, lifestyles, and secular rights. In his opinion, the amendment was important for future dealings with Northern Ireland and its Protestant majority (Coakley, 1987). However, according to the social identity theory (please see Chapter One, Section 3.2.2), voters might perceive it as almost impossible to concede individually from their own group, i.e. from Catholic-nationalists toward the other group, i.e. the Protestant-unionists. This is a situation involving an intense conflict of interests, in which it is extremely difficult for voters to even imagine betraying their own group by making concessions to the other group (Tajfel and Turner, 1986). Thus, the concept of social identity can explain the intergroup behavior of rejecting the legislation of divorce.

Other reasons for the rejection can be found in the well-planned and effective campaign of the divorce opponents. The numerous Catholic organizations argued that divorce was immoral and against God's law. However, they also used the negative material effects of divorce as an argument against it. They stated that pensions and welfare claims of divorced partners were uncertain and reinforced voters' fears of losing property in the case of divorce (Alioth, 1986).

Politicians in Northern Ireland who opposed any ties with the Republic of Ireland labeled the outcome of the referendum a stranglehold of the Roman Catholic Church on the Irish Republic. They were confirmed in their prejudices that the values and convictions of all Irish were not respected by the voters in the Republic. After the referendum, the moderates in the North also began to doubt whether their individual liberty would be respected by the Catholic majority (Clines, 1986; Alioth, 1986). In vain, the political representatives of the Catholic minority in Northern Ireland had pleaded with voters to vote for yes which they had wanted to cite as proof that the South was ready for concessions in the interest of unity (Alioth, 1986).

Political analysts of that time stated that the rejection of the voters was partly based on the opposition of the Catholic leaders but mainly on the failure of political parties to clarify the impact of divorce on economic matters (Alioth, 1986; Kissane, 2003). The economic stagnation was not helpful to this situation. With knowledge of the historical background, the crucial arguments in the debate of the referendum were not the spiritual arguments or respect of the values regarding Northern Ireland's minority, but the effect that divorce would have on personal property rights. This was the decisive issue in a country where land ownership was denied for centuries under British colonial rule (Clarity, 1995).

According to Hardiman and Whelan (1998) it can be concluded conversely to aforementioned arguments that a country, which was stagnating economically for decades, was more likely to live according to traditional religious and moral values (Hardiman and Whelan, 1998). Consequently, the poor economic situation in the Republic also influenced the behavior of the voters with regard to the referendum in 1986 when they preferred to hold on to their traditions including religious doctrines. A representative of the Catholic Church argued in 1986 that Ireland remained the last Catholic country in Europe because its people were remote, rural, and poor (Christopher, 1997).

4.2 The Environment of the Divorce Referendum 1995

In 1995, the Northern Ireland conflict also played a role in the divorce referendum. The Taoiseach (Prime Minister) at the time argued that voting for change would reflect Ireland's image as a friendly and tolerant place and would support efforts toward peace in Northern Ireland. In addition to this, the Irish people would have to find a way of governing that included both communities, also the minority. Therefore, the Irish voters should demonstrate tolerance for minorities. Further, he rebutted the argument of the anti-divorce groups who claimed that divorce was non-Christian and would destabilize Irish society in stating that Christian values are the virtue of charity and forgiveness. Thus, he considered it wrong not to allow Irish law to express forgiveness to those whose consciences allow them to remarry (Clarity, 1995).

A representative of the Catholic Church emphasized the importance of Catholicism for Irish voters due to their historical experience because for centuries, they suffered injustice by the British who violated their human rights. Thus, a religious position was defended with secular arguments, but it shows how tenaciously Irish conservatism was still willing to defend aspects of a constitution that were considered anachronistic by many people (Kissane, 2003).

In 1995, the economic situation in Ireland had changed significantly compared to 1986. One year before the referendum of 1995, the country was labeled the Celtic Tiger. The economic boom led to employment-intensive growth with unemployment declining steadily down to 12% in 1995 and a tendency of further decrease. Thus, per capita income increased significantly (Fink, 2008). Consequently, many Irish had shared in the growing prosperity which was triggered in particular by the construction boom. As mentioned before, the overall economic development led to a heightened autonomy of individuals regarding the development of their own values and norms (Hardiman and Whelan, 1998). All these factors together might have led to the development of people's values and norms toward a more secularized worldview inspired by their European neighbors, such as the UK, in which divorce is legally possible and relatively easy. The economic development along with modernization could also have influenced the decision of the voters to make concessions to Northern Ireland and the rights of its religious minority.

5 The Social Ecological Micro-Level Analysis

Micro-level analysis refers to both the intrapersonal and interpersonal levels of interpretation and construction of meaning and is closest to the individual. It contains the structures with which the individual has direct contact. It represents the complex of relations and interrelations between the developing individual and his or her environment, meaning the direct setting containing that individual, for instance, church, or neighborhood (Bronfenbrenner, 1977; Rogoff, 2003).

A possible example for this is that an individual was part of a pro- or anti-divorce campaign or member of a political party with a pro-divorce attitude in both the referendum of 1986 and 1995. However, in the following, the analysis focuses on the time period after the referendum of 1995. It analyzes the effects of the result for the micro-level, see figure 36.

Although the result of the referendum in 1995 led to approval of divorce through legislation, the Constitution made it difficult by stating that the dissolution of a marriage could only be granted when the couple had lived apart for four out of the preceding five years (Coulter, 2015). The director of the Catholic marriage-counseling agency agreed that this legislation made divorce extremely difficult. The very existence of this state-funded counseling agency was part of the social remedy that the government had promised to help minimize what some people considered as the social scourge of divorce (Holmquist, 2015a).

A woman who was divorced and remarried was questioned in an interview for *The Irish Times* about the economic, legislative, and social difficulties of her divorce. She stated that her divorce had cost €500 paid to an agency that did the paperwork. However, she owned inherited land and had to pay her former husband a lump sum. Therefore, she was forced to sell property to fund a separation that cost her €17,000 in order to pay off her former husband. Nevertheless, in her opinion, it had been worth spending the money because she had been very unhappy, although she admitted that the divorce also involved a huge personal and emotional struggle. In addition to this, she experienced Irish family law courts as humiliating because the whole process dragged on for four years costing her a lot of energy. In her experience, people were ostracized by their former social circle because of being divorced (Holmquist, 2015b). This is supported by the results of a study, which reveals that 45% of divorced people say that their status makes them feel stigmatized in Irish society (Meagher, 2015). Brendan Madden, a psychotherapist and former Director of *Relationships Ireland*, a counseling agency offering couple and family counseling, states that it takes years to proceed to divorce and points out the psychological wounds caused by this long period of time. In contrast, a divorce process in the UK is much faster (Holmquist, 2015b). An uncontested divorce can take as little as four months in England and Wales (Citizens Advice, 2019).

Separation and divorce can cost a couple from €500 up to €100,000 for a highly contested one. The typical costs for having a divorce in Ireland are €12,000 to €20,000. Thus, financial difficulties due to high legal fees can make divorce almost impossible for low income couples wishing to separate (Holmquist, 2015b; Meagher, 2015). Thus, it may not come as a surprise that the economic development and the associated personal prosperity, including employment and income of the individuals, play a significant role. The numbers support this assumption because the amount of divorces granted peaked in 2007 and has been in decline in the eight years since then. However, now that the economy has recovered, the number of divorces has also risen significantly, again (Coulter, 2015; Meagher, 2015).

6 The Individual in the Social Ecological Perspective

In the following, the analysis focuses on the time period after the referendum of 1995. It analyzes the effects of the result for the individual, see figure 36. Religion seems to be one of the most important factors for the Irish because they define their identity over Catholicism (Elliott, 2009). Hofstede (2003) argues that of all European countries with Catholic majorities, only Ireland and Poland do not have a Latin past, i.e. never were part of the Roman Empire. The Irish use their "Catholicism as a source of identity to protect them against powerful non-Catholic occupants" (Hofstede, 2003, p. 113). This implies a societal significance of stating to be Catholic. Catholicism is part of the identity and serves as a clear distinction between invaders and oppressors. Therefore, economic and cultural sovereignty is demonstrated by Catholicism.

The results of the EVS show that the percentage of people who believe in God is almost the same with 97% in 1981 opposed to 96% in 1999 (Atlas of European

Values, 2011d). However, the percentage of people who say the church offers adequate answers to the moral problems and needs of the individual decreased significantly from 56% in 1981 to 31% in 1999 (Atlas of European Values, 2011e). Also, the percentage of people who say the church offers adequate answers to the problems of family life decreased significantly from 52% in 1981 to 27% in 1999 (Atlas of European Values, 2011f). In fact, more than 90% of the Irish are still Catholic, but the values and aspirations of 1937 have changed (Kissane, 2003). The figures imply that the Irish held on to their attitude toward God but that the power of the Catholic Church had faded. In general, a process of secularization took place in Ireland. For those, whose outlook on life was shaped by the doctrines of the Catholic Church, much had indeed changed. For instance, the change away from a total ban on divorce to the possibility of legal divorce. However, the narrow margin of the victory in 1995 is a measure of not only the change in Irish attitudes, but also the persistence of traditional values regarding the place of the family in society and the guidelines of the Catholic Church, and of how weak the impulse toward secularization has been since the end of WWI (Christopher, 1997; Kissane, 2003). Nevertheless, the introduction of divorce implies a strong bottom-up effect and shows a tendency to separate church and state (Kissane, 2003).

The Irish have always had a unique approach to Christianity. For centuries, Christianity practiced in Ireland had nothing to do with the mainstream and hardly ever conformed to the doctrines of the Catholic Church. Christianity instead endured throughout the centuries as "an informal, ceremonial, unofficial but intense, deeply spiritual, passionate expression of a profound relationship with the Almighty" (McCaffrey, 2006, p. 262). For the Irish, religion lies in the spiritual expression. Religion was practiced outside the tight strictures of the Roman Catholic Church's authority. The rigid religion that Catholicism became at the beginning of self-government and the usage for political reasons is comprehensible considering the historical and political background of that time. The Irish may have moved away from the Catholic Church's conventions but the Christian values are still there (McCaffrey, 2006).

Chapter 8: Conclusions and Discussion

This chapter deals in Section 1 with the answers of the research questions which were formulated in the introduction. Section 2 provides a discussion about the theoretical and practical implications of the application of the layered perspective and provides recommendations for further research.

1 Conclusion

The main objective of this dissertation is testing the application of a multi-level framework in order to reveal the ecological influences on human behavior and decision-making processes that impact social and economic development. Additionally, it is tested whether a multi-level framework is able to reveal links between social and economic development and cultural change. This is investigated from a cultural-anthropological perspective and, therefore, the basic assumption is that culture is an all-encompassing influencing factor. The three research questions, first raised in the introduction in 'Objective and Problem Statement,' were:

- As mentioned, influences on behavior and decision-making processes are always multi-layered and multi-contextual (Oetzel, 2009). Behavior and decision-making processes determine the direction of social and economic developments. Consequently, the first research question arose. Which influences on behavior and decision-making processes have which effects on societal development?
- Second, which influences on behavior and decision-making processes have an impact on economic development? The motivation was to find explanations, in particular, for the economic crisis in Ireland of 2007. Therefore, it is specifically examined which influences affected behavior and decision-making processes and in this way contributed to Ireland's economic crisis.
- Finally, the interrelations of social and economic development are examined. According to Minkov (2011), a relation between economic development and cultural change exists. Inglehart and Oyserman (2004) also assume relations when emphasizing that economic development facilitates cultural change. Therefore, the third research question discusses how far economic developments have an impact on society and cultural values.

Therefore, all analyzing chapters (Chapter Five, Six, and Seven – each chapter deals with one of the research questions) show that a multi-level framework is able to provide answers to each of the research questions.

In the analysis in Chapter Five, 'A Layered Perspective on Social Ecology of Ireland' the chosen examples reveal important influences on, and provide explanations for the behavior and decision-making processes and show its effects on the social development of Ireland. This demonstrates that a multi-level model can also make a valuable contribution to the field of social studies, such as the EVS and ESS.

In the analysis in Chapter Six, 'A Layered Perspective on Economic Ecology of Ireland' the chosen examples reveal important influences on, and provide explanations for the behavior and decision-making processes and show how the behavior and decisions contributed to Ireland's economic crisis. This indicates that a multi-level model can also make a valuable contribution to economic analysis by integrating the human factor, for instance by the research field of behavioral economics.

The analysis in Chapter Seven, 'A Layered Perspective on Economic Development and Cultural Change of Ireland' reveals the influences of economic development on social development and cultural change over time. This demonstrates that a multi-level model can also make a valuable contribution to the field of cultural anthropology.

In conclusion, this dissertation shows the application of a model that reveals the interaction of social, economic, and cultural mechanisms.

2 Discussion

The approach of a layered perspective requires the integration of other disciplines, such as psychology, anthropology, archaeology, and history in order to leave the confinement of pure economics in favor of a progressive holistic analysis of the ecology in which economy takes place.

Various factors, such as geography, history, and culture, have an impact on individuals. This dissertation focuses on historical and cultural aspects. The results of a historical analysis together with the results of a cultural analysis provide the context in which a society and economy develop. Thus, the argument is put forward that rather than employing merely an economic analysis it is necessary to integrate interdisciplinarity to understand economic and social development (Spash, 2011).

2.1 Implications and Limitations of the Layered Perspective

Lejano and Stokols (2013) state that the interaction between multiple dimensions, such as culture and economy, is most deeply analyzed by a layered perspective and thus understood in context. Therefore, economic issues can best be analyzed and understood with the help of a multi-level framework. There is no free-standing economic system. Therefore, economic developments, such as crises, cannot be understood by simply looking at some indicators and neglecting others. Several different influences have to be considered in order to receive a holistic picture and understanding of the causes and effects of the crisis. Lejano and Stokols (2013) refer to failures in analyses that are based on only one aspect and at the same time exclude others, as well as systems that operate in one dimension without reference to the others. In the case of economic development, it is important to not only look at the economic indicators but also at culture. All humans are influenced by culture because there is no cultural-free area. As a result, culture influences human behavior and decision-making, also with regard to economic issues. However, a multilevel model also has limitations regarding its applicability.

2.1.1 Implications and Limitations for the Practical Application of a Layered Perspective

One challenge was to find a suitable model that reveals the influences on behavior and decision-making processes which contributed significantly to social and economic turning points. Another challenge of this dissertation was to find a model that reveals and provides explanations for changes in behavior and decision-making processes.

After presenting and examining various theoretical frameworks on human values and behavior (please see Chapter Two) it became clear that a model with a multi-layered perspective is most suitable to examine these issues. The dissertation also demonstrates that a multi-layered perspective can be applied in different ways, such as revealing bottom-up, top-down, and interactive effects but also as an analysis of layers taking into account time.

Chapter Five examines the behavior and decision-making processes that contributed to the development of the Irish society. This is achieved by placing the Irish society at the center of consideration. The central issue is how and why the Irish society developed in a certain direction. This section examines the influences that affected the behavior and decisions of key-decision makers and also analyzes the consequences of these decisions for the Irish society. It is shown that an interplay of multiple influences exists, for instance, legislation, politics, religious affiliation, and history which all affected the societal development of the Irish.

This holistic view is limited by the fact that it is not possible to fully consider every piece of information that is relevant for a perspective.

This chapter also reveals the influences of societal change, for instance, away from a traditional worldview towards more secularity. This is exemplified by the change of the Constitution. Changes in jurisprudence have a significant impact on the functioning of a society. Consequently, a layered perspective helps to gain a better understanding of the development of the Irish society by considering legal, social, religious, political, and economic areas. It becomes clear that Irish national identity has gone through many changes since the foundation of Ireland and that the social ecological model is able to explain how and why these changes occurred over time.

Taking into account time presupposes the setting of a specific timeframe. As a consequence, the model is limited to the selected time period. However, effects of events that influence legal, social, religious, political and economic developments cannot be clearly differentiated into time periods.

Chapter Six focuses particularly on Ireland's dramatic economic slump, also known as the fall of the Celtic Tiger. The analysis reveals the influences on the behavior and decisions of key-decision-makers that finally contributed to the fall of the Celtic Tiger. This is achieved by placing the various institutions, such as banks, politics, and control authorities at the center of consideration. Then, important influencing factors from various sources are identified, including reports of commissions of investigation that examined the fall of the Celtic Tiger and reports from investigative journalism concerning this topic. Therefore, this analyzing chapter shows that a layered perspective helps to gain a better understanding of the reasons and origins of behavior and decision-making processes that significantly contributed to the economic crisis. It shows that there were characteristics that apply specifically to the Irish, such as property ownership for historical reasons. However, many mistakes were also made by key-decision makers, for instance, in politics and banks. These were a consequence of false incentives created by the institutions that resulted in conflicts of interest.

Thus, from a cultural-anthropological perspective, the model has limitations regarding complete objectivity because the behavior of key-decision makers is taken into account. This behavior is not only based on their cultural background but also influenced by individual psychological factors.

Chapter Seven reveals cultural change in light of economic developments by taking into account a framework that focuses on the subsystems of the human ecological surroundings, as well as on the ways in which these subsystems interact with and influence each other, that is macro-, exo-, meso-, micro-system, and the individual. This part also includes the chronosystem. By taking into account the factor 'time' in this section, the layered perspective is able to show changes in behavior and decision-making processes, and also cultural change. This is achieved by comparing the behavior and decision-making processes with regard to the change of legislation concerning divorce rights in Ireland at two different points in time.

At each level, the divorce referendums also show top-down effects, such as the influence of cultural values on the individual as well as bottom-up effects, such as the effort of many individuals to mobilize others to vote. There were also multiple reciprocal and interactive effects at all levels. For instance, at the macro-level, the dissertation examines the environment in which the Constitution was created. It shows that the Constitution reflects the minds of its designers and society at that time. The Constitution, per definition, embodies the all-encompassing basic rules which guide a society. Finally, the dissertation discloses which factors led to cultural change in Ireland and thus provides explanations for cultural change. This is also illustrated by the decline of a traditional worldview, for instance with reference to the Constitution which originally did not accept divorce and the people's decision to change the Constitution. It shows that economic development also played a significant role for a different outcome in the second divorce referendum.

As it approached the 21st century, the Irish society evolved rapidly into a modern country. This is also due to the detachment from the conventions of the Catholic Church. A demonstrative affiliation to the Catholic Church to differentiate the Irish from their Protestant occupiers is seemingly not as important in light of the membership of the European Union. For example, Ireland revised laws that denied the same rights to all, in particular, concerning the issues of homosexuality, divorce rights, or abortion. As a consequence, church membership has declined. The dissertation finds that economic development encourages changes in society and the transformation of cultural values. Thus, the layered perspective helps to gain a better understanding of the interrelations of economic development and the forces that lead to societal and cultural change.

In conclusion, the various parts of the analysis show different applications of a layered perspective. Although these analyses were all carried out using the example of Ireland (society and economy), it can be assumed that the framework is transferrable and can also be applied to other issues and other societies and/ or economies. The prerequisite for this is a precise analysis of culture and especially history. Culture permeates every system, such as the economic system. According to DiMaggio (1994), aspects of culture shape economic institutions and affairs. This indicates the importance of cultural-anthropology not only for social but also for economic analyses. Furthermore, the historical knowledge about the development of the Republic of Ireland provides the basis for the whole analysis in Chapter Five, Six, and Seven.

This dissertation modifies the social ecological model so that it can contribute to answering research questions in many fields of research. The possibilities of the application of this modified model were demonstrated in the analyzing Chapters Five, Six, and Seven.

The modified model is applied in such a way that the individual is not at the center of consideration as is the case in the social ecological model, but instead an issue is at the center of consideration, such as a culture, a society, or the economy. Then, this modified model examines the influences on this observation object with respect to a specific question. At the beginning of such an analysis, the observation object has to be defined and the specific research question has to be formulated. Then, the influences of each layer on the object of observation are examined in the direction of the yellow arrows while taking into account the research question (please see figure 37).

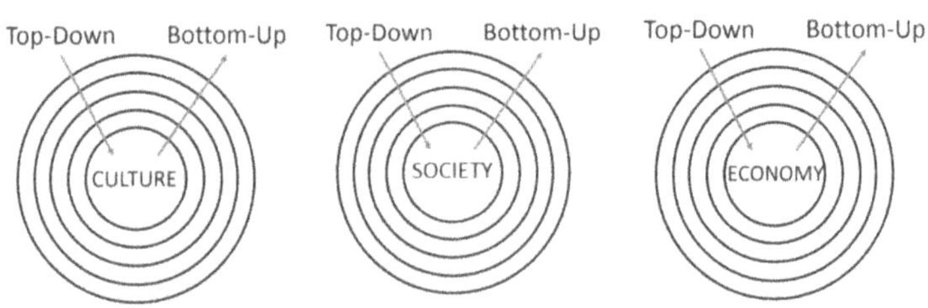

Figure 37: Examination model using the examples of culture, society, and economy

Now, if the focus is on examining changes of an observation object over time, it can be examined at different points in time and the results then compared (please see figure 38).

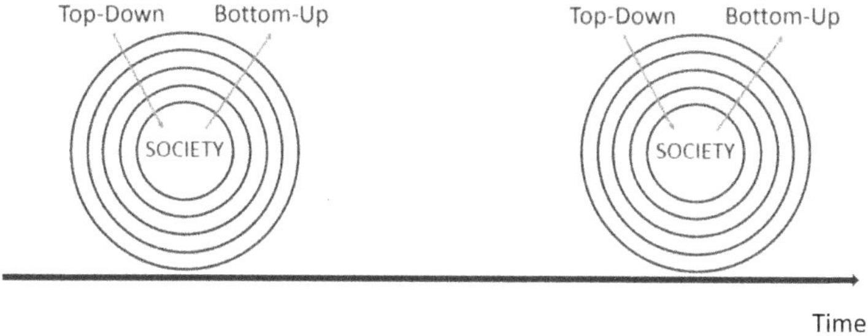

Figure 38: Examination model using the example of society in comparison to two different points in time

This dissertation shows relations between social and economic issues with the help of a layered perspective and analyzes developments. The application of an ecological model to also find explanations for economic issues includes a variety of interdisciplinary fields. Thus, the analysis is a bridge across not only ecology and economics but also psychology, anthropology, archaeology, and history, because it is necessary to show a more holistic picture of how humans have interacted with their environment in the past and how they could interact with it in the future (Costanza, 2010). Therefore, the model offers a valuable contribution to various research fields, such as social ecology, behavioral economics, and ecological economics.

2.1.2 Implications and Limitations for the Theoretical Application of a Layered Perspective

Tudge et al. (2009) state that there should be a tight connection between a theory, the methods used, and the analytic strategy. The meaning of 'theory' is to provide a framework within which to explain connections among the phenomena under study and to provide insights leading to the discovery of new connections. The goal of much empirical work is to test the accuracy and goodness-of-fit of theories that aim at describing the phenomena under study. It is important to make the theoretical framework on which the research is based explicit. Tudge et al. (2009) found out that many scientific analyses that claim to use Bronfenbrenner's model actually use an older version instead of the mature one. Bronfenbrenner had already been critical toward his own model. He was always aware of the limitations of his model and therefore continued to further develop it, as mentioned in Chapter Two, Section 3. Thus, an analysis should clearly state whether it strictly follows his model, in which case his most recent version should be used, or if not, it should explain why an earlier version is used and which one exactly (Tudge et al., 2009).

Whether or not Bronfenbrenner's model is applied, the application of a layered perspective framework generally offers many advantages while at the same time it poses challenges and sets limitations.

Advantages are first of all that focusing on only a single layer, such as individual behavior, carries the risk of underestimating the effect of other contexts, such as historical incidents and economic systems. When using a layered perspective framework, contexts are taken into account and provide explanations for individual behavior and decisions by illuminating reciprocal contextual influences (Oetzel, 2009). Thus, one benefit of a layered perspective is that it helps to gain a more comprehensive understanding of the multi-layered influences on behavior and decision-making processes which in turn influence, for instance, social and economic developments.

Second, a layered perspective is able to reveal cultural change in contrast to cultural models which only display a singular data collection of cultural dimensions. The layered perspective also helps to identify how certain contexts support or inhibit behavioral change (Oetzel, 2009). This is illustrated in the analyzing part by comparing different decisions concerning the same issue at different points in time while taking into account the ecological changes.

Third, a layered perspective framework is also able to provide valuable contributions to the various social surveys, such as EVS and ESS. These surveys which collect data and are able to reveal changes due to their periodic repetition cannot explain why the data has changed. A layered perspective framework, however, allows the interpretation of the data as it provides explanations for why the data has changed.

One limitation regarding the applicability of this model, which is also a main point of criticism of the layered perspective framework, is that it is too extensive. The construction of the framework is such that it takes into account multiple issues. Yet, this does not mean that everything matters. Instead, with regard to a certain issue, some factors matter more than others so that these factors must be emphasized. It is a challenge of the application of a layered perspective framework to determine its theoretical limits because expanding these limits further enhances the explanatory nature of this heuristic theoretical framework. Additionally, it is a challenge to keep all the information well-ordered since the layered perspective is not linear due to the many different interlacing factors that influence behavior and decision-making processes.

Second, this framework does not claim completeness, which, given the unlimited perspectives, cannot be achieved at all. Thus, the object of investigation and its limits have to be clearly defined. However, even though not all influences can be revealed, the analysis highlights very important influencing factors underpinned by evidence and explains the relationships to the other layers. Although the consequences of decisions taken by key figures are discussed as examples in the analysis section, the layered perspective approach helps to avoid blaming someone for all of his or her behavioral choices. The approach considers various influencing factors and places behavior in context rather than simply viewing behavior as a series of individual choices (Oetzel, 2009). However, the restriction that not all factors can be taken into account does not excuse poor behavior by not considering individual responsibility. Instead, it highlights other explanatory factors as well. The approach recognizes the importance of individual responsibility for behavioral choices and thus, brings up ethical consideration for explaining behavior (Oetzel, 2009).

Third, this dissertation shows that history has a significant impact on behavior and decision-making. History shapes, among others, cultural identity, social relations, and social structures. For instance, events that go back hundreds of years can still have an impact on the present. At this point it should be acknowledged that such an extensive consideration is not always easy to implement. Thus, it has to be said that the inclusion of different disciplines, such as history, also requires an in-depth examination of these disciplines. Such an in-depth investigation can set limits, because the knowledge of non-experts is limited. For this, the results of previous research are very important, even if these topics are challenging to understand for non-experts.

Last but not least, the dissertation shows how important it is in future analyses to include a cultural-anthropological perspective. As shown, no system can be adequately explained if culture or the human factor is not taken into account. However, according to Minkov (2011) culture is not an easy topic. Even though many people are aware of the fact that different societies often have different cultures, education and training is necessary to be able to express a professional view in this area.

2.2 Recommendations for Further Research

To apply a social ecological framework to economic issues is a transdisciplinary approach that looks at the full range of interrelationships between ecological and economic systems. This broad approach is essential to understand and manage human behavior and decision-making processes in the face of increasing challenges regarding interdependent global social and economic development. There should be an increasing awareness that economic decisions made on the basis of local, narrow, short-term criteria can produce disastrous results in the long run on a global level as seen with the global economic crisis. There should also be an increasing awareness that traditional economic models and concepts fall short in their ability to deal with these challenges (Costanza, 1991). Additionally, there should be an awareness of the mutual dependence between economic development and social change.

Current economic analyses are not very efficient in revealing and including ecological influences on human behavior and decision-making processes. What use are the economic analyses when the hitherto existing economic institutions, such as banks and rating agencies, provide incentives from which individuals can benefit for themselves in the short-term, but these incentives do not support action that promotes a sustainable and healthy economic growth over the long-term, as was shown in the lending practices of the banks. It was shown that these incentives provoked actions that did not harmonize with the market signals, such as the pretended good economic situation that firms and individuals adjusted their behavior to and on which basis they made decisions. There is a need to explore alternatives to current control mechanisms and management systems. Likewise, uncertainty about local and transnational ecological influences should be included as factors when modifying these control mechanisms (Costanza, 1991). Many existing institutions have not optimally used market and non-market knowledge in the creation of their processes. Some reasons for this are the bureaucratic structures of many modern institutions. For example, the removal of authority to make decisions of the central bank and the creation of a new regulatory body did not help to avert the crisis. Institutions should be de-bureaucratized so that they can effectively respond to the upcoming challenges of achieving social and economic development (Costanza, Daly and Bartholomew, 1991).

There is a need to broaden economic and ecological research topics by including non-economic factors. While the economy has developed many useful analysis tools, it has mostly focused these tools on economic issues without taking into account other ecological influences on the economic actors. In particular, there is a need to better understand influences on behavior and decision-making, also over time. Additionally, there is a need to understand how individual behavior and decision-making as opposed to group behavior and decision-making may differ. So far, too little attention was paid to ecological influences in economic analyses, otherwise the global economic crisis might not have occurred (Costanza, Daly and Bartholomew, 1991).

There is a need to broaden economic and ecological education which includes a broader general knowledge of fields, such as psychology, anthropology, and history. The current education system is characterized by overspecialization and disciplinary isolation. Instead, transdisciplinary curricula as well as job and academic support systems should be developed for both specialization and generalization. This should be combined with an emphasis on the value of general education and personal development as opposed to the more narrow training of professional economic specialists. An ecological economics core curriculum and degree granting programs that embody the skills of both economics and ecology could be helpful. This implies a curriculum with some blending of anthropological, historical and psychological sciences and economics. Within this curriculum, quantitative methods are essential but they should be problem-directed rather than just mathematical tools or economic models. Education programs have to be developed that effectively transfer information between ecology, social and economic development (Costanza, Daly and Bartholomew, 1991).

This dissertation provides a comprehensive theory and practical examples and therefore, a solid basis upon which further research can be built. To understand a whole system it is not possible to only look at parts of it. In the end, a developing economy and developing society can only be understood when ecological influences are taken into account.

References

Adler, N. J., & Gundersen, A. (2008). *International dimensions of organizational behavior* (5th ed.). Mason, OH: Thomson South-Western.

Agnew, P. (2015, May 26). Vatican calls Irish referendum a 'defeat for humanity'. *irishtimes.com*. Retrieved from http://www.irishtimes.com/news/politics/marriage-referendum/vatican-calls-irish-referendum-a-defeat-for-humanity-1.2226957

Ahearne, A. G., Ammer, J., Doyle, B. M., Kole, L. S., & Martin, R. F. (2005). *House prices and monetary policy: A cross-country study* (International Finance Discussion Papers No. 841). Retrieved from Board of Governors of the Federal Reserve System website: https://www.federalreserve.gov/pubs/ifdp/2005/841/ifdp841.pdf

AHK Japan. (2018). *Japanknigge*. Retrieved from http://japan.ahk.de/japan-tipps/auf-geschaeftsreisen/japanknigge/

Alderman, L. (2010, June 28). In Ireland, a picture of the high cost of austerity. *nytimes.com*. Retrieved from http://www.nytimes.com/2010/06/29/business/global/29austerity.html?_r=4&

Alioth, M. (1986, July 4). Die Iren wollen keine Scheidung. *zeit.de*. Retrieved from http://www.zeit.de/1986/28/die-iren-wollen-keine-scheidung?print

Alioth, M. (Author) (2009, November 11). *Die Wut kocht: Irland verordnet den öffentlichen Kassen drastisches Sparen* [Television broadcast]. Deutschlandfunk. Retrieved from http://www.dradio.de/dlf/sendungen/europaheute/1067676/

Allport, G. W. (1979). *The nature of prejudice* (Unabridged, 25th anniversary ed.). Reading, MA: Addison-Wesley Pub. Co.

Anderson, P., Møller, L., & Galea, G. (2012). *Alcohol in the European Union: Consumption harm and policy approaches*. Copenhagen, Denmark: World Health Organization. Retrieved from www.euro.who.int/__data/assets/pdf_file/0003/160680/e96457.pdf

Arnold, B. (2001). *Halloween customs in the Celtic world*. Retrieved from https://people.uwm.edu/barnold/2001/10/31/halloween-customs-in-the-celtic-world/

Ascarelli, S. (2016). *The more we earn, the more often we drink: If your household income tops $75,000, you're very likely to have had a drink in the past 24 hours*. Retrieved from http://www.marketwatch.com/story/the-more-we-earn-the-more-often-we-drink-2016-03-08?link=sfmw_fb

Asch, R. G. (1994). Kulturkonflikt und Recht: Irland, das Common Law, und die Ancient Constitution. *Ius Commune Zeitschrift für Europäische Rechtsgeschichte, 21*, 169–212. Retrieved from http://www.rg.mpg.de/948306/ic21_05_asch.pdf

Atlas of European Values. (2011a). *Percentage of people that say family is very or quite important in their lives*. Retrieved from http://www.atlasofeuropeanvalues.eu/new/europa.php?ids=2&year=2008&country=IE

Atlas of European Values. (2011b). *Opinion on a scale of 0 to 100: homosexuality can be justified (0 = never 100 = always)*. Retrieved from http://www.atlasofeuropeanvalues.eu/new/europa.php?ids=240&year=2008&country=IE

Atlas of European Values. (2011c). *Percentage of people that attend religious services (apart from weddings, funerals and christenings) at least once a week*. Retrieved from http://www.atlasofeuropeanvalues.eu/new/europa.php?ids=109&year=1981&country=IE

Atlas of European Values. (2011d). *Percentage of people that believe in God*. Retrieved from http://www.atlasofeuropeanvalues.eu/new/europa.php?ids=119&year=2008&country=IE

Atlas of European Values. (2011e). *Percentage of people that say churches in their country are giving adequate answers to the moral problems and needs of the individual*. Retrieved from http://www.atlasofeuropeanvalues.eu/new/europa.php?ids=115&year=2008&country=IE

Atlas of European Values. (2011f). *Percentage of people that say churches in their country are giving adequate answers to the problems of family life*. Retrieved from http://www.atlasofeuropeanvalues.eu/new/europa.php?ids=116&year=2008&country=IE

Aujean, M. (2001). *Company taxation in the internal market*. Retrieved from http://ec.europa.eu/taxation_customs/sites/taxation/files/resources/documents/company_tax_study_en.pdf

Bacon, P., MacCabe, F., & Murphy, A. (1999). *The housing market: An economic review and assessment: Report submitted to the Minister for Housing and Urban Renewal*. Dublin. Retrieved from The Irish Council for Social Housing website: http://www.environ.ie/en/Publications/DevelopmentandHousing/Housing/FileDownLoad,2071,en.pdf

Bailey, G. A., & Peoples, J. G. (2014). *Essentials of cultural anthropology* (3rd ed.). Belmont, CA: Wadsworth/Cengage Learning.

Barnes, M., & Rowe, J. (2013). *Child, youth and family health: Strengthening communities* (2nd ed.). Chatswood, NSW: Elsevier Australia.

Barnlund, D. C. (1989). *Communicative styles of Japanese and Americans: Images and realities*. Belmont, CA: Wadsworth Publishing.

Barrett, A., Kearney, I., & O'Brien, M. (2007). *Quarterly economic commentary* (ESRI Forecasting Series). Dublin, Ireland.

Barro, R. J. (1991). Economic growth in a cross section of countries. *The quarterly Journal of Economics, 106*(2), 407–443.

Barro, R. J., Grilli, V. (1996). *Makroökonomie: Europäische Perspektive. Wolls Lehr- und Handbücher der Wirtschafts- und Sozialwissenschaften*. München, Deutschland: Oldenbourg.

Barro, R. J., & Sala-i-Martin, X. (1992). Convergence. *Journal of Political Economy, 100*(2), 223–251.

Barwell, R. (2017). *Macroeconomic policy after the crash: Issues in microprudential and macroprudential policy* (1st ed.). Dartford, United Kingdom: Palgrave Macmillan.

Becker, B. H. (1881). *Disturbed Ireland: Being the letters written during the winter of 1880–81*. London, United Kingdom: MacMillan and Co.

Becker, J., Stolberg, S. G., & Labaton, S. (2008, December 21). Bush drive for home ownership fueled housing bubble. *nytimes.com*. Retrieved from http://www.nytimes.com/2008/12/21/business/worldbusiness/21iht-admin.4.18853088.html?_r=0

Beckett, J. C. (2008). *The making of modern Ireland, 1603–1923*. London, United Kingdom: Faber and Faber.

Bender, T. (2006). *A nation among nations: America's place in world history* (1st ed.). New York, NY: Hill and Wang.

Benedict, R. (2005). *Patterns of culture* (1st Mariner books ed.). Boston, MA: Houghton Mifflin.

Berger, D. (2015, July 20). Das ist die wahre Ursache für Homosexualität. *huffingtonpost.de*. Retrieved from http://www.huffingtonpost.de/david-berger/wahre-ursache-fuer-homosexualitaet_b_7828530.html

Bernal, M. E., & Knight, G. P. (Eds.) (1993). *SUNY series, United States Hispanic studies. Ethnic identity: Formation and transmission among Hispanics and other minorities*. Albany, NY: State University of New York Press.

Berry, J. W. (2005). Acculturation: Living successfully in two cultures. *International Journal of Intercultural Relations, 29*(6), 697–712. doi:10.1016/j.ijintrel.2005.07.013

Bieler, L. (1993). *Clavis Patricii II: Libri epistolarum sancti Patricii episcopi*. Introduction, text and commentary by Ludwig Bieler (The Royal Irish Academy, Ed.). Dublin, Ireland: W. & G. Baird Ltd.

Binchy, D. A. (1962). Patrick and his biographers: Ancient and modern. *Studia Hibernica*, (2), 7–173.

Birkhan, H. (1997). *Kelten: Versuch einer Gesamtdarstellung ihrer Kultur.* Wien, Österreich: Verlag der Österreichischen Akademie der Wissenschaften.

Blodget, H. (2011, August 19). Moody's analyst breaks silence: Says ratings agency rotten to core with conflicts. *businessinsider.com.* Retrieved from http://www.businessinsider.com/moodys-analyst-conflicts-corruption-and-greed-2011-8?IR=T

Blom, H., & Meier, H. (2017). *Interkulturelles Management: Interkulturelle Kommunikation, Internationales HR-Management, Interkulturelle Teams und Führung, Managing Diversity* (3., überarbeitete und erweiterte Auflage). *NWB Studium Betriebswirtschaft.* Herne, Deutschland: nwb Studium.

Blum, L. A. (2002). *I'm not a racist, but…: The moral quandary of race.* Ithaca, NY: Cornell University Press.

Board of Trinity College Dublin (2011). *Book of Armagh – Liber Ardmachanus (L.A.).* Retrieved from http://www.confessio.ie/manuscripts/dublin#1

Boss, P. Doherty, W. J., LaRossa, R., Schumm, W. R., & Steinmetz, S. K. (Eds.). (2009). *Sourcebook of family theories and methods: A contextual approach.* Saint Paul, MN: Springer.

Boutell, C. (1914). The Handbook to English heraldry (11th ed.). London, United Kingdom: Reeves & Turner. Retrieved from http://www.gutenberg.org/files/23186/23186-h/23186-h.htm

Boyce, D. G., & O'Day, A. (Eds.). (1997). *The making of modern Irish history: Revisionism and the revisionist controversy.* London, United Kingdom: Routledge.

Brasse, H. (2014). Maya. Retrieved from https://www.planet-wissen.de/kultur/voelker/maya_ein_ewiges_raetsel/index.html

Breadun, D. De (2009, November 30). Ahern says Government critics should 'dig the garden or grow bluebells'. *irishtimes.com.* Retrieved from http://www.irishtimes.com/news/ahern-says-government-critics-should-dig-the-garden-or-grow-bluebells-1.780939

Breen, M. J., & Healy, A. E. (2016). *Changing values, attitudes and behaviours in Ireland: An analysis of European social survey data in Ireland, 2002–2012.* Newcastle upon Tyne, United Kingdom: Cambridge Scholars Publishing.

Breen, M. J., & Reynolds, C. (2011). The rise of secularism and the decline of religiosity in Ireland: The pattern of religious change in Europe. *The International Journal of Religion and Spirituality in Society, 1 Issue 2,* 195–212.

Brennock, M. (1998, May 8). RTE decision to deny free broadcasts to treaty campaigners timid, says lecturer. *irishtimes.com.* Retrieved from http://www.irishtimes.com/news/rte-decision-to-deny-free-broadcasts-to-treaty-campaigners-timid-says-lecturer-1.150232

Brinkbäumer, K., Goos, H., Hornig, F., Ludwig, U., & Pauly, C. (2009). Gorillas Spiel: Warum finden die Finanzmärkte – trotz billionenschwerer staatlicher Schutzschirme – nicht zurück zur Normalität? Weil die Pleite der New Yorker Bank Lehman Brothers das Vertrauen zwischen den Banken ruiniert hat und die Welt kollabieren ließ. Die Geschichte eines Jahrhundertfehlers. *Der Spiegel*, (11), 40–52.

Brislin, R. W. (1993). *Understanding culture's influence on behavior.* Fort Worth, TX: Harcourt Brace Jovanovich College Publishers.

Bronfenbrenner, U. (1975). Reality and research in the ecology of human development. *Proceedings of the American Philosophical Society, 119*(6), 439–469.

Bronfenbrenner, U. (1977). Toward an experimental ecology of human development. *American Psychologist, 32,* 513–531.

Bronfenbrenner, U. (1979). *The ecology of human development: Experiments by nature and design.* Cambridge, MA: Harvard University Press.

Bronfenbrenner, U. (1992). Ecological systems theory. In R. Vasta (Ed.), *Six theories of child development. Revised Formulations and Current Issues* (pp. 187–250). London, United Kingdom: Jessica Kingsley.

Bronfenbrenner, U. (1994). Ecological models of human development. In T. Husén & T. N. Postlethwaite (Eds.), *The international encyclopedia of education* (2nd ed., pp. 1643–1647). Oxford, United Kingdom: Pergamon.

Bronfenbrenner, U., & Ceci, S. J. (1994). Nature-nurture reconceptualized in developmental perspective: A bioecological model. *Psychological Review, 101*(4), 568–586. doi:10.1037/0033-295X.101.4.568

Bronfenbrenner, U., & Morris, P. A. (1998). The ecology of developmental processes. In R. M. Lerner (Ed.), *Handbook of child psychology* (5th ed., pp. 993–1023). New York, NY: Wiley.

Bronfenbrenner, U., & Morris, P. A (2006). The bioecological model of human development. In W. Damon & R. M. Lerner (Eds.), *Handbook of child psychology: vol. 1. Theoretical models of human development* (6th ed., pp. 793–828). Hoboken, NJ: John Wiley & Sons.

Brown, T. (2003). 'Bloomsday'. In B. Lalor (Ed.), *The encyclopedia of Ireland* (pp. 98–99). New Haven, CT: Yale University Press.

Brown, T. (2015). *The Irish Times: 150 Years of influence.* London, United Kingdom: Bloomsbury Publishing Plc.

Browne, V. (2011, April 6). Let's own up to our part in the burst bubble. *irishtimes.com.* Retrieved from http://www.irishtimes.com/opinion/let-s-own-up-to-our-part-in-the-burst-bubble-1.564844?via=mr

Bubolz, M. M., & Sontag, M. S (2009). Human ecology theory. In P. Boss, W. J. Doherty, R. LaRossa, W.R. Schumm, & S.K. Steinmetz, (Eds.) (2009).

Sourcebook of family theories and methods: A contextual approach (pp. 419–447). Saint Paul, MN: Springer.

Budzinski, O. & Michler, A. (2014). *Subprime-Krise*. Retrieved from http://wirtschaftslexikon.gabler.de/Archiv/72525/subprime-krise-v9.html

Bundesministerium der Finanzen (2016). *Stabilisierung des Euroraums: Chronologie der Stabilisierung der Wirtschafts- und Währungsunion*. Retrieved from http://www.bundesfinanzministerium.de/Content/DE/Standardartikel/Themen/Europa/Stabilisierung_des_Euro/2010-06-04-chronologie-euro-stabilisierung.html

Bunting, M. (2009, May 21). An abuse too far by the Catholic church. *The Guardian. theguardian.com*. Retrieved from https://www.theguardian.com/commentisfree/belief/2009/may/21/catholic-abuse-ireland-ryan

Burke, K. (1966). *Language as symbolic action: Essays on life, literature, and method*. Berkeley and Los Angeles, CA: University of California Press, Ltd.

Burnand, F. (1882). *The Irish Frankenstein. "The baneful and blood-stained Monster yet was it not my Master to the very extent that it was my Creature? Had I not breathed into it my own spirit?"*. Retrieved from https://punch.photoshelter.com/image/I0000xxAezHq7rx4

Bury, J. B. (1902). Tírechán's memoir of St. Patrick. *The English Historical Review, 17*(66), 235–267. Retrieved from http://ehr.oxfordjournals.org/content/XVII/LXVI/235.citation

Buti, M. (2008). The economy of Ireland: whither the Celtic Tiger? *European Economy News*, (11), 12–13. Retrieved from http://ec.europa.eu/archives/economy_finance/een/pdf/een_011_en.pdf

Caesar, G. I. (2005). *Der gallische Krieg* (Oberbreyer, M., Ed.). Köln, Deutschland: Anaconda.

Cahill, C., & Casey, M. R (Author) (2015, October 12). *History of St. Patrick's day videos: Why wear green on St. Patrick's day?* [Television broadcast]. A&E Television Networks, LLC. Retrieved from http://www.history.com/topics/st-patricks-day/history-of-st-patricks-day/videos/why-wear-green-on-st-patricks-day

Callanan, F. (2003). Parnell, Charles Stewart. In B. Lalor (Ed.), *The encyclopedia of Ireland* (p. 858). New Haven, CT: Yale University Press.

Calomiris, C. (2008). *The subprime turmoil: What's old, what's new, and what's next*. Retrieved from http://www.imf.org/external/np/res/seminars/2008/arc/pdf/cwc.pdf

Cambrensis, G. (1982). *The history and topography of Ireland. Penguin classics*. London, United Kingdom: Penguin Books.

Campbell, J. (2008). *The hero with a thousand faces* (3rd rev. ed.). *Bollingen series: Vol. 17.* Novato, CA: New World Library.

Campbell, J. Y., & Cocco, J. F. (2011). *A model of mortgage default*. Cambridge, MA. Retrieved from National Bureau of Economic Research website: http://www.nber.org/papers/w17516.pdf

Carolan, M. (2016, April 15). Central bank failed to act on property lending alert, court hears: Former chief economist says 'senior people within the bank simply did not wish to know about the problems or, if they did know, they did not wish to do anything about them'. *irishtimes.com*. Retrieved from http://www.irishtimes.com/business/economy/central-bank-failed-to-act-on-property-lending-alert-court-hears-1.2612399

Carrillo, R., & Tello, J. (2008). *Family violence and men of color: Healing the wounded male spirit* (2nd ed.). *Springer Series, Focus on Men*. New York, NY: Springer Publishing Company.

Carswell, S. (2010, June 11). Report highlights how inadequately financial regulation is resourced. *irishtimes.com*. Retrieved from http://www.irishtimes.com/business/report-highlights-how-inadequately-financial-regulation-is-resourced-1.676680

Casey, M. (2007, May 14). Inevitable recession awaits poll winners. *irishtimes.com*. Retrieved from http://www.irishtimes.com/opinion/inevitable-recession-awaits-poll-winners-1.1205810

Casey, M. (2008, October 14). Is financial regulation in Ireland a fair-weather activity? *irishtimes.com*. Retrieved from http://www.irishtimes.com/opinion/is-financial-regulation-in-ireland-a-fair-weather-activity-1.895536

Castle, S. (2013, November 14). Ireland Is to exit its bailout, and without a safety net. *nytimes.com*. Retrieved from http://www.nytimes.com/2013/11/15/business/international/ireland-to-end-reliance-on-bailout-lifeline.html

Cathcart, B. (1994, June 11). Rear window: Punch lines that kept the Irish in their place: Taking the mick. *independent.co.uk*. Retrieved from http://www.independent.co.uk/voices/rear-window-punch-lines-that-kept-the-irish-in-their-place-taking-the-mick-1422052.html

Cavendish, R. (2014). Brian Boru, High King of Ireland, killed. *History Today, 64*(4). Retrieved from http://www.historytoday.com/richard-cavendish/brian-boru-high-king-ireland-killed

CBFSAI. (2007a). *Annual Report 2006: Report of the central bank and financial services authority of Ireland for the year ended 31 December 2006*. Dublin, Ireland. Retrieved from Central Bank & Financial Services Authority of Ireland website: http://centralbank.ie/docs/default-source/publications/annual-reports/2006-cbfsai-annual-report.pdf?sfvrsn=12

CBFSAI. (2007b). *Financial stability report 2007.* Dublin, Ireland.

Ceci, S. J. (2006). Urie Bronfenbrenner (1917–2005). *American Psychologist, 61*(2), 173–174. doi:10.1037/0003-066X.61.2.173

Central Bank of Ireland (1999). *Report of the Implementation advisory group on the establishment of a single regulatory authority.* Dublin, Ireland. Retrieved from http://www.financialregulator.ie/press-area/press-releases/Pages/ReportoftheImplementationAdvisoryGroupontheestablishmentofaSingleRegulatoryAuthority.aspx

Central Bank of Ireland (2003). *Central bank and financial services authority of Ireland.* Dublin, Ireland. Retrieved from http://www.ifsc.ie/company.aspx?idcompany=124

Charles, G. (2011). Tullamore Dew unveils fresh global ad campaign: William Grant & Sons is rolling out a new global ad campaign for Tullamore Dew as part of a wholesale revamp of the Irish whiskey brand. *campaignlive.co.uk.* Retrieved from http://www.campaignlive.co.uk/article/1094953/tullamore-dew-unveils-fresh-global-ad-campaign#

Chatterton Newman, R. (2011). *Brian Boru: King of Ireland.* Cork, Ireland: Mercier Press.

Cheney, G., May, S., & Munshi, D. (Eds.) (2011). *International communication association (ICA). handbook series. The handbook of communication Ethics.* New York, NY: Routledge.

Cheprasov, A. (2003). *History 301: Historiography & historical methods: What is historical memory? – Biases & examples.* Retrieved from https://study.com/academy/lesson/what-is-historical-memory-biases-examples.html

Chhokar, J. S., Brodbeck, F. C., & House, R. J. (2007). Methodology. In J. S. Chhokar, F. C. Brodbeck, & R. J. House (Eds.), *Culture and leadership across the world. The GLOBE book of in-depth studies of 25 societies* (pp. 17–30). New York, NY: Routledge.

Chhokar, J. S., Brodbeck, F. C., & House, R. J. (Eds.) (2007). *Culture and leadership across the world: The GLOBE book of in-depth studies of 25 societies. Lea's organization and management series.* New York, NY: Routledge.

Christopher, A. J. (1997). The Irish divorce referendum of 1995. *Geography, 82*(1), 79–90.

Chubb, B. (1982). *The government and politics of Ireland* (2nd ed.). Stanford, CA: Stanford University Press.

Cialdini, R. B. (2018). Why the World Is Turning to Behavioral Science. In A. Samson (Ed.), *The Behavioral Economics Guide 2018* (pp. VI–XIV).

Citizens Advice. (2019). *Getting a divorce*. Retrieved from https://www.citizensadvice.org.uk/family/ending-a-relationship/how-to-separate/getting-a-divorce/

Clarity, J. F. (1995, November 20). Premier urges Irish to vote for legalizing of divorce. *nytimes.com*. Retrieved from http://www.nytimes.com/1995/11/20/world/premier-urges-irish-to-vote-for-legalizing-of-divorce.html

Clarke, H. B., Ní Mhaonaigh, M., & Ó Floinn, R. (Eds.) (1998). *Ireland and Scandinavia in the early Viking Age*. Blackrock, Portland, OR: Four Courts Press.

Cleary, J., & Connolly, C. (2005). *The Cambridge companion to modern Irish culture*. Cambridge, United Kingdom: Cambridge University Press.

Clines, F. X. (1986, June 28). The Irish uphold ban on divorce by 3-to-2 margin. *nytimes.com*. Retrieved from http://www.nytimes.com/1986/06/28/world/the-irish-uphold-ban-on-divorce-by-3-to-2-margin.html

Coakley, J. (1987). Moral consensus in a secularising society: The Irish divorce referendum of 1986. *West European Politics, 10*(2), 291–296. doi:10.1080/01402388708424632

Coakley, J. (1998). Religion, ethnic identity and the protestant minority in the Republic. In W. J. Crotty & D. E. Schmitt (Eds.), *Ireland and the politics of change*. Harlow, United Kingdom: Addison Wesley Longman.

Cohen, A. (1974). *Two-dimensional man: An essay on the anthropology of power and symbolism in complex society*. London, United Kingdom: Routledge & Kegan Paul.

Coleman, M. C. (2009). *American Indians, the Irish, and government schooling: A comparative study. Indigenous education*. Lincoln, NE: University of Nebraska Press.

Collins, M. & Volmer, H. (2015). *Irland und Griechenland: "Die Erholung kam erst nach der Austerität". n-tv.de*. Retrieved from http://www.n-tv.de/politik/Die-Erholung-kam-erst-nach-der-Austeritaet-article15440071.html

Cone, P., Grossman, A., & Ascherl, J. P. (Eds.) (1978). *Treasures of early Irish art 1500 B.C. to 1500 A.D.: from the collections of the National Museum of Ireland, Royal Irish Academy, Trinity College, Dublin*, Ireland. Exhibited at the Metropolitan Museum of Art, the Fine Arts Museum of San Francisco: M.H. de Young Memorial Museum, Museum of Art, Carnegie Institute, Pittsburgh, Museum of Fine Arts, Boston, Philadelphia Museum of Art. Verona, Italy: Arnoldo Mondadori Editore.

Costanza, R. (Ed.). (1991). *Complexity in ecological systems series. Ecological economics: The science and management of sustainability*. New York, NY: Columbia University Press.

Costanza, R. (1991). Ecological economics: A research agenda. *Structural Change and Economic Dynamics, 2*(2), 335–357. doi:10.1016/S0954-349X(05)80007-4

Costanza, R., Daly, H. E., & Bartholomew, J. A. (1991). Goals, agenda, and policy recommendations for ecological economics. In R. Costanza (Ed.), *Complexity in ecological systems series. Ecological economics. The science and management of sustainability* (pp. 1–20). New York, NY: Columbia University Press.

Costanza, R. (2010, May 11). Interview by T. O'Callahan [https://insights.som.yale.edu/insights/what-is-ecological-economics]. New Haven, CT.

Constitution Review Group. (1996). *Report of the Constitution Review Group.* Dublin, Ireland. Retrieved from Government of Ireland website: http://archive.constitution.ie/reports/crg.pdf

Coogan, T. P. (2001). *1916: The Easter rising.* London, United Kingdom: Cassell.

Coogan, T. P. (2012). *The famine plot: England's role in Ireland's greatest tragedy* (1st ed.). New York, NY: Palgrave Macmillan.

Corcoran, J. (2008, September 21). Lenihan lash at Joe Duffy banks panic: Finance Minister rang RTE's director general over 'run on banks' fear after liveline broadcast. *independent.ie.* Retrieved from http://www.independent.ie/business/irish/lenihan-lash-at-joe-duffy-banks-panic-26478869.html

Cotterill, J. (2011, February 11). World's best bank (2006 vintage). *Financial Times Alphaville.* Retrieved from https://ftalphaville.ft.com/2011/02/11/485311/worlds-best-bank-2006-vintage/

Coulter, C. (2015, January 20). Ireland's divorce regime: long, cumbersome and expensive. *irishtimes.com.* Retrieved from http://www.irishtimes.com/life-and-style/ireland-s-divorce-regime-long-cumbersome-and-expensive-1.2071474

Creswell, J. W. (2013). *Research Design: Qualitative, Quantitative, and Mixed Methods Approaches* (4th ed.). Thousand Oaks, CA: Sage Publications.

Cronin, M., & Adair, D. (2006). *The wearing of the green: A history of St. Patrick's Day.* London, United Kingdom: Routledge.

Crotty, W. J., & Schmitt, D. E. (Eds.) (1998). *Ireland and the politics of change.* Harlow, United Kingdom: Addison Wesley Longman.

Crown (1800; 2002). *Union with Ireland act 1800.* Retrieved from http://www.legislation.gov.uk/apgb/Geo3/39-40/67

Csipek, G. (2007). *Bestimmungsfaktoren kurzfristiger Wechselkursbewegungen. Europäische Hochschulschriften / 5: Bd. 3280.* Frankfurt a. M., Berlin, Bern, Bruxelles, New York, Oxford, Wien: Lang.

Cumiskey, G. (2003). Amhrán na bhFiann. In B. Lalor (Ed.), *The encyclopedia of Ireland* (pp. 22–23). New Haven, CT: Yale University Press.

Cussen, M., Kelly, J., & Phelan, G. (2008). The impact of asset price trends on Irish households. *Central Bank and Financial Services Authority of Ireland, Quarterly Bulletin* (3), 70–81.

DAFM – The Department of Agriculture, Food and the Marine (2016). *[Landing Page]*. Retrieved from https://www.agriculture.gov.ie/

Dalby, D. (2012, March 22). 15-year inquiry faults ex-leader and finds corruption widespread in Irish politics. *nytimes.com*. Retrieved from http://www.nytimes.com/2012/03/23/world/europe/15-year-inquiry-finds-corruption-widespread-in-irish-politics.html

Dalton, P., & Cavan, N. (2014). *Census 2011 Ireland and Northern Ireland*. Cork. Retrieved from Central Statistics Office, Information Section (Cork) and the Northern Ireland Statistics and Research Agency website: http://www.cso.ie/en/media/csoie/census/documents/north-south-spreadsheets/Census2011IrelandandNorthernIrelandwebversion1.pdf

Daly, M. (1997). Revisionism and Irish history: The Great Famine. In D. G. Boyce & A. O'Day (Eds.), *The making of modern Irish history. Revisionism and the revisionist controversy* (pp. 71–89). London, United Kingdom: Routledge.

Damon, W., & Lerner, R. M. (Eds.) (2006). *Handbook of child psychology: v. 1. Theoretical models of human development* (6th ed.). Hoboken, NJ: John Wiley & Sons.

Darnton, R. (2003). *George Washington's false teeth: An unconventional guide to the eighteenth century* (1st ed.). New York, NY: W.W. Norton.

Dauderstädt, M. (2001). Irland, der »keltische Tiger«: Vorbild oder Warnung für ein wachsendes Europa? *ifo Schnelldienst, 54*, 34–41.

Davies, M. (2015). *How we are structured: What is 'PwC'?* Retrieved from http://www.pwc.com/gx/en/about/corporate-governance/network-structure.html

Department of Health and Children (2009). *Report of the commission to inquire into child abuse, 2009: Implementation plan*. Dublin, Ireland: Stationery Office.

Department of Housing, Planning, Community and Local Government (2014). *Construction 2020: A strategy for a renewed construction sector.* Dublin, Ireland. Retrieved from http://www.merrionstreet.ie/en/wp-content/uploads/2014/05/Construction-Strategy-14-May-20141.pdf

Department of Justice and Equality (Ed.) (2009). *Report by commission of investigation into Catholic archdiocese of Dublin*. Dublin, Ireland. Retrieved from http://www.justice.ie/en/JELR/Pages/PB09000504

Department of the Taoiseach (2010). *Constitution of Ireland – BUNREACHT NA hÉIREANN*. Retrieved from http://www.taoiseach.gov.ie/eng/Publications/Publications_Archive/Publications_2010/March%202010%20Version%20-%20Constitution%20of%20Ireland.pdf

Department of the Taoiseach (2013). *Historical information: National anthem*. Retrieved from http://www.taoiseach.gov.ie/eng/Historical_Information/The_National_Anthem/

Department of the Taoiseach (2016). *Historical information: The national flag*. Retrieved from http://www.taoiseach.gov.ie/eng/Historical_Information/The_National_Flag/The_National_Flag.pdf

Deutsche Bundesbank. (2006). Konzentrationsrisiken in Kreditportfolios: Monatsbericht Juni 2006. Retrieved from https://www.bundesbank.de/resource/blob/692476/33f86ed72eb459ffddd4e9d0ec318bb0/mL/2006-06-konzentrationsrisiken-data.pdf

Dewatripont, M., Rochet, J.-C. & Tirole, J. (2010). *Balancing the banks: Global lessons from the financial crisis*. Princeton, NJ: Princeton University Press.

Diamond, J. M. (2014). *Kollaps: Warum Gesellschaften überleben oder untergehen* (3. Aufl., erw. Neuausgabe). *Fischer-Taschenbücher: Vol. 19258*. Frankfurt am Main, Deutschland: Fischer-Taschenbuch-Verlag.

Dieter, H. (2002). *Ostasien nach der Krise: Interne Reformen, neue Finanzarchitektur und monetärer Regionalismus*. Retrieved from http://www.bpb.de/apuz/25449/ostasien-nach-der-krise-interne-reformen-neue-finanzarchitektur-und-monetaerer-regionalismus?p=all

Dill, A. (2009). *Der Grosse Raubzug: Wie im Windschatten der Weltfinanzkrise die Staatskasse geplündert werden*. München, Deutschland: FinanzBuch Verlag.

DiMaggio, P. (1994). Culture and economy. In N. J. Smelser & R. Swedberg (Eds.), *The handbook of economic sociology* (pp. 27–57). Princeton, NJ: Princeton University Press; Russell Sage Foundation.

Dineley, T., Shirley, E. P., & Prendergast, J. P. (1856). Extracts from the journal of Thomas Dineley, Esquire, giving some account of his visit to Ireland in the reign of Charles II. *The Journal of the Kilkenny and South-East of Ireland archaeological society, 1*(1), 143–146; 170–188.

DJEI – Department of Jobs, Enterprise and Innovation (2016). *Protection and use of state emblems – DJEI*. Retrieved from https://www.djei.ie/en/

Donovan, D., & Murphy, A. E. (2014). *The fall of the Celtic Tiger: Ireland and the euro debt crisis*. Oxford, United Kingdom: Oxford University Press.

Dovidio, J. F., Glick, P. S., & Rudman, L. A. (2005). *On the nature of prejudice: Fifty years after Allport*. Malden, MA: Blackwell Pub.

Downham, C. (2005). The battle of Clontarf in Irish history and legend. *History Ireland, 13*(5), 19–23.

DTTAS – The Department of Transport, Tourism and Sport (2013). *[Landing Page]*. Retrieved from http://www.dttas.ie/

Duffy, S. (2014a, April 10). What did Brian Boru ever do for us?: For generations of Irish people he is the hero who secured the country's freedom. The truth is more complicated. *irishtimes.com*. Retrieved from http://www.irishtimes.com/culture/heritage/what-did-brian-boru-ever-do-for-us-1.1755758

Duffy, S. (2014b). *Brian Boru and the battle of Clontarf*. Dublin, Ireland: Gill & Macmillan Ltd.

Duffy, S. (2014c). Brian Boru: Imperator scotorum. *History Ireland, 22*(2). Retrieved from http://www.historyireland.com/volume-22/brian-boru-imperator-scotorum/

Dühnfort, E. (2012). *Irische Sagen und Legenden: Von Helden, Heiligen, Elfen und Druiden*. Köln, Deutschland: Anaconda.

Dunne, J. (2001, June 23). Boston, or Berlin. *irishtimes.com*. Retrieved from http://www.irishtimes.com/news/boston-or-berlin-1.314552

Durkheim, É. (2008). *The elementary forms of the religious life*. Mineola, NY: Dover Publications, Inc.

Dwyer, C. (2008, October 19). Ann and Katherine say it loud: Ann Louise Gilligan is a former nun, her partner Katherine is a Washington-born academic – and together they brought a case of same-sex recognition to the High Court. Ciara Dwyer meets the fun-loving lesbian theologians who are living life to the full. *independent.ie*. Retrieved from http://www.independent.ie/style/sex-relationships/ann-and-katherine-say-it-loud-26486166.html

Dwyer, R. (2011, April 11). The illusion of power. *irishexaminer.com*. Retrieved from http://www.irishexaminer.com/ireland/the-illusion-of-power-151017.html

Economist (2002). America's current-account deficit: The O'Neill doctrine. *economist.com*. Retrieved from http://www.economist.com/node/1098936

Edles, L. D., & Appelrouth, S. (2015). *Sociological theory in the classical era: Text and readings* (3rd ed.). Thousand Oaks, CA: Sage Publications.

Egan, B. (2009, September 20). Bertie Ahern: 'I don't consider myself a romantic person, mabye that was the problem': Ahern doesn't rule out running for the presidency as he reveals his difficulty with relationships. *independent.ie*. Retrieved from http://www.independent.ie/irish-news/

bertie-ahern-i-dont-consider-myself-a-romantic-person-mabye-that-was-the-problem-26567641.html

Eichengreen, B. (2015). *Hall of mirrors: The Great Depression, the Great Recession, and the uses-and misuses-of history.* New York, NY: Oxford University Press Inc.

Eisenberg, P., & Schneider, J. G. (2011). *Richtiges und gutes Deutsch: Das Wörterbuch der sprachlichen Zweifelsfälle* (7., vollständig überarbeitete Aufl.). *Duden: Vol. 9.* Mannheim [u.a.], Deutschland: Dudenverlag.

Elkink, J. A., Farrell, D. M., Reidy, T., & Suiter, J. (2016). Understanding the 2015 marriage referendum in Ireland: context, campaign, and conservative Ireland. *Irish Political Studies,* 1–21. doi:10.1080/07907184.2016.1197209

Elliott, M. (2009). *When God took sides: Religion and identity in Ireland. Unfinished History.* New York, NY: Oxford University Press Inc.

Endres, A. (2013, June 3). Irland ist das Steuerparadies der US Konzerne: Apple wusste die Steuerschlupflöcher in Irland zu nutzen. Deswegen wird das Land nicht sein System ändern. Ohnehin kann Irland allein wenig tun. *zeit.de.* Retrieved from http://www.zeit.de/wirtschaft/2013-06/apple-irland-unternehmenssteuer/komplettansicht?print

Erdoes, R., & Ortiz, A. (1984). *American Indian myths and legends* (1st ed.). *Pantheon fairy tale & folklore library.* New York, NY: Pantheon Books.

Eringa, K., Caudron, L. N., Rieck, K., Xie, F., & Gerhardt, T. (2015). How relevant are Hofstede's dimensions for inter-cultural studies? A replication of Hofstede's research among current international business students. *Research in Hospitality Management, 5*(2), 187–198. doi:10.1080/22243534.2015.11828344

ESS (2015). *European Social Survey.* Retrieved from http://www.europeansocialsurvey.org/about

Ettel, A., & Zschäpitz, H. (2015, August 6). Italien ist der eigentliche Euro-Wackelkandidat. *welt.de.* Retrieved from https://www.welt.de/wirtschaft/article144873286/Italien-ist-der-eigentliche-Euro-Wackelkandidat.html

European Commission (2011). *European economy: The economic adjustment programme for Ireland* (European economy: Occasional papers No. 76). Brussels. Retrieved from http://ec.europa.eu/economy_finance/publications/occasional_paper/2011/pdf/ocp76_en.pdf

European Central Bank. (2006). *Financial stability review: December 2006.* Frankfurt am Main, Deutschland. Retrieved from European Central Bank website: https://www.ecb.europa.eu/pub/pdf/other/financialstabilityreview200612en.pdf

European Central Bank (2007). *Financial stability review: June 2007.* Frankfurt am Main, Deutschland. Retrieved from https://www.ecb.europa.eu/pub/pdf/other/financialstabilityreview200706en.pdf

European Central Bank. (2011). *The monetary policy of the ECB.* Frankfurt am Main, Deutschland. Retrieved from https://www.ecb.europa.eu/pub/pdf/other/monetarypolicy2011en.pdf

European Union. (1992). *Treaty on European Union, signed at Maastricht* (No. C 191/14). Luxembourg. Retrieved from http://eur-lex.europa.eu/legal-content/EN/TXT/PDF/?uri=OJ:C:1992:191:FULL&from=DE

European Union. (2012). *Consolidated version of the treaty on the functioning of the European Union* (No. C 326/47). Brussels, Belgium. Retrieved from http://eur-lex.europa.eu/legal-content/EN/TXT/PDF/?uri=CELEX:12012E/TXT&from=EN

European Values Study. (2015a). About EVS. Retrieved from http://www.europeanvaluesstudy.eu/page/about-evs.html

European Values Study. (2015b). History. Retrieved from http://www.europeanvaluesstudy.eu/page/history.html

European Values Study. (2015c). Life. Retrieved from http://www.europeanvaluesstudy.eu/page/life.html

European Values Study. (2015d). Family. Retrieved from http://www.europeanvaluesstudy.eu/page/family.html

European Values Study. (2015e). Work. Retrieved from http://www.europeanvaluesstudy.eu/page/work.html

European Values Study. (2015f). Religion. Retrieved from http://www.europeanvaluesstudy.eu/page/religion.html

European Values Study. (2015g). Politics. Retrieved from http://www.europeanvaluesstudy.eu/page/politics.html

European Values Study. (2015h). Society. Retrieved from http://www.europeanvaluesstudy.eu/page/society.html

EY (2017). *Building a better working world for our clients: At EY, we are committed to delivering exceptional client service across our four service lines – assurance, tax, advisory and transaction advisory services. See how we can help build a better working world for you.* Retrieved from http://www.ey.com/uk/en/services/services

Fahey, T. (1998). Progress or decline? Demographic change in political context. In W. J. Crotty & D. E. Schmitt (Eds.), *Ireland and the politics of change* (pp. 51–65). Harlow, United Kingdom: Addison Wesley Longman.

Fahey, T., Hayes, B. C., & Sinnott, R. (2005). *Conflict and consensus: A study of values and attitudes in the Republic of Ireland and Northern Ireland*. Dublin, Ireland: Institute of Public Administration.

Fanning, R. (2015). *Éamon de Valera: A will to power*. London, United Kingdom: Faber & Faber.

Fedec, A. & Sousa, A. (2012). *Ireland Government Debt To GDP: 1980–2016*. Retrieved from https://d3fy651gv2fhd3.cloudfront.net/charts/ireland-government-debt-to-gdp.png?s=irldebt2gdp&v=201707031822v&d1=19170101&d2=20171231

Feehan, C. (2013, June 28). Anglo executive's five-star escape. *independent.ie*. Retrieved from http://www.independent.ie/business/irish/anglo/anglo-executives-fivestar-escape-29380242.html

Fehr, B. (2008). *Der Weg in die Krise. faz.net*. Retrieved from http://www.faz.net/aktuell/wirtschaft/wirtschaftspolitik/analyse-der-weg-in-die-krise-1516156.html?printPagedArticle=true#pageIndex_2

Ferraro, G. (2008). *Cultural anthropology: An applied perspective* (7th ed.). Belmont, CA: Thomson/Wadsworth.

Ferraro, G. P., & Andreatta, S. (2014). *Cultural anthropology: An applied perspective* (10th ed.). Stamford, CT: Cengage Learning.

Ferry, D. (2014, July 17). Fresh Anglo tape recordings reveal David Drumm joking and laughing about banks' finances ahead of economic collapse: The disgraced banker also tells executive John Bowe that he would give Anglo's board "the ladybird" version of bank's finances. *irishmirror.ie*. Retrieved from http://www.irishmirror.ie/news/irish-news/fresh-anglo-tape-recordings-reveal-3872317

Fink, P. (2008). *Länderanalyse Irland: Ein Erfolgsmodell auf dem Prüfstand* ([Electronic ed.]). *Internationale Politikanalyse*. Berlin: Friedrich-Ebert-Stiftung. Retrieved from http://library.fes.de/pdf-files/id/ipa/05351.pdf

Fischer, S., & Rotemberg, J. J. (Eds.) (1994). *NBER macroeconomics annual 1994, Volume 9*. Cambridge, MA: MIT Press.

Fitch Ratings (2006). *Fitch: Banking systems stronger; rapid credit growth still a concern in some countries*. London, United Kingdom. Retrieved from https://www.fitchratings.com/site/pr/287991

Fitch Ratings (2014). *Fitch ratings – definitions of ratings and other forms of opinion*. Retrieved from https://www.fitchratings.com/web_content/ratings/fitch_ratings_definitions_and_scales.pdf

Flood, F., & Mahon, A. (2013). *Tribunal of inquiry into certain planning matters and payments*. Dublin, Ireland. Retrieved from https://planningtribunal.ie/wp-content/uploads/2016/11/sitecontent_1257.pdf

Fogarty, M. P., Ryan, L., & Lee, J. (1984). *Irish values & attitudes: The Irish report of the European value systems study.* Dublin, Ireland: Dominican Publications.

Fong, M., & Chuang, R. (2004). *Communicating ethnic and cultural identity.* Lanham, MD: Rowman & Littlefield Publishers.

Foster, R. F. (Ed.) (2000). *The Oxford illustrated history of Ireland* (Reissued ed.). Oxford, United Kingdom: Oxford University Press.

Fox, L., Alvarez, S., Braunstein, S., Emerson, M., Johnson, J., Johnson, K., … Stockton, D. (2005). *The Federal Reserve System: Purposes & functions* (9th ed.). Washington, D.C.

Freeman, P. (2014). *The world of Saint Patrick.* New York, NY: Oxford University Press Inc.

Frentz, C. von (2003). Die Chronik einer Kapitalvernichtung: Knapp sechs Jahre nach dem Start am 10. März 1997 ist der Neue Markt endgültig gescheitert. Das einst hochgelobte "Wachstums-Segment" wird abgeschafft. Ein Rückblick. *manager-magazin.de.* Retrieved from http://www.manager-magazin.de/finanzen/artikel/a-186368.html

Frerk, C. (2017). *Religiöse und Nicht-Religiöse in Irland.* Retrieved from https://fowid.de/meldung/religioese-und-nicht-religioese-irland

Friedman, M., & Schwartz, A. J. (1963). *A monetary history of the United States, 1867–1960. National Bureau of Economic Research. Studies in business cycles: Vol. 12.* Princeton, NJ: Princeton University Press.

Frisell, L. (2015, May). *Address by advisor to the Governor, Lars Frisell to the financial safety net conference in Stockholm, 19 May 2015.* The Swedish House of Finance, Stockholm. Retrieved from https://www.centralbank.ie/news-media/press-releases/lars-frisell-financial-safety-net-conference-in-stockholm

FTD (2008, September 30). Marktturbulenzen: Irland springt für Einlagen der Banken ein. *ftd.de.* Retrieved from https://archive.is/20120804014455/http://www.ftd.de/politik/international/:Marktturbulenzen-Irland-springt-f%FCr-Einlagen-der-Banken-ein/420110.html#selection-1079.0-1079.42

FTD (2009, April 14). Lehman Brothers und die Atombombe: Die insolvente US-Investmentbank sitzt auf einem Schuldenberg von 200 Mrd. $. Vermögenswerte hat das Geldhaus kaum noch – abgesehen von einer halben Million Pfund Uran, mit dem sich eine Atombombe bauen ließe. *ftd.de.* Retrieved from https://web.archive.org/web/20090417031644/http://www.ftd.de/unternehmen/finanzdienstleister/:Gewaltiger-Uranvorrat-Lehman-Brothers-und-die-Atombombe/499823.html

Fujishin, R. (2009). *Creating communication: Exploring and expanding your fundamental communication skills*. Lanham, MD: Rowman & Littlefield Publishers.

Gallagher, C. (2016, April 8). David Drumm to face two trials over alleged offences during time at Anglo Irish bank. *irishmirror.ie*. Retrieved from http://www.irishmirror.ie/news/irish-news/david-drumm-face-two-trials-7714990

Gallagher, T. (2001). The value orientations method: A tool to help understand cultural differences. *Journal of Extension (JOE), 39*(6), 6TOT1. Retrieved from https://www.joe.org/joe/2001december/tt1.php

Garber, P. M. (1990). Famous first bubbles. *The Journal of Economic Perspectives, 4*(2), 35–54.

Garber, P. M. (2000). *Famous first bubbles: The fundamentals of early manias*. Cambridge, MA: MIT Press.

Gardiner, K. (1994). The Irish economy: A Celtic Tiger? In Morgan Stanley Euroletter (Ed.), *Ireland: Challenging for Promotion* (pp. 9–21).

Gilroy, J. (2000). *Tlachtga: Celtic fire festival*. Cork, Ireland: Pikefield Publications.

Gleeson, C. (2015a, March 4). Government actions 'led to increase in property prices': Economist Dr Peter Bacon says housing report proposals were reversed too early. *irishtimes.com*. Retrieved from http://www.irishtimes.com/business/government-actions-led-to-increase-in-property-prices-1.2125629

Gleeson, C. (2015b, March 4). Alan Ahearne warned Lenihan about banks before guarantee: Economist stressed the importance of having a 'very accurate picture of the banks'. *irishtimes.com*. Retrieved from http://www.irishtimes.com/business/alan-ahearne-warned-lenihan-about-banks-before-guarantee-1.2125742

Gleeson, C. (2015c, June 10). Central Bank had to 'pull punches' despite indicators: Inquiry went into private session after claims of 'lack of credibility'. *irishtimes.com*. Retrieved from http://www.irishtimes.com/business/financial-services/central-bank-had-to-pull-punches-despite-indicators-1.2244862

Government of Ireland (Ed.). (1861). *Offences against the person act, 1861*. Retrieved from http://www.irishstatutebook.ie/eli/1861/act/100/enacted/en/print.html

Government of Ireland (Ed.). (1961). *Dairy produce marketing act, 1961*. Dublin, Ireland. Retrieved from http://www.irishstatutebook.ie/eli/1961/act/1/section/4/enacted/en/html

Government of Ireland (Ed.). (2002). *Residential institutions redress act, 2002* (No. 13). Dublin, Ireland. Retrieved from http://www.irishstatutebook.ie/eli/2002/act/13/enacted/en/print

Government of Ireland (Ed.). (2003). *Central Bank and Financial Services Authority of Ireland act 2003* (No. 12). Dublin, Ireland. Retrieved from http://www.irishstatutebook.ie/eli/2003/act/12/enacted/en/html

Grant, R. G. (2011). *1001 Battles that changed the course of history*. London, United Kingdom: Cassell Illustrated.

Green, S. K. (2014). *The Separation of Church and State in the United States*. Oxford, United Kingdom: Oxford University Press.

Gudykunst, W. B. (2004). *Bridging differences: Effective intergroup communication* (4th ed.). Thousand Oaks, CA: Sage Publications.

Gudykunst, W. B. (2005). *Theorizing about intercultural communication*. Thousand Oaks, CA: Sage Publications.

Gwynn, J. (1913). *The Book Of Armagh*. Dublin, Ireland: Hodges Figgis & Co. Ltd. Retrieved from http://www.confessio.ie/sites/confessio.ie/files/pdfs/print_gwynn_transcription.pdf

Haas, H.-D. & Neumair, S.-M. (2013). *Gabler Wirtschaftslexikon, Stichwort: Tigerstaaten*. Retrieved from http://wirtschaftslexikon.gabler.de/Archiv/8355/tigerstaaten-v7.html

Haeckel, E. H. P. A. (1906). *Prinzipien der generellen Morphologie der Organismen: Wörtlicher Abdruck eines Teiles der 1866 erschienen Generellen Morphologie (allgemeine Grundzüge der organischen Formen-Wissenschaft, mechanisch begründet durch die von Charles Darwin reformierte Deszendenz-Theorie)*. Berlin: Georg Reimer. Retrieved from https://archive.org/details/prinzipiendergen00haec

Hall, E. T. (1959). *The silent language*. New York, NY: Doubleday.

Hall, E. T. (1977, 1989). *Beyond culture* (Anchor Books ed.). New York, NY: Anchor Books.

Hall, E. T. (1969, 1990). *The silent language*. New York, NY: Anchor Books.

Halman, L., Sieben, I., & Zundert, M. van (2012). *Atlas of European values: Trends and traditions at the turn of the century. European Values Studies*. Leiden, Netherlands: Koninklijke Brill.

Halman, L., & Vloet, A. (1994). *Measuring and comparing values in 16 countries of the Western World: Documentation of the European values study 1981–1990 in Europe and North America. Worc Report: Vol. 94.11.001*. Tilburg, Netherlands: WORC.

Hancock, C. (2015, May 29). Banking inquiry: Patrick Neary argued for blanket guarantee. *irishtimes.com*. Retrieved from http://www.irishtimes.com/business/financial-services/banking-inquiry-patrick-neary-argued-for-blanket-guarantee-1.2229973

Hancock, C., & Minihan, M. (2015, May 28). Banking inquiry: 'The system failed and I regret that': Former regulator Patrick Neary says he relied on banks for risk analysis. *irishtimes.com*. Retrieved from http://www.irishtimes.com/business/financial-services/banking-inquiry-the-system-failed-and-i-regret-that-1.2229123

Harbison, P. (1988). *Pre-Christian Ireland: From the first settlers to the early Celts*. London, United Kingdom: Thames and Hudson.

Hardes, H.-D., Schmitz, F., & Uhly, A. (2002). *Grundzüge der Volkswirtschaftslehre* (8th ed.). München, Deutschland: Oldenbourg.

Hardiman, N., & Whelan, C. (1998). Changing values. In W. J. Crotty & D. E. Schmitt (Eds.), *Ireland and the politics of change* (pp. 107–121). Harlow, United Kingdom: Addison Wesley Longman.

Harrison, L. E., & Huntington, S. P. (2000). *Culture matters: How values shape human progress* (1st ed.). New York, NY: Basic Books.

Harrison, S. (Author) (2013, June 25). *Irish shock and anger as tapes reveal bankers' behaviour* [Television broadcast]. BBC News. Retrieved from http://www.bbc.com/news/world-europe-23049191

Haughton, J. (1995). The historical background. In J. W. O'Hagan (Ed.), *The economy of Ireland. Policy and performance of a small European country* (pp. 1–49). New York, NY: St. Martin's Press.

Haughton, J. (1998). The dynamics of economic change. In W. J. Crotty & D. E. Schmitt (Eds.), *Ireland and the politics of change* (pp. 27–65). Harlow, United Kingdom: Addison Wesley Longman.

Haviland, W. A., Prins, H. E. L., McBride, B., & Walrath, D. (2013). *Cultural anthropology: The human challenge* (14th ed.). Belmont, CA: Wadsworth Publishing.

Hawley, A. H. (1986). *Human ecology: A theoretical essay*. Chicago, IL: The University of Chicago Press.

Hayes, I. (2016, September 7). Former Anglo chief David Drumm loses bid to relax bail conditions. *independent.ie*. Retrieved from http://www.independent.ie/irish-news/courts/former-anglo-chief-david-drumm-loses-bid-to-relax-bail-conditions-35029412.html

Hämäläinen, T. J., & Heiskala, R. (Eds.) (2007). *Social innovations, institutional change, and economic performance: Making sense of structural adjustment processes in industrial sectors, regions, and societies*. Cheltenham, United Kingdom: Edward Elgar.

Hecht, M. L., Warren, J. R., Jung, E., & Krieger, J. L. (2005). The communication theory of identity: Development, theoretical perspective, and future development. In W. B. Gudykunst (Ed.), *Theorizing about intercultural communication* (pp. 257–278). Thousand Oaks, CA: Sage Publications.

Hederman O'Brien, M., Carroll, D., Chambers, D., Gallagher, J., Harmon, C., Murphy, D.,… Louden Ryan, W. J. (1982). *First report of the commission on taxation: Direct taxation July 1982*. Dublin, Ireland. Retrieved from Foundation For Fiscal Studies website: http://fiscal.ie/wp-content/uploads/2015/10/First-Report-July-1982.pdf

Heidt, E. U. (1987). *Mass media, cultural tradition, and national identity: The case of Singapore and its television programmes. Bielefelder Studien zur Entwicklungssoziologie Bielefeld Studies on the Sociology of Development: Vol. 35*. Saarbrücken, Deutschland: Breitenbach.

Heizer, R. F. (1962). The background of Thomsen's three-age system. *Technology and culture, 3*(3), 259. doi:10.2307/3100819

Helmreich, W. B. (1982). *The things they say behind your back*. Garden City, NY: Doubleday & Company.

Herbermann, C. G., Pace, E., Pallen, C., Shahan, T., & Wynne, J. (Eds.) (1913). *The Catholic encyclopedia; an international work of reference on the constitution, doctrine, discipline, and history of the Catholic Church*. New York, NY: The Encyclopedia Press. Retrieved from https://archive.org/details/catholicencyclop11herbuoft

Hermans, J. M. M., & Nelissen, M. (Eds.) (2005). *Charters of foundation and early documents of the Universities of the Coimbra Group* (2nd revised ed.). Leuven, Belgium: Leuven University Press.

Hickman, M. J. (2005). Migration and diaspora. In J. Cleary & C. Connolly (Eds.), *The Cambridge companion to modern Irish culture* (pp. 117–136). Cambridge, United Kingdom: Cambridge University Press.

Hinner, M. B. (Ed.) (2014). *Freiberger Beiträge zur interkulturellen und Wirtschaftskommunikation: Vol. 8. Chinese culture in a cross-cultural comparison* (1st ed.). Frankfurt a. M., Deutschland: Peter Lang GmbH.

Hofstede, G. (1980). *Culture's consequences: International differences in work-related values*. Thousand Oaks, CA: Sage Publications.

Hofstede, G. H. (2003). *Culture's consequences: Comparing values, behaviors, institutions, and organizations across nations* (2nd ed.). Thousand Oaks, CA: Sage Publications.

Hofstede, G. H. (2006). What did GLOBE really measure? Researchers' minds versus respondents' minds. *Journal of International Business Studies, 37*(6), 882–896. doi:10.1057/palgrave.jibs.8400233

Hofstede, G. (2011). Dimensionalizing cultures: The Hofstede model in context. *Online Readings in Psychology and Culture, 2*(1). doi:10.9707/2307-0919.1014

Hofstede, G., & Bond, M. H. (1988). The confucius connection: From cultural roots to economic growth. *Organizational Dynamics, 16*(4), 5–21. doi:10.1016/0090-2616(88)90009-5

Hofstede, G., Hofstede, G. J., & Minkov, M. (2010). *Cultures and organizations: Software of the mind: intercultural cooperation and its importance for survival* (Revised and expanded 3rd ed.). New York, NY: McGraw-Hill.

Holmquist, K. (2015a, January 17). Divorce, Irish style: Almost 20 years ago, after a bitter debate, Ireland voted for the introduction of divorce. Almost 100,000 people have availed of the law since then. How have they fared, and what's life like after marriage breakdown? *irishtimes.com*. Retrieved from http://www.irishtimes.com/life-and-style/divorce-irish-style-1.2068656

Holmquist, K. (2015b, January 17). My divorce. Aoife: 'I've never been so happy'. *irishtimes.com*. Retrieved from http://www.irishtimes.com/life-and-style/people/my-divorce-aoife-i-ve-never-been-so-happy-1.2068643

Honohan, P., Gorecki, P. K., Donovan, D., Mottiar, R., Cadden, N., Kinsella, S., . . . McKenna, I. (2010). *The Irish banking crisis regulatory and financial stability policy 2003–2008: A report to the Minister for Finance by the Governor of the Central Bank*. Dublin, Ireland. Retrieved from http://www.bankinginquiry.gov.ie/The%20Irish%20Banking%20Crisis%20Regulatory%20and%20Financial%20Stability%20Policy%202003-2008.pdf

Honohan, P., & Walsh, B. (2002). Catching up with the leaders: The Irish hare. *Brookings Papers on Economic Activity*, (1), 1–77. Retrieved from https://www.brookings.edu/wp-content/uploads/2002/01/2002a_bpea_honohan.pdf

Horn, W. W., Marshall, J. W., Rourke, G. D., O'Leary, P., & Snodgrass, L. (2002). *The forgotten hermitage of Skellig Michael* (2nd ed.). *California studies in the history of art. Discovery series: Vol. 2*. Berkeley, CA: University of California Press.

Horvath, M. (2013). *Arbeitslosenquote*. Retrieved from http://wirtschaftslexikon.gabler.de/Archiv/2157/arbeitslosenquote-v12.html

House, R. J., Hanges, P. J., Javidan, M., Dorfman, P. W., & Gupta, V. (2004). *Culture, leadership, and organizations: The GLOBE Study of 62 societies*. Thousand Oaks, CA: Sage Publications.

Houses of the Oireachtas (2016). *1950s – Mother and child scheme: Proposals for improved and extended health services 1952*. Retrieved from http://www.oireachtas.ie/parliament/about/libraryresearchservice/onlinecataloguecollections/documentslaidthroughthedecades/1950s-motherandchildscheme/

Hückmann, C. (2003). *Kreditrating der Mittel- und Kleinbetriebe: Eine Orientierungs- und Entscheidungshilfe zu den Verfahren der Kreditinstitute und*

Agenturen (2., neubearb. und erw. Aufl). *Grundlagen und Praxis des Bank- und Börsenwesens: Vol. 41.* Berlin, Deutschland: Erich Schmidt.

Hudson, M. (2014). *Der Krieg der Banken gegen die Welt: Warum wir vor dem Kapitalismus kapitulieren.* Stuttgart, Deutschland: Klett-Cotta.

Humphries, T. (2003, October 5). Sticks and thrones. *theguardian.com.* Retrieved from https://www.theguardian.com/sport/2003/oct/05/features.sportmonthly1

Huntington, S. P. (1996). The West unique, not universal. *Foreign Affairs, 75*(6), 28–46. doi:10.2307/20047828

Husén, T., & Postlethwaite, T. N. (Eds.) (1994). *The international encyclopedia of education* (2nd ed.). Oxford, United Kingdom: Pergamon.

Hutton, R. (1993). *The pagan religions of the ancient British Isles: Their nature and legacy.* Oxford, United Kingdom: Blackwell Publishing.

Imahori, T. T., & Cupach, W. R. (2005). Identity management theory: Face work in intercultural relations. In W. Gudykunst (Ed.), *Theorizing about intercultural communication* (pp. 195–210). Thousand Oaks, CA: Sage Publications.

IMF (2003). *International Monetary Fund: Ireland.* Staff Report for the 2003 Article IV Consultation (No. 03/242). Washington, D.C. Retrieved from International Monetary Fund website: https://www.imf.org/external/pubs/ft/scr/2003/cr03242.pdf

IMF (2006a). *Ireland: Financial system stability assessment update* (No. 06/292). Washington, D.C. Retrieved from International Monetary Fund website: https://www.imf.org/~/media/Websites/IMF/imported-full-text-pdf/external/pubs/ft/scr/2006/_cr06292.ashx

IMF (2006b). *Ireland: 2006 Article IV Consultation—Staff Report; staff supplement; and public information notice on the executive board discussion* (No. 06/293). Washington, D.C. Retrieved from https://www.imf.org/external/pubs/ft/scr/2006/cr06293.pdf

IMF (2007). *World economic outlook: Spillovers and cycles in the global economy.* Washington, D.C. Retrieved from International Monetary Fund website: http://www.imf.org/~/media/Websites/IMF/imported-flagship-issues/external/pubs/ft/weo/2007/01/pdf/_textpdf.ashx

IMF (2014). *About the IMF.* Retrieved from http://www.imf.org/external/about.htm

Ingber, H. (2015, May 22). For one Irish couple, backing gay marriage is a matter of family values. *nytimes.com.* Retrieved from http://www.nytimes.com/2015/05/23/world/europe/for-one-irish-couple-backing-gay-marriage-is-a-matter-of-family-values.html?_r=0

Inglehart, R. F. (2007). The worldviews of Islamic publics in global perspective. In M. Moaddel (Ed.), Values and perceptions of the Islamic and Middle Eastern publics (pp. 25–46). Basingstoke, United Kingdom: Palgrave Macmillan.

Inglehart, R., & Oyserman, D. (2004). Individualism, autonomy and self-expression: The human development syndrome. In H. Vinken, J. Soeters, & P. Ester (Eds.), *International studies in sociology and social anthropology: Vol. 93. Comparing cultures. Dimensions of culture in a comparative perspective* (pp. 74–96). Boston, MA: Brill.

Inglis, T. (2005). Religion, identity, state and society. In J. Cleary & C. Connolly (Eds.), *The Cambridge companion to modern Irish culture* (pp. 59–77). Cambridge, United Kingdom: Cambridge University Press.

Irish Examiner (2008, May 2). Who shot the Celtic Tiger? Well, don't blame me and George Lee. *irishexaminer.com*. Retrieved from http://www.irishexaminer.com/archives/2008/0502/opinion/who-shot-the-celtic-tiger-well-donapost-blame-me-and-george-lee-61749.html

Irish Independent (2015, March 14). Faughart couplc back gay marriage in YouTube video. *independent.ie*. Retrieved from http://www.independent.ie/regionals/argus/news/faughart-couple-back-gay-marriage-in-youtube-video-31055521.html

Irish Times (1997, March 8). Roof over our heads. *irishtimes.com*. Retrieved from http://www.irishtimes.com/opinion/roof-over-our-heads-1.50309

Irish Times (2015, July 1). Banking inquiry: Charlie McCreevy defends policies: Former minister for finance appears before Oireachtas committee. *irishtimes.com*. Retrieved from http://www.irishtimes.com/business/financial-services/banking-inquiry-charlie-mccreevy-defends-policies-1.2269529

Irwin-Zarecka, I. (1994). *Frames of remembrance: The dynamics of collective memory* (2nd ed.). London, United Kingdom: Routledge Taylor & Francis Group.

Irwin, N. (2013). *Die Alchemisten: Die geheime Welt der Zentralbanker*. Berlin, Deutschland: Econ.

Jasper, J. (2013). *Inflationsrate*. Retrieved from http://wirtschaftslexikon.gabler.de/Archiv/6907/inflationsrate-v6.html

Javidan, M., House, R. J., Dorfman, P. W., Hanges, P. J., & Sully de Luque, M. (2006). Conceptualizing and measuring cultures and their consequences: a comparative review of GLOBE's and Hofstede's approaches. *Journal of International Business Studies, 37*(6), 897–914. doi:10.1057/palgrave.jibs.8400234

Jenkins, R. (2008). *Social identity* (3rd ed.). *Key Ideas*. London, United Kingdom: Routledge.

Joyce, J. (2013). *Ulysses* (5. Auflage). *Suhrkamp Taschenbuch: Vol. 3816*. Frankfurt am Main, Deutschland: Suhrkamp.

Kassin, S. M., Fein, S., & Markus, H. R. (2014). *Social psychology* (9th ed.). Belmont, CA: Wadsworth, Cengage Learning.

Keating, M. A., & Martin, G. S. (2007). Leadership and culture in the Republic of Ireland. In J. S. Chhokar, F. C. Brodbeck, & R. J. House (Eds.), *Culture and leadership across the world. The GLOBE book of in-depth studies of 25 societies* (pp. 361–396). New York, NY: Routledge.

Kee, R. (2000). *The green flag: A history of Irish nationalism*. London, United Kingdom: Penguin Books.

Keena, C. (2016, June 1). Anglo case: Willie McAteer and John Bowe found guilty of conspiracy: Jury still deliberating in case of IL&P's Peter Fitzpatrick and Denis Casey. *irishtimes.com*. Retrieved from http://www.irishtimes.com/business/financial-services/anglo-case-willie-mcateer-and-john-bowe-found-guilty-of-conspiracy-1.2668466

Kehse, U., & Witte, S. (2015). Wurzeln der Homosexualität: Wie entsteht die Neigung zur gleichgeschlechtlichen Liebe? Forscher vermuten, dass bestimmte körperliche Vorgänge vor der Geburt sie auslösen. *geo.de*, (43). Retrieved from http://www.geo.de/magazine/geo-kompakt/964-rtkl-sex-leseprobe-wurzeln-der-homosexualitaet

Kelleher, R. (1999, July 15). McDowell defends regulator recommendation. *irishtimes.com*. Retrieved from http://www.irishtimes.com/business/mcdowell-defends-regulator-recommendation-1.206756

Keller, E. v (1982). *Management in fremden Kulturen: Ziele, Ergebnisse und methodische Probleme der kulturvergleichenden Managementforschung. Veröffentlichungen der Hochschule St. Gallen für Wirtschafts- und Sozialwissenschaften. Schriftenreihe Betriebswirtschaft: Vol. 10*. Bern, Schweiz: Paul Haupt.

Kelly, F. (2015a, March 10). Simon Carswell of 'Irish Times' appears at banking inquiry: Journalist discusses 'cosy' relationship between political parties and property sector. *irishtimes.com*. Retrieved from http://www.irishtimes.com/news/politics/simon-carswell-of-irish-times-appears-at-banking-inquiry-1.2133906

Kelly, F. (2015b, November 7). Central Bank cut property bubble warning from report: Banking inquiry: Ex-director general says 'things were going crazy' as early as 2001. *irishtimes.com*. Retrieved from http://www.irishtimes.com/news/politics/central-bank-cut-property-bubble-warning-from-report-1.2420489

Kelly, J. (2012). *The graves are walking: The Great Famine and the saga of the Irish people*. New York, NY: Henry Holt.

Kelly, M. (2006, December 28). How the housing corner stones of our economy could go into a rapid freefall. *irishtimes.com*. Retrieved from http://www.irishtimes.com/business/how-the-housing-corner-stones-of-our-economy-could-gointo-a-rapid-freefall-1.1042463

Kelly, M. (2007). On the likely extent of falls in Irish house prices. In *Quarterly Economic Commentary* (ESRI Forecasting Series, pp. 42–54). Dublin, Ireland: The Economic and Social Research Institute. Retrieved from https://www.esri.ie/pubs/QEC2007Sum.pdf

Kelly, J., Cussen, M., & Phelan, G. (2007). The net worth of Irish households — An update. *Central Bank and Financial Services Authority of Ireland, Quarterly Bulletin*(3), 109–122.

Kenna, P. (2011). *Housing law, rights & policy*. Dublin, Ireland: Clarus Press.

Kennedy, M., Girouard, N., André, C., & van den Noord, P. (2005). *OECD economics department working papers: III. Recent house price developments: The role of fundamentals* (Vol. 475). Paris, France. Retrieved from https://www.oecd.org/eco/monetary/35756053.pdf

Kenny, C. (2015, May 22). Emigrants take planes, trains and automobiles #HomeToVote: Irish citizens are travelling back from as far afield as Canada, Australia and Africa to cast their ballot. *irishtimes.com*. Retrieved from http://www.irishtimes.com/life-and-style/abroad/generation-emigration/emigrants-take-planes-trains-and-automobiles-hometovote-1.2222151

Kiberd, D. (2009, June 16). Ulysses, modernism's most sociable masterpiece: There are good reasons why Dublin has taken Bloomsday, the celebration of Joyce's classic novel, to its heart. *theguardian.com*. Retrieved from https://www.theguardian.com/books/2009/jun/16/jamesjoyce-classics

Kimball, C. A. (2008). *When religion becomes evil*. New York, NY: HarperCollins.

Kindleberger, C. P., & Aliber, R. Z. (2005). *Manias, panics, and crashes: A history of financial crises* (5th ed.). *Wiley investment classics*. Hoboken, NJ: John Wiley & Sons.

Kinealy, C. (2004). *Geschichte Irlands*. Essen, Deutschland: Magnus.

Kinealy, C. (2006). *This great calamity: The Irish Famine 1845–52* (2., illustriert, überarbeitet). Dublin, Ireland: Gill & Macmillan.

Kirby, P., Gibbons, L., & Cronin, M. (Eds.) (2002). *Reinventing Ireland: Culture, society, and the global economy*. London, United Kingdom: Pluto Press.

Kirby, P., Gibbons, L., & Cronin, M. (2002). Introduction: The reinvention of Ireland: A critical perspective. In P. Kirby, L. Gibbons, & M. Cronin (Eds.) (2002). *Reinventing Ireland: Culture, society, and the global economy* (pp. 1–18). London, United Kingdom: Pluto Press.

Kirchhoff, S., & Hagenbaugh, B. (2004, February 24). Greenspan says ARMs might be better deal. *usatoday.com*. Retrieved from http://usatoday30.usatoday.com/money/economy/fed/2004-02-23-greenspan-debt_x.htm

Kirschbaum, C. (2008). *Biopsychologie von A bis Z. Springer-Lehrbuch*. Heidelberg, Deutschland: Springer.

Kissane, B. (2003). The illusion of state neutrality in a secularising Ireland. *West European Politics, 26*(1), 73–94. doi:10.1080/01402380412331300207

Klein, K., Tosi, H., & Cannella, A. A. (1999). Multilevel theory building: Benefits, barriers, and new developments. *The Academy of Management Review, 24*(2), 243–248.

Kloepfer, I. (2008, September 21). Finanzkrise: Der Schock an der Wall Street. *faz.net*. Retrieved from http://www.faz.net/aktuell/wirtschaft/finanzkrise-der-schock-an-der-wall-street-1697880.html?printPagedArticle=true#pageIndex_0

Kluckhohn, F. R., & Strodtbeck, F. L. (1961). *Variations in value orientations*. Evanston, IL: Row, Peterson.

Kluge, F., & Seebold, E. (2002). *Etymologisches Wörterbuch der deutschen Sprache* (24., durchgesehene und erweiterte. Auflage). Berlin, Deutschland: De Gruyter.

Koczy, F., 2019, custom design.

Konner, M. (2011). *The evolution of childhood: Relationships, emotion, mind*. Cambridge, MA: Harvard University Press.

Korostelina, K. (2008). History Education and Social Identity. *Identity, 8*(1), 25–45. doi:10.1080/15283480701787327

Kostick, C. (2005). Laudabiliter: a new interpretation by Professor Anne Duggan. *History Ireland, 13*(3). Retrieved from http://www.historyireland.com/early-modern-history-1500-1700/laudabiliter-a-new-interpretation-by-professor-anne-duggan/

Kroeber, A. L., & Kluckhohn, C. (1952). *Culture: A critical review of concepts and definitions*. Papers of the Peabody Museum of American Archæology and Ethnology, Harvard University, vol. 47, no. 1. Cambridge, MA: The Museum.

Kuckenburg, M. (2010). *Die Kelten* (2., stark erweiterte und komplett überarbeitete Neuauflage). Stuttgart, Deutschland: Theiss.

Kunkel, J. H. (1970). *Society and economic growth: A behavioral perspective of social change*. London, United Kingdom: Oxford University Press.

Kutschker, M., & Schmid, S. (2011). *Internationales Management* (7., überarbeitete und aktualisierte Auflage). München, Deutschland: Oldenbourg.

Laeven, L., & Valencia, F. (2008). *Systemic banking crises: A new database* (No. WP/08/224). Retrieved from International monetary fund website: http://www.imf.org/external/pubs/ft/wp/2008/wp08224.pdf

Lalor, B. (2003). General post office. In B. Lalor (Ed.), *The encyclopedia of Ireland* (pp. 433–434). New Haven, CT: Yale University Press.

Lalor, B. (2003). *The encyclopedia of Ireland*. New Haven, CT: Yale University Press.

Lang, R., & Baldauf, N. (2016). *Interkulturelles Management. Studienwissen kompakt*. Wiesbaden, Deutschland: Springe Gabler.

Larkin, E. J. (1984). *The historical dimensions of Irish Catholicism*. Washington, D.C: Catholic University of America Press.

La Roche, J. (2013, June 24). Busted: Bankers caught on tape, joking about bailout, and how they'd never pay it back. *businessinsider.com*. Retrieved from http://www.businessinsider.com/anglo-irish-bank-tapes-2013-6?IR=T

Larosière, J. De (2009). *The high-level group on financial supervision in the EU*. Brussels, Belgium. Retrieved from http://ec.europa.eu/internal_market/finances/docs/de_larosiere_report_de.pdf

LaRossa, W. R. Schumm, & S. K. Steinmetz (Eds.), *Sourcebook of family theories and methods. A contextual approach* (pp. 419–450). New York, NY: Plenum Press.

Lee, G. (Author) (March 2009). *How we blew the boom* [Television broadcast]. RTÉ One. Retrieved from http://www.rte.ie/tv/boom/

Lee, J. J. (1989). *Ireland, 1912–1985: Politics and society*. Cambridge, NY: Cambridge University Press.

Lee, J. (2008). *The modernisation of Irish society 1848–1918*. Dublin, Ireland: Gill & MacMillan Ltd.

Lee-Peuker, M.-Y., Scholtes, F., & Schumann, O. J. (Eds.). (2007). *Wirtschafts- und Unternehmensethik: Vol. 18. Kultur – Ökonomie – Ethik* (1. Aufl). München, Deutschland: Hampp.

Lejano, R. P., & Stokols, D. (2013). Social ecology, sustainability, and economics. *Ecological Economics, 89*, 1–6. doi:10.1016/j.ecolecon.2013.01.011

Lemon, M. (1848). *The British lion and the Irish monkey. Monkey (Mr. Mitchell). "One of us MUST be 'Put Down.'"*. Retrieved from https://punch.photoshelter.com/image/I0000c1E5Q7ELdBI

Lennihan, M. (2010). *"9/15" -die-Lehman Pleite: Was damals wirklich geschah*. Retrieved from https://diepresse.com/home/wirtschaft/finanzkrise/503750/915-die-LehmanPleite_Was-damals-wirklich-geschah#slide-503750-0

Leo XIII (1888). *SAEPE NOS: Encyclical of Pope Leo XIII on boycotting in Ireland*. Retrieved from http://w2.vatican.va/content/leo-xiii/en/encyclicals/documents/hf_l-xiii_enc_24061888_saepe-nos.html

Lequiller, F., & Blades, D. (2014). *Understanding national accounts* (2nd ed.). Paris, France: OECD Publishing.

Lerner, G. (1997). *Why history matters: Life and thought*. New York, NY: Oxford University Press Inc.

Lerner, R. M. (Ed.) (1998). *Handbook of child psychology* (5th ed.). New York, NY: Wiley.

Lerner, R. M. (2012). *Concepts and theories of human development* (3rd ed.). New York, NY: Routledge.

Leubecher, M. (2014, May 21). Kaum Steuerlast: Wie Starbucks den deutschen Staat austrickst. *welt.de*. Retrieved from http://www.welt.de/128247128

Lewis, M. (2011). When Irish eyes are crying: Crash course. *vanityfair.com*. Retrieved from http://www.vanityfair.com/news/2011/03/michael-lewis-ireland-201103

Lin, T. C. W. (2011). A Behavioral Framework for Securities Risk. *Seattle University Law Review, 34*(2), 325–378. Retrieved from https://digitalcommons.law.seattleu.edu/cgi/viewcontent.cgi?article=2001&context=sulr

Loewen, J. W. (2000). *Lies across America: What our historic sites get wrong* (1st ed.). New York, NY: Simon & Schuster.

Logan, F. D. (1992). *The Vikings in history* (2nd ed.). London, United Kingdom: Routledge.

Lonergan, A. (2017, March 17). McDonald's apologises for St. Patrick's Day ad featuring 'Irishman' playing bagpipes in front of Stonehenge. *irishpost.co.uk*. Retrieved from http://irishpost.co.uk/mcdonalds-apologises-st-patricks-day-ad-irishman-bagpipes-stonehenge/

Lüpke, M. von (2014, January 17). Geschichte der Homosexualität: Gleichgeschlechtliche Liebe war in Ordnung, Sex verboten. *zeit.de*. Retrieved from http://www.zeit.de/wissen/geschichte/2014-01/geschichte-der-homosexualitaet-schwule-lesben-verfolgung/komplettansicht

Luyendijk, J. (2012, December 17). Ex-Moody's analyst: 'By 2006 it was toxic everywhere'. *theguardian.com*. Retrieved from https://www.theguardian.com/commentisfree/2012/dec/17/ex-moodys-analyst-william-harrington

Lynch, B. (2003). Ulster Cycle. In B. Lalor (Ed.), *The encyclopedia of Ireland* (pp. 1089–1090). New Haven, CT: Yale University Press.

Lynch, C., Doherty, P., Higgins, J., McGrath, M., Murphy, E., O'Donnell, K., . . . O'Keeffe, S. (2015). *Report of the Joint Committee of inquiry into the banking crisis: Volume 3: Evidence*. Witness statements and hearing transcripts. Dublin, Ireland. Retrieved from Houses of the Oireachtas website: https://inquiries.oireachtas.ie/banking/hearings-evidence/

Lynch, C., Doherty, P., Higgins, J., McGrath, M., Murphy, E., O'Donnell, K., … O'Keeffe, S. (2015a). Peter Bacon. The housing market in Ireland in the run up to banking crisis. In R*eport of the Joint Committee of inquiry into the banking crisis. Volume 3: Evidence. Witness statements and hearing transcripts* (pp. 13–435). Dublin, Ireland: Houses of the Oireachtas. Retrieved from https://inquiries.oireachtas.ie/banking/hearings/peter-bacon-the-housing-market-in-ireland-in-the-run-up-to-banking-crisis/

Lynch, C., Doherty, P., Higgins, J., McGrath, M., Murphy, E., O'Donnell, K., … O'Keeffe, S. (2015b). Charlie McCreevy. Former Minister for Finance. In *Report of the Joint Committee of inquiry into the banking crisis. Volume 3: Evidence. Witness statements and hearing transcripts* (pp. 936–1900). Dublin, Ireland: Houses of the Oireachtas. Retrieved from https://inquiries.oireachtas.ie/banking/hearings/charlie-mccreevy-former-minister-for-finance/

Lynch, C., Doherty, P., Higgins, J., McGrath, M., Murphy, E., O'Donnell, K., … O'Keeffe, S. (2015c). Alan Ahearne. Early warnings, divergent & contrarian views. In *Report of the Joint Committee of inquiry into the banking crisis. Volume 3: Evidence. Witness statements and hearing transcripts* (pp. 436–735). Dublin, Ireland: Houses of the Oireachtas. Retrieved from https://inquiries.oireachtas.ie/banking/hearings/alan-ahearne-early-warnings-divergent-contrarian-views/

Lynch, C., Doherty, P., Higgins, J., McGrath, M., Murphy, E., O'Donnell, K., … O'Keeffe, S. (2015d). Simon Carswell. Relationships between state authorities, political parties … In *Report of the Joint Committee of inquiry into the banking crisis. Volume 3: Evidence. Witness statements and hearing transcripts* (pp. 13–375). Dublin, Ireland: Houses of the Oireachtas. Retrieved from https://inquiries.oireachtas.ie/banking/hearings/simon-carswell-relationships-between-state-authorities-political-parties-elected-representatives-supervisory-authorities-banking-institutions-the--property-sector/

Lynch, C., Doherty, P., Higgins, J., McGrath, M., Murphy, E., O'Donnell, K., … O'Keeffe, S. (2015e). Statement by Patrick Neary. In *Report of the Joint Committee of inquiry into the banking crisis. Volume 3: Evidence. Witness statements and hearing transcripts* (pp. 1–21). Dublin, Ireland: Houses of the Oireachtas. Retrieved from https://inquiries.oireachtas.ie/banking/wp-content/uploads/2015/05/Patrick-Neary-Opening-Statement.pdf

Lyons, T. (2016). 'Inciting the lawless and profligate adventure'—THE HEDGE SCHOOLS OF IRELAND. *History Ireland, 24*(6), 28–31.

Macalister, R. A. S. (1921). *Ireland in pre-Celtic times*. Dublin, Ireland: Maunsel and Roberts.

MacCann, L., Courtney, T. B., & Daly, E. (2008). *Companies acts, 1963–2006* (2008 ed.). Haywards Heath, United Kingdom: Tottel Pub.

Macfadyen, A. (Ed.) (1974). *Advances in ecological research* (8th ed.). London, United Kingdom: Elsevier.

Mac Ginty, R. (Ed.) (2013). *Routledge handbook of peacebuilding*. New York, NY: Routledge.

Macinnes, A. I. (2011). *Acts of Union: The creation of the United Kingdom*. Retrieved from http://www.bbc.co.uk/history/british/empire_seapower/acts_of_union_01.shtml#five

Mackie, J. D. (1907). *Pope Adrian IV: The Lothian Essay*. 1907. Oxford: Simpkin, Marshall & Co. Limited. Retrieved from https://archive.org/details/popeadrianivlot00mackgoog

Mac Mathúna, S. (2006). *Collins Irish dictionary* (2nd ed.). Glasgow, Scotland: HarperCollins.

MacNeill, M. (1982). *The festival of Lughnasa: A study of the survival of the Celtic festival of the beginning of harvest. Scríbhinní béaloidis/Folklore studies: Vol. 11*. Dublin, Ireland: Comhairle Bhéaloideas Èireann, University College.

Macrae, C. N., Stangor, C., & Hewstone, M. (1996). *Stereotypes and stereotyping*. New York, NY: Guilford Press.

Maher, D. (2016, June 1). Two former Anglo Irish bank chiefs found guilty of conspiring to defraud the public: John Bowe, 52, and 65-year-old Willie McAteer denied trying to mislead investors. *irishmirror.ie*. Retrieved from http://www.irishmirror.ie/news/irish-news/two-former-anglo-irish-bank-8098295

Maier, B. (2001). *Die Religion der Kelten: Götter, Mythen, Weltbild*. München, Deutschland: Beck.

Mandelbaum, D. G. (1965). Alcohol and culture. *Current anthropology, 6*(3), 281–293.

Marks, K. (1997, June 2). Blair issues apology for Irish potato famine. *independent.co.uk*. Retrieved from http://www.independent.co.uk/news/blair-issues-apology-for-irish-potato-famine-1253790.html

Marlow, J. (1973). *Captain Boycott and the Irish*. London, United Kingdom: Saturday Review Press.

Martin, C. L., & Fabes, R. A. (2009). *Discovering child development* (2nd ed.). Boston, MA: Houghton Mifflin Co.

Martin, J. N., & Nakayama, T. K. (2013). *Intercultural communication in contexts* (6th ed.). New York, NY: McGraw-Hill.

Massard, J. A. (2009a). 300 Jahre Kartoffel in Luxemburg: Europa entdeckt die Kartoffel – Teil 1. *Lëtzebuerger Journal*, (15), 23. Retrieved from https://

www.yumpu.com/de/document/view/18119603/300-jahre-kartoffel-in-luxemburg-jos-a-massard/3

Massard, J. A. (2009b). 300 Jahre Kartoffel in Luxemburg: Europa entdeckt die Kartoffel – Teil 2. *Lëtzebuerger Journal*, (16), 10. Retrieved from https://www.yumpu.com/de/document/view/18119603/300-jahre-kartoffel-in-luxemburg-jos-a-massard/3

Mayer, C., & Schwepcke, B. (1995). Irland: Scheidung auf Irisch: Regierung und Volk kratzen an den katholischen Grundlagen der Verfassung. *focus.de*, (48). Retrieved from http://www.focus.de/politik/ausland/irland-scheidung-auf-irisch_aid_156036.html

Mayes, E. (2013). *Áras an Uachtaráin: A history of the President's House*. Retrieved from http://www.president.ie/en/explore-visit/official-residence

McCaffrey, C. (2006). *In search of Ireland's heroes: The story of the Irish from the English invasion to the present day*. Chicago, IL: Ivan R. Dee.

McCaffrey, C., & Eaton, L. (2002). *In search of ancient Ireland: The origins of the Irish, from Neolithic times to the coming of the English*. Chicago, IL: New Amsterdam Books.

McCarthy, P. (2011). *My name is Patrick. I am a sinner, a simple country person and the least of all believers: Read St. Patrick in his own words*. Dublin, Ireland: The Royal Irish Academy.

McConnel, J. (2011). *Irish Home Rule: An imagined future*. Retrieved from http://www.bbc.co.uk/history/british/victorians/home_rule_movement_01.shtml

McDermott, P. (2010, December 14). Less dogma, more dialogue needed in economics. *irishecho.com*. Retrieved from http://irishecho.com/2010/12/less-dogma-more-dialogue-needed-in-economics/

McDonald, F. (2016, February 20). George Redmond among most corrupt officials in Irish history: Senior council official showed ill-disguised contempt for Dublin's architectural heritage. *irishtimes.com*. Retrieved from https://www.irishtimes.com/news/ireland/irish-news/george-redmond-among-most-corrupt-officials-in-irish-history-1.2541848

McDonnell, M. J., & Pickett, S. T. (1990). Ecosystem structure and function along urban-rural gradients: An unexploited opportunity for ecology. *Ecology, 71*(4), 1232–1237. doi:10.2307/1938259

McDowell, M. (1999). *Report of the Implementation Advisory Group on the establishment of a single regulatory authority for the financial services sector*. Dublin, Ireland: Stationery Office.

McEwen, M., & Wills, E. M. (2014). *Theoretical basis for nursing* (4th ed.). Philadelphia, PA: Wolters Kluwer Health | Lippincott Williams & Wilkins.

McLaren, L., & Hawe, P. (2005). Ecological perspectives in health research. *Journal of Epidemiology & Community Health, 59*(1), 6–14. doi:10.1136/jech.2003.018044

McLeroy, K. R., Bibeau, D., Steckler, A., & Glanz, K. (1988). An ecological perspective on health promotion programs. *Health Education Quarterly, 15*(4), 351–377. doi:10.1177/109019818801500401

McMahon, A. (2015, June 2). Catholic Church 'bereavement' after same-sex marriage vote. *irishtimes.com*. Retrieved from http://www.irishtimes.com/news/politics/marriage-referendum/catholic-church-bereavement-after-same-sex-marriage-vote-1.2234500

McManus, J. (2006, July 28). Irish Times buys myhome.ie for €50m. *irishtimes.com*. Retrieved from http://www.irishtimes.com/business/irish-times-buys-myhome-ie-for-50m-1.1263303

McNeill, W. H. (1985). *Why study history?* Retrieved from https://www.historians.org/about-aha-and-membership/aha-history-and-archives/archives/why-study-history-(1985)

McQuinn, K., & O'Reilly, G. (2006). Assessing the role of income and interest rates in determining Irish house prices. In Central Bank of Ireland (Ed.), *Financial Stability Report 2006* (pp. 123–131). Dublin, Ireland. Retrieved from https://www.centralbank.ie/publications/Documents/Part%203%20-%20Assessing%20the%20Role%20of%20Income%20and%20Interest%20Rates%20in%20Determining%20Irish%20House%20Prices%20Kieran%20McQuinn%20Gerard%20O'Reilly.pdf

McSweeney, B. (2002). Hofstede's model of national cultural differences and their consequences: A triumph of faith – a failure of analysis. *Human Relations, 55*(1), 89–118. doi:10.1177/0018726702551004

Meagher, J. (2015, November 22). Why does Ireland have the lowest divorce rate in the EU?: Two decades on from the referendum that legalised divorce in Ireland, we still have the lowest divorce rate in the EU. *independent.ie*. Retrieved from http://www.independent.ie/life/family/family-features/why-does-ireland-have-the-lowest-divorce-rate-in-the-eu-34217513.html

Mekhova, E. P. (1999). *Financial sector assessment program (FSAP)*. Retrieved from http://www.worldbank.org/en/programs/financial-sector-assessment-program.print

Memery, C. (2000). Foreword. In Threshold and St. Pancras Housing Association (Ed.), *The Private Rented Sector in the 21st Century: Policy Choices* (pp. vii–x). Dublin, Ireland. Retrieved from http://www.threshold.ie/download/pdf/private_rented_sector_in_the_21st_century.pdf

Menand, L. (2012, July 2). Silence, exile, punning: James Joyce's chance encounters. *newyorker.com*. Retrieved from http://www.newyorker.com/magazine/2012/07/02/silence-exile-punning

Meyer, T. (2004). *Cultural difference, citizenship and global cooperation: The challenge of today: The politics of cultural identity*. Retrieved from http://library.fes.de/pdf-files/bueros/singapur/04601/d+c2004-2.pdf

Miller, J. R., Lerner, R. M., Schiamberg, L. B., & Anderson, P. M. (2003). *Encyclopedia of human ecology*. Santa Barbara, CA: ABC-CLIO.

Milmo, C. (2006, March 17). St. Patrick's Day: The legend of the shamrock. *independent.co.uk*. Retrieved from http://www.independent.co.uk/news/uk/this-britain/st-patricks-day-the-legend-of-the-shamrock-6106550.html

Minkov, M. (2011). *Cultural differences in a globalizing world*. Bingley, United Kingdom: Emerald.

Minkov, M., & Hofstede, G. (2013). *Cross-cultural analysis: The science and art of comparing the world's modern societies and their cultures*. Thousand Oaks, CA: Sage Publications.

Minneapolis Institute of Art (MIA) (2016). *Curtain, 5th-6th century*. Retrieved from https://collections.artsmia.org/art/3149/curtain-coptic

Minter, S. (2013). *Staatsschulden*. Retrieved from http://wirtschaftslexikon.gabler.de/Archiv/8058/staatsschulden-v9.html

Moaddel, M. (Ed.). (2007). *Values and perceptions of the Islamic and Middle Eastern publics*. Basingstoke, United Kingdom: Palgrave Macmillan.

Moane, G. (2002). Colonialism and the Celtic Tiger: Legacies of history and the quest for vision. In P. Kirby, L. Gibbons, & M. Cronin (Eds.) (2002). *Reinventing Ireland: Culture, society, and the global economy* (pp. 109–123). London, United Kingdom: Pluto Press.

Monaghan, P. (2004). *The encyclopedia of Celtic mythology and folklore. Facts on file library of religion and mythology*. New York, NY: Facts On File.

Moran, P. F (1913). Patrick, Saint, Apostle of Ireland. In C. G. Herbermann, E. Pace, C. Pallen, T. Shahan, & J. Wynne (Eds.), *The Catholic encyclopedia; an international work of reference on the constitution, doctrine, discipline, and history of the Catholic Church* (Vol. 11, pp. 554–559). New York, NY: The Encyclopedia Press.

Morgan Stanley Euroletter (Ed.) (1994). *Ireland: Challenging for promotion.*

Mullen, K., Williams, R., & Hunt, K. (1996). Irish descent, religion, and alcohol and tobacco use. *Addiction, 91*(2), 243–254. doi:10.1046/j.1360-0443.1996.9122436.x

Müller, S., & Gelbrich, K. (2004). *Interkulturelles Marketing. Vahlens Handbücher der Wirtschafts- und Sozialwissenschaften*. München, Deutschland: Vahlen.

Mulraney, F. (2017, March 12). McDonald's shamrock shake ad features Stonehenge and bagpipes – oops! *irishcentral.com*. Retrieved from https://www.irishcentral.com/culture/food-drink/mcdonald-s-shamrock-shake-ad-features-stonehenge-and-bagpipes-oops

Mulvihill, M. (2012). *Why this plant is a bit of a sham. irishtimes.com*. Retrieved from http://www.irishtimes.com/news/science/why-this-plant-is-a-bit-of-a-sham-1.482086

Murdoch, A. (1997, May 23). Obituary: Dr Noel Browne. *independent.co.uk*. Retrieved from http://www.independent.co.uk/news/people/obituary-dr-noel-browne-1262981.html

Murphy, B. (2013, January 6). Was the Famine genocide by the British? *independent.ie*. Retrieved from https://www.independent.ie/entertainment/books/was-the-famine-genocide-by-the-british-28954929.html

Murphy, D. (Author) (2013, June 24). *Two Anglo executives deny misleading Central Bank over funding* [Television broadcast]. RTÉ News Raidió Teilifís Éireann. Retrieved from http://www.rte.ie/news/business/2013/0624/458433-anglo-central-bank/

Murray, S. (2016, December 16). Bank of Ireland confirms it overcharged on almost 4,000 mortgages: The bank says it will commence refunding customers from the beginning of 2017. *thejournal.ie*. Retrieved from http://www.thejournal.ie/bank-ireland-overcharging-3144674-Dec2016/

Murray Brown, J. (2009, October 15). Ahern admits to part in Irish crisis. *ft.com*. Retrieved from https://www.ft.com/content/becb8b70-b917-11de-98ee-00144feab49a

Murtagh, P. (2016, January 30). Ulster Bank predicted fall of 20% in house prices before crash: Analysts appeared to have bought into the 'soft landing' scenario popular at the time. *irishtimes.com*. Retrieved from http://www.irishtimes.com/business/financial-services/ulster-bank-predicted-fall-of-20-in-house-prices-before-crash-1.2515959

Nanda, S., & Warms, R. L. (2014). *Cultural anthropology* (11th ed.). Belmont, CA: Cengage Learning.

National Museum of Ireland (2016a). *The Faddan More psalter*. Retrieved from http://www.museum.ie/Archaeology/Exhibitions/Current-Exhibitions/The-Treasury/Gallery-1-Iron-Age-to-12th-Century/Gallery-2-The-Faddan-More-Psalter-(1)

National Museum of Ireland (2016b). *The bell of St. Patrick and its shrine*. Retrieved from http://www.museum.ie/Archaeology/Exhibitions/

Current-Exhibitions/The-Treasury/Gallery-1-Iron-Age-to-12th-Century/The-Bell-of-St-Patrick-and-its-Shrine-(1)

National Stamp Duty Office (2016). *Former rates of stamp duty applicable to residential property.* Retrieved from http://www.revenue.ie/en/tax/stamp-duty/index.html

Neate, R. (2011, August 22). Ratings agencies suffer 'conflict of interest,' says former Moody's boss. *theguardian.com.* Retrieved from http://www.theguardian.com/business/2011/aug/22/ratings-agencies-conflict-of-interest

NESC (National Economic and Social Council) (Ed.) (2014). *Homeownership and rental: What road is Ireland on?* (No. 140). Retrieved from NESC – National economic and social council website: http://files.nesc.ie/nesc_reports/en/140_Homeownership_and_Rental.pdf

Newman, K. L., & Nollen, S. D. (1996). Culture and congruence: The fit between management practices and national culture. *Journal of International Business Studies, 27*(4), 753–779. doi:10.1057/palgrave.jibs.8490152

Nier, H. (2017). *Homosexualität: Wo gleichgeschlechtliche Liebe verboten ist.* Retrieved from https://de.statista.com/infografik/10471/wo-gleichgeschlechtliche-liebe-verboten-ist/

NTMA (2012). *Eligible liabilities guarantee scheme: Frequently asked questions.* Retrieved from http://www.ntma.ie/download/elg_scheme/ELGSchemeFAQs24Dec2012.pdf

NTMA (2013). *Ending of the ELG Scheme: frequently asked questions.* Retrieved from http://www.ntma.ie/download/elg_scheme/FrequentlyAskedQuestionsELGScheme26Feb2013.pdf

Nyberg, P. (2011). *Misjudging risk: Causes of the systemic banking crisis in Ireland: Report of the Commission of Investigation into the banking sector in Ireland.* Dublin, Ireland. Retrieved from http://opac.oireachtas.ie/Data/Library3/NybergMisjudingRisk_124409.pdf

O'Brien, D. (2015, January 25). Irish home ownership is in decline: Hail to the renters. *independent.ie.* Retrieved from http://www.independent.ie/opinion/columnists/dan-obrien/irish-home-ownership-is-in-decline-hail-to-the-renters-30934495.html

O'Brien, J., & Harbison, P. (1996). *Das alte Irland: Von der Frühgeschichte bis ins späte Mittelalter.* Frankfurt, Deutschland: Bechtermünz.

O'Carroll, S. (2013, June 24). The Anglo tapes: 9 jaw-dropping quotes from before the bailout: There have been calls for a fresh banking inquiry following the revelations in the Irish Independent this morning. *thejournal.ie.* Retrieved from http://www.thejournal.ie/

the-anglo-tapes-9-jaw-dropping-quotes-from-before-the-bailout-964097-Jun2013/

O'Connell, H. (2014, September 24). What role did the media have in the financial crisis? The banking inquiry wants to find out: Terms of reference for the investigation into the collapse of the Irish banking system were finalised today. *thejournal.ie*. Retrieved from http://www.thejournal.ie/banking-inquiry-media-role-1687910-Sep2014/

O'Connor, J. S. (2007a). Social innovation and institutional change in Ireland in the late 20th century: From 'the poorest of the rich' to 'Europe's shining light'. In T. J. Hämäläinen & R. Heiskala (Eds.), *Social innovations, institutional change, and economic performance. Making sense of structural adjustment processes in industrial sectors, regions, and societies* (pp. 280–303). Cheltenham, United Kingdom: Edward Elgar.

O'Connor, B. (2007b, July 29). The smart, ballsy guys are buying up property right now. *independent.ie*. Retrieved from http://www.independent.ie/opinion/analysis/the-smart-ballsy-guys-are-buying-up-property-right-now-26307728.html

Ó Corráin, D. (2008). Irland, Wales, die Insel Man und die Hebriden. In P. H. Sawyer (Ed.), *Die Wikinger. Geschichte und Kultur eines Seefahrervolkes* (pp. 93–119). Hamburg, Deutschland: Nikol.

Ó Corráin, D., & O'Riordan, T. (2011). *Ireland, 1815–70: Emancipation, famine and religion*. Dublin, Ireland: Four Courts Press.

O'Donnell, M. L. (2012). Death of an icon: Deconstructing the Irish harp emblem in the Celtic Tiger years. *Journal of the Society for Musicology in Ireland, 8*, 21–39. Retrieved from http://www.academia.edu/3769457/Death_of_an_Icon_Deconstructing_the_Irish_Harp_Emblem_in_the_Celtic_Tiger_Years

O'Donnell, M. L. (2013). *Tuning the harp to suit a changing Ireland. irishtimes.com*. Retrieved from http://www.irishtimes.com/culture/art-and-design/tuning-the-harp-to-suit-a-changing-ireland-1.961769

O'Donnell, M. L. (2015a). *Ireland's harp: The shaping of Irish identity, c. 1770–1880*. Dublin, Ireland: UCD Press.

O'Donnell, M. L. (2015b). *The history of the Irish harp – the symbol of Ireland. irishpost.co.uk*. Retrieved from http://irishpost.co.uk/history-irish-harp-symbol-ireland/

O Grádá, C. (2000). *Black '47 and beyond: The great Irish famine in history, economy, and memory* (4th print., 1st pbk. print. [af 1999]). *The Princeton economic history of the Western world*. Princeton, NJ: Princeton University Press.

Oerter, R., & Montada, L. (2002). *Entwicklungspsychologie* (5., vollständig überarbeitete Auflage). *Lehrbuch*. Weinheim [u.a.], Deutschland: Beltz PVU.

Oetzel, J. G. (2009). *Intercultural communication: A layered approach*. New York, NY: Pearson.

Ó Gráda, C., & O'Rourke, K. (1995). Economic growth: Performance and explanations. In J. W. O'Hagan (Ed.), *The economy of Ireland. Policy and performance of a small European country* (pp. 198–227). New York, NY: St. Martin's Press.

O'Hagan, J. W. (Ed.) (1995). *The economy of Ireland: Policy and performance of a small European country*. New York, NY: St. Martin's Press.

O'Hearn, D. (1998). *Inside the Celtic Tiger: The Irish economy and the Asian model. Contemporary Irish studies*. London, United Kingdom: Pluto Press.

Orbe, M. P., & Harris, T. M. (2015). *Interracial communication: Theory into practice* (3rd ed.). Thousand Oaks, CA: Sage Publications.

Ó Riain, P. (2003). Brigid. In B. Lalor (Ed.), *The encyclopedia of Ireland* (p. 123). New Haven, CT: Yale University Press.

O'Regan, M. (2016, December 26). Dr Noël Browne: 'The furthest thing from a career politician'. *irishtimes.com*. Retrieved from https://www.irishtimes.com/news/politics/dr-no%C3%ABl-browne-the-furthest-thing-from-a-career-politician-1.2917820

O'Riain, S. (2014). *The rise and fall of Ireland's Celtic Tiger: Liberalism, boom and bust*. Cambridge, United Kingdom: Cambridge University Press.

Ornua Co-operative Limited. (2017a). *Ornua: Our group*. Retrieved from http://www.ornua.com/our-group

Ornua Co-operative Limited. (2017b). *Ornua: What we do*. Foods. Retrieved from http://www.ornua.com/what-we-do/foods

Ornua Co-operative Limited. (2017c). *Unternehmen: Kerrygold Historie*. Retrieved from https://www.kerrygold.de/unternehmen/kerrygold-historie.html

Owen, J. (2014). Did St. Patrick Really drive snakes out of Ireland?: It's the stuff of legend: The reptiles never existed on the emerald isle. *nationalgeographic.com*. Retrieved from http://news.nationalgeographic.com/news/2014/03/140315-saint-patricks-day-2014-snakes-ireland-nation/

Page, J. (1994). The East Asian miracle: Four lessons for development policy. In S. Fischer & J. J. Rotemberg (Eds.), *NBER Macroeconomics Annual 1994, Volume 9* (pp. 219–282). Cambridge, MA: MIT Press.

Paor, L. de (1978). The Christian triumph: The Golden Age. In P. Cone (Ed.), *Treasures of Early Irish art 1500 B.C. to 1500 A.D. from the collections of the*

National Museum of Ireland, Royal Irish Academy, Trinity College, Dublin. exhibited at the Metropolitan Museum of Art, the Fine Arts Museum of San Francisco: M.H. de Young Memorial Museum, Museum of Art, Carnegie Institute, Pittsburgh, Museum of Fine Arts, Boston, Philadelphia Museum of Art (pp. 93–143). Verona, Italy: Arnoldo Mondadori Editore

Parsons, M. (2010). *Psalter to go on display in 2011. irishtimes.com.* Retrieved from http://www.irishtimes.com/news/psalter-to-go-on-display-in-2011-1.640349

Parsons, T., & Shils, E. (Eds.) (1951). *Toward a general theory of action.* Cambridge, MA: Harvard University Press.

Parsons, T., & Shils, E. (1951). Values, motives, and systems of action. In T. Parsons & E. Shils (Eds.), *Toward a general theory of action* (pp. 45–275). Cambridge, MA: Harvard University Press.

Pašeta, S. (2003). *Modern Ireland: A very short introduction. Very short introductions: Vol. 85.* Oxford, United Kingdom: Oxford University Press.

Peet, J. (2004). The luck of the Irish: A survey of Ireland | October 16th 2004. *The Economist,* 1–10.

Phinney, J. S. (1993). A three-stage model of ethnic identity development in adolescence. In M. E. Bernal & G. P. Knight (Eds.), *SUNY series, United States Hispanic studies. Ethnic identity. Formation and transmission among Hispanics and other minorities* (pp. 61–80). Albany, NY: State University of New York Press.

Powell, Elinor D. U. (2007). *The High Crosses of Ireland: Inspirations in stone.* Dublin, Ireland: Liffey Press.

PwC (2009). *Project Atlas – Anglo Irish bank corporation plc: Summary report extracts.* Dublin, Ireland. Retrieved from PricewaterhouseCoopers website: http://www.finance.gov.ie/sites/default/files/Anglopwc.pdf

Quinlan, R. (2014, July 20). Incinerate Morgan Kelly – the most shocking Anglo tape yet. *independent.ie.* Retrieved from http://www.independent.ie/business/irish/anglo/incinerate-morgan-kelly-the-most-shocking-anglo-tape-yet-30444629.html

Quinn, E. (2010). *focus Migration: Länderprofil Irland* (No. 19). Hamburg. Retrieved from http://focus-migration.hwwi.de/Irland.6269.0.html

Rafter, K. (2013, November 12). The Tiger years: How well did Irish media hold financial elites to account? *irishtimes.com.* Retrieved from http://www.irishtimes.com/business/the-tiger-years-how-well-did-irish-media-hold-financial-elites-to-account-1.1593451

Rajan, R. G. (2005). *Has financial development made the world riskier?* (No. 11728). Cambridge, MA. Retrieved from National Bureau of Economic Research website: http://www.nber.org/papers/w11728.pdf

Reddan, F. (2016, December 21). What does the tracker mortgage scandal mean for you? *irishtimes.com*. Retrieved from http://www.irishtimes.com/business/financial-services/what-does-the-tracker-mortgage-scandal-mean-for-you-1.2914156

Reilly, G. (2012, March 22). Mahon: Liam Lawlor "hopelessly compromised" by payments from developers: The 25-year TD "conducted a personal business" where he sold his influence for personal reward, the Mahon Tribunal finds. *thejournal.ie*. Retrieved from https://www.thejournal.ie/mahon-liam-lawlor-hopelessly-compromised-by-payments-from-developers-392575-Mar2012/

Reinhart, C. M., & Rogoff, K. S. (2009). *This time is different: Eight centuries of financial folly*. Princeton, NJ: Princeton University Press.

Rieke, S. (2015). *Verrechnungspreise im Spannungsfeld zwischen Konzernsteuerung und internationalem Steuerrecht*. Wiesbaden, Deutschland: Springer Gabler.

Rimmer, J. (1964). The morphology of the Irish harp. *The Galpin Society Journal, 17*, 39. doi:10.2307/841312

Roach, J. (2014). St. Patrick's Day 2014: Facts, myths, and traditions: The march holiday signals the start of spring for many. *nationalgeographic.com*. Retrieved from http://news.nationalgeographic.com/news/2014/03/140314-saint-patricks-day-2014-culture-nation-ireland/

Robinson, W. E. (1842). *St. Patrick and the Irish: An oration, pronounced before the Hibernian provident society of New Haven*. New Haven, CT: Hitchcock and Stafford. Retrieved from https://archive.org/details/stpatrickandiri00socigoog

Robinson-Hammerstein, H. (2005). Dublin: 1592. In J. M. M. Hermans & M. Nelissen (Eds.), *Charters of foundation and early documents of the universities of the Coimbra group* (2nd ed., pp. 40–41). Leuven, Belgium: Leuven University Press.

Rodriguez, G. G. (1999). *Raising nuestros niños: Bringing up Latino children in a bicultural world*. New York, NY: Fireside.

Rogers, E. M., & Steinfatt, T. M. (1999). *Intercultural communication*. Prospect Heights, IL: Waveland Press.

Rogers, S. (2010, June 10). Deaths in the Northern Ireland conflict since 1969. *theguardian.com*. Retrieved from https://www.theguardian.com/news/datablog/2010/jun/10/deaths-in-northern-ireland-conflict-data

Rogoff, B. (2003). *The Cultural nature of human development*. New York, NY: Oxford University Press, Inc.

Rokeach, M. (1973). *The nature of human values*. New York, NY: Free Press.

Rolle, R. (2005). *Homo oeconomicus: Wirtschaftsanthropologie in philosophischer Perspektive*. Würzburg: Königshausen und Neumann.

Rolleston Gwynn, D. (2016). *Eamon de Valera*. Retrieved from http://www.britannica.com/biography/Eamon-de-Valera

Ross, M. H. (2013). The politics of memory and peacebuilding. In R. Mac Ginty (Ed.), *Routledge Handbook of Peacebuilding* (pp. 91–101). New York, NY: Routledge.

Ross, S. (2004, December 19). Ahoy, a toff at helm of BoI. *independent.ie*. Retrieved from http://www.independent.ie/business/irish/ahoy-a-toff-at-helm-of-boi-26227732.html

Ross, S. (2009). *The bankers: How the banks brought Ireland to its knees*. Dublin, Ireland: Penguin Ireland.

Rothbard, M. N. (1994). *The case against the Fed*. Auburn, AL: Ludwig von Mises Institute.

RTÉ. (2007). *Myhome.ie sold to Irish Times for €50m*. Retrieved from https://www.rte.ie/news/business/2006/0728/78794-myhome/

RTÉ. (2012). *Micheál Martin accepts Mahon findings against FF members*. Retrieved from https://www.rte.ie/news/2012/0327/315153-mahon/

Saint Patrick (1993). Liber primus: Confessio. In L. Bieler (Ed.): *Dictionary of Medieval Latin from Celtic Sources, Clavis Patricii II. Libri Epistolarum Sancti Patricii Episcopi. Introduction, text and commentary by Ludwig Bieler.*, pp. 56–91. Dublin, Ireland: W. & G. Baird Ltd. Retrieved from www.confessio.ie/sites/confessio.ie/files/pdfs/print_bieler.pdf

Saint Patrick (2011). Confessio. In P. McCarthy (Ed.), *My name is Patrick. I am a sinner, a simple country person and the least of all believers. Read St. Patrick in his own words*. Dublin, Ireland: The Royal Irish Academy.

Samovar, L. A., Porter, R. E., McDaniel, E. R., & Roy, C. S. (2013). *Communication between cultures* (8th ed.). *Wadsworth series in communication studies*. Boston, MA: Cengage Learning.

Samson, A. (Ed.). (2018). *The Behavioral Economics Guide 2018*. Retrieved from https://www.behavioraleconomics.com/download/4601/

Samuelson, P. A., & Nordhaus, W. D. (2010). *Volkswirtschaftslehre: Das internationale Standardwerk der Makro- und Mikroökonomie* (4., aktualisierte Auflage). München: mi-Wirtschaftsbuch.

Sawyer, P. H. (Ed.) (2008). *Die Wikinger: Geschichte und Kultur eines Seefahrervolkes*. Hamburg, Deutschland: Nikol.

Scarisbrick, J. J. (1997). *Henry VIII*. New Haven, CT: Yale University Press.

Schneider, M., & Stokols, D. (2009). Multilevel theories of behavior change: A social ecological framework. In S. A. Shumaker, J. K. Ockene, & K. A.

Riekert (Eds.), *The handbook of health behavior change* (3rd ed., pp. 85–105). New York, NY: Springer.

Schulz, B. (2010, September 6). Anglo Irish Bank wird wohl nicht fortgeführt: Die verstaatlichte Bank erscheint wie ein Fass ohne Boden. Pläne, nur mit den guten Teilen des Instituts weiterzumachen, gelten als chancenlos. In Sorge um die Kosten setzt sich die irische Regierung für eine langsame Abwicklung ein. *faz.net*. Retrieved from http://www.faz.net/aktuell/wirtschaft/wirtschaftspolitik/rekordverluste-anglo-irish-bank-wird-wohl-nicht-fortgefuehrt-11036249.html

Schwab, K. (Ed.). (2010). *The global competitiveness report 2010–2011*. Geneva, Switzerland. Retrieved from World Economic Forum website: http://www3.weforum.org/docs/WEF_GlobalCompetitivenessReport_2010-11.pdf

Selz, G. J. (2016). *Sumerer und Akkader: Geschichte – Gesellschaft – Kultur* (3., aktualisierte Auflage). München: C.H. Beck.

Sen, A. K. (2007a). How does culture matter? In M.-Y. Lee-Peuker (Ed.), *Wirtschafts- und Unternehmensethik: Vol. 18. Kultur – Ökonomie – Ethik* (1st ed., pp. 29–61). München, Mering: Hampp.

Sen, A. (2007b). *Identity and violence: The illusion of destiny. Issues of our time*. New York, NY: W.W. Norton.

Sheehy, C. (2015, July 2). Defiant McCreevy denies his policies fuelled bubble. *independent.ie*. Retrieved from http://www.independent.ie/business/irish/banking-inquiry/defiant-mccreevy-denies-his-policies-fuelled-bubble-31345888.html

Sheils McNamee, M. (2015, January 19). Timeline: A history of gay rights in Ireland: Leo Varadkar becoming Ireland's first openly gay minister comes 22 years after the decriminalisation of homosexuality in Ireland. *thejournal.ie*. Retrieved from http://www.thejournal.ie/gay-rights-ireland-history-varadkar-history-1890129-Jan2015/

Shiller, R. J. (2000). *Irrational exuberance*. Princeton, NJ: Princeton University Press.

Shiller, R. J. (2008). *The subprime solution: How today's global financial crisis happened, and what to do about it*. Princeton, NJ: Princeton University Press.

Shumaker, S. A., Ockene, J. K., & Riekert, K. A. (Eds.). (2009). *The handbook of health behavior Change* (3rd ed.). New York, NY: Springer.

Shweder, R. A., & LeVine, R. A. (1984). *Culture theory: Essays on mind, self, and emotion*. Cambridge, MA: Cambridge University Press.

Siggins, L. (2014, January 8). NUIG law lecturer leads EU survey on housing evictions. *irishtimes.com*. Retrieved from http://www.irishtimes.com/news/ireland/irish-news/nuig-law-lecturer-leads-eu-survey-on-housing-evictions-1.1646271

Slater, M. D., Snyder, L., & Hayes, A. F. (2006). Thinking and modeling at multiple levels: The potential contribution of multilevel modeling to communication theory and research. *Human Communication Research, 32*(4), 375–384. doi:10.1111/j.1468-2958.2006.00292.x

Smelser, N. J., & Swedberg, R. (Eds.) (op. 1994). *The handbook of economic sociology*. Princeton, NJ: Princeton University Press; Russell Sage Foundation.

Smiljanic, M. (2016). *Wie unser Gehirn die Welt sortiert: Schubladen für das Denken*. Retrieved from https://www.deutschlandfunk.de/wie-unser-gehirn-die-welt-sortiert-schubladen-fuer-das.1148.de.html?dram:article_id=364463

Smith, E. R., & Mackie, D. M. (2007). *Social psychology* (3rd ed.). New York, NY: Psychology Press.

Smith, P. B., Fischer, R., Vignoles, V. L., & Bond, M. H. (2013). *Understanding social psychology across cultures: Engaging with others in a changing world* (Second edition). Thousand Oaks, CA: Sage Publications.

Somerville, R. A. (2007). Housing tenure in Ireland. *The Economic and Social Review, 38*(1), 107–134.

Søndergaard, M. (1994). Research note: Hofstede's consequences: A study of reviews, citations and replications. *Organization Studies, 15*(3), 447–456. doi:10.1177/017084069401500307

Søndergaard, M. (2002). *In my opinion-Mikael Søndergaard on cultural differences*. Retrieved from http://geert-hofstede.international-business-center.com/Sondergaard.shtml

Spash, C. L. (2011). Social ecological economics: Understanding the past to see the future. *American Journal of Economics and Sociology, 70*(2), 340–375. doi:10.1111/j.1536-7150.2011.00777.x

Spielmann, M. H. (1895). *The history of "Punch": With numerous illustrations*. London, Paris, Melbourne: Cassell and Company, Limited. Retrieved from http://www.gutenberg.org/files/23881/23881-h/23881-h.htm

Squire, C. (1910). *Celtic myth and legend, poetry and romance*. London, United Kingdom: The Gresham Publishing Company. Retrieved from https://archive.org/details/celticmythlegend00squi

Stalley, R. (1994). Review: The High Crosses of Ireland, an iconographical and photographic survey by Peter Harbison. *Irish Arts Review Yearbook, 10*, 258–260.

Standard & Poor's Financial Services LLC (2016). *S&P global ratings definitions*. Retrieved from http://www.standardandpoors.com/en_US/web/guest/article/-/view/sourceId/504352

Stangor, C., & Lange, J. (1993). Mental representations of social groups: Advances in understanding stereotypes and stereotyping. In M. P. Zanna (Ed.), *Advances in experimental social psychology: Vol. 26. Advances in experimental social psychology* (pp. 357–416). San Diego, CA: Academic Press.

Stanley, T. (2015, May 23). Ireland has said yes to gay marriage and no to Catholicism. *telegraph.co.uk*. Retrieved from http://www.telegraph.co.uk/news/religion/11625907/Ireland-has-said-yes-to-gay-marriage-and-no-to-Catholicism.html

Statista. (2018). *Retail expenditure on Halloween products in the United Kingdom (UK) from 2013 to 2018 (in million GBP)*. Retrieved from https://www.statista.com/statistics/330279/halloween-products-expenditure-in-the-united-kingdom-uk-forecast/

Statistische Ämter des Bundes und der Länder (Ed.). (2012). *Zensus 2011: Vielfältiges Deutschland*. Endgültige Ergebnisse. Düsseldorf, Deutschland. Retrieved from www.statistikportal.de

Statistisches Bundesamt (Destatis) (2013). *Bruttoinlandsprodukt (BIP)*. Retrieved from https://www.destatis.de/DE/ZahlenFakten/GesamtwirtschaftUmwelt/

VGR/Methoden/BIP.html;jsessionid=2840E8D8D0145A546F4CF7573D52B007.cae1

Stearns, P. N. (1998). *Why study history?* Washington, DC Retrieved from American Historical Association website: http://www.historians.org/about-aha-and-membership/aha-history-and-archives/archives/why-study-history-(1998)

Steffler, A. W. (2002). *Symbols of the Christian faith*. Grand Rapids, MI: W.B. Eerdmans Pub.

Steindorff, E. (2013). *Europa-Recht: Europäische Union (EUV/AEUV), Charta der Grundrechte, Gerichtsbarkeit, Europarat-Satzung, EMRK, Begleitgesetze* (25., neubearbeitete Auflage, Stand: 1. März 2013.). *Beck-Texte im dtv*. Muenchen, Deutschland: Deutscher Taschenbuch Verlag.

Stokols, D. (1992). Establishing and maintaining healthy environments: Toward a social ecology of health promotion. *American Psychologist, 47*(1), 6–22.

Stokols, D. (1996). Translating social ecological theory into guidelines for community health promotion. *American Journal of Health Promotion, 10*(4), 282–298.

Sumner, W. G. (2014). *Folkways: A study of the sociological importance of usages, manners, customs, mores, and morals*. North Charleston, SC: CreateSpace Independent Publishing Platform.

Sunday Tribune (2010, January 24). Anyone can be like Fintan O'Toole and follow the consensus: Be for the poor and against the rich. *tribune.ie*.

Retrieved from https://web.archive.org/web/20100127183842/http://www.tribune.ie:80/magazine/article/2010/jan/24/anyone-can-be-like-fintan-otoole-and-follow-the-co/

Susser, M., & Susser, E. (1996). Choosing a future for epidemiology: II. From black box to Chinese boxes and eco-epidemiology. *American Journal of Public Health, 86*(5), 674–677. doi:10.2105/AJPH.86.5.674

Tajfel, H., & Turner, J. C. (1986). The social identity theory of intergroup behavior. In S. Worchel & W. G. Austin (Eds.), *Psychology of intergroup relations* (pp. 7–24). Chicago, IL: Nelson-Hall.

Taylor, L. J. (1993). Peter's Pence: Official Catholic discourse and Irish nationalism in the nineteenth century. *History of European ideas, 16*(1–3), 103–107. doi:10.1016/S0191-6599(05)80107-X

TCD (2014). *The battle of Clontarf: The Brian Boru harp*. Retrieved from http://dh.tcd.ie/clontarf/The%20Brian%20Boru%20Harp

Ternès, A., & Towers, I. (Eds.). (2017). *Interkulturelle Kommunikation: Länderporträts – Kulturunterschiede – Unternehmensbeispiele* (1st ed.). Wiesbaden, Deutschland: Springer Gabler.

Terpstra, V., & David, K. H. (1991). *The cultural environment of international business* (3rd ed.). Mason, OH: South-Western.

Thaler, R. H. (2016). *Misbehaving: The making of behavioral economics*. New York, NY: W. W. Norton & Company.

Theurer, M. (2010, November 23). Irland und die Euro-Krise: Das Sündenregister des keltischen Tigers. *faz.net*. Retrieved from http://www.faz.net/aktuell/wirtschaft/eurokrise/irland-und-die-euro-krise-das-suendenregister-des-keltischen-tigers-11070004.html

Theurer, M., & Plickert, P. (2013, June 25). Verräterische Telefonmitschnitte Irische Pleitebanker haben den Staat betrogen: Telefongespräche führender irischer Bankmanager zeigen: Die Anglo Irish Bank hat mit falschen Angaben staatliche Milliardenhilfe erlangt. Die von der Bank genannte Zahl von 7 Milliarden Euro sei einfach „aus dem Arsch gezogen" worden. *faz.net*. Retrieved from http://www.faz.net/aktuell/wirtschaft/verraeterische-telefonmitschnitte-irische-pleitebanker-haben-den-staat-betrogen-12244082.html

Ting-Toomey, S. (1999). *Communicating across cultures. The Guilford communication series*. New York, NY: Guilford Press.

Ting-Toomey, S. (2011). Intercultural communication ethics: Multiple layered issues. In G. Cheney, S. May, & D. Munshi (Eds.), *International communication association (ICA). handbook series. The handbook of communication ethics* (pp. 335–352). New York, NY: Routledge.

Towers, I., & Peppler, A. (2017). Geert Hofstede und die Dimensionen einer Kultur. In A. Ternès & I. Towers (Eds.), *Interkulturelle Kommunikation. Länderporträts – Kulturunterschiede – Unternehmensbeispiele* (1st ed., pp. 15–19). Wiesbaden, Deutschland: Springer Gabler.

Tögel, C. (2006, April). *Die Bedeutung der Religion im Leben von Sigmund Freud.* Katholische Akademie in Bayern. Tagung der Katholischen Akademie in Bayern zum Thema »Psychoanalyse und Religion. Zum 150. Geburtstag von Sigmund Freud«., München, Deutschland. Retrieved from http://www.freud-biographik.de/Toegel%20-%20Die%20Bedeutung%20der%20Religion%20im%20Leben%20von%20Sigmund%20Freud.pdf

Trautmann, P. & Mäkelä, M. (2017a). *Mikroprudenzielle Aufsicht.* Retrieved from https://www.bundesbank.de/Redaktion/DE/Glossareintraege/M/mikroprudenzielle_aufsicht.html

Trautmann, P. & Mäkelä, M. (2017b). *Makroprudenzielle Überwachung.* Retrieved from https://www.bundesbank.de/Redaktion/DE/Glossareintraege/M/makroprudenzielle_ueberwachung.html

Traynor, I. (2013, July 28). Anglo Irish bank scandal damages democracy, Angela Merkel says: German chancellor delivers a strong condemnation of the revelations that the Irish bank's executives mocked the country's role in Anglo's bailout. *theguardian.com*. Retrieved from https://www.theguardian.com/business/2013/jun/28/angela-merkel-anglo-irish-bank-scandal

Tregaskis, S. (2015). Into the woods: How a father's queries sparked a new theory of human development. *Human Ecology, 43*(1), 12–18.

Trompenaars, F. (1993). *Riding the waves of culture: Understanding cultural diversity in business*. London, United Kingdom: Economist Books.

Tudge, J., Mokrova, I., Hatfield, B. E., & Karnik, R. B. (2009). Uses and misuses of Bronfenbrenner's bioecological theory of human development. *Journal of Family Theory & Review, 1*(4), 198–210. doi:10.1111/j.1756-2589.2009.00026.x

Turner, E. R. (1917). Opposition to Home Rule. *The American Political Science Review, 11*(3), 448–460. Retrieved from https://www.jstor.org/stable/1944247

Turner, J. C., Oakes, P. J., Haslam, S. A., & McGarty, C. (1994). Self and collective: Cognition and social context. *Personality and Social Psychology Bulletin, 20*(5), 454–463. doi:10.1177/0146167294205002

Turner, J. C., & Oakes, P. J. (1986). The significance of the social identity concept for social psychology with reference to individualism, interactionism and social influence. *British Journal of Social Psychology, 25*(3), 237–252. doi:10.1111/j.2044-8309.1986.tb00732.x

Tylor, E. B. (1920). *Primitive culture: Researches into the development of mythology, philosophy, religion, language, art, and custom* (6th ed.). London,

United Kingdom: John Murray. Retrieved from https://archive.org/stream/primitiveculture01tylouoft#page/n7/mode/2up

ui Ógáin, R. (2003). Cú Chulainn. In B. Lalor (Ed.), *The encyclopedia of Ireland* (p. 261). New Haven, CT: Yale University Press.

United States (2011). *The financial crisis inquiry report: Final report of the national commission on the causes of the financial and economic crisis in the United States*. Seattle, WA: Pacific Publishing Studio.

Vasta, R. (Ed.) (1992). *Six theories of child development: Revised formulations and current issues*. London, Philadelphia: J. Kingsley.

Venaik, S., & Brewer, P. (2016). National culture dimensions: The perpetuation of cultural ignorance. *Management Learning, 47*(5), 563–589. doi:10.1177/1350507616629356

Vinken, H., Soeters, J., & Ester, P. (Eds.) (2004). *International studies in sociology and social anthropology: Vol. 93. Comparing Cultures: Dimensions of Culture in a Comparative Perspective*. Boston, MA: Brill.

Vygotsky, L. S., & Cole, M. (1978). *Mind in society: The development of higher psychological processes*. Cambridge, MA: Harvard University Press.

Waddell, J. (1991). The question of the Celticization of Ireland. *Emania: Bulletin of the Navan Research Group*, (9), 5–16.

Waddell, J. (1998). *The prehistoric archaeology of Ireland*. Galway, Ireland: Galway University Press.

Waddell, J. (2014, April). *Archaeology and Celtic myth: An exploration*. Society of Antiquaries of Scotland. 2014 Rhind Lecture 1: Confronting Ancient Myth, the Royal Society of Edinburgh, 22–28 George Street, Edinburgh EH2 2PQ.

Waddell, J., & Twohig, E. S. (1995). *Ireland in the Bronze Age: Proceedings of the Dublin conference, April 1995*. Dublin, Ireland: The Stationery Office.

Wade, J. (2012, March 29). Census 2011: 1.77m say they are able to speak Irish. *thejournal.ie*. Retrieved from http://www.thejournal.ie/census-2011-1-77m-say-they-are-able-to-speak-irish-400442-Mar2012/

Wahl, H.-M. (1997). *Die Jakobserzählungen: Studien zu ihrer mündlichen Überlieferung, Verschriftung und Historizität. Beihefte zur Zeitschrift für die alttestamentliche Wissenschaft: Bd. 258*. Berlin, New York, NY: Walter de Gruyter.

Wall, C. J. (1905; 2015). *Shrines of british saints (classic reprint)*. London, United Kingdom: FORGOTTEN Books.

Waxman, O. B. (2017). How green became associated with St. Patrick's Day and all things Irish. *time.com*. Retrieved from http://time.com/4699771/green-irish-st-patricks-day-color/

Webster (Ed.) (1996). *Webster's new encyclopedic dictionary* (2nd ed.). *Webster's*. New York, NY: Black Dog & Leventhal Publishers.

Weinberg, H. (2014). *Paradox of internet groups: Alone in the presence of others. New international library of group analysis series*. London, United Kingdom: Karnac Books.

Wetzel, J. (2014, January 28). Ehe-Annullierungen in der katholischen Kirche: Als wäre nie etwas gewesen. *sueddeutsche.de*. Retrieved from http://www.sueddeutsche.de/muenchen/ehe-annullierungen-in-der-katholischen-kirche-als-waere-nie-etwas-gewesen-1.1873323

Wexler, L. (2009). The importance of identity, history, and culture in the well-being of indigenous youth. *The Journal of the History of Childhood and Youth, 2*(2), 267–276. doi:10.1353/hcy.0.0055

Whelan, K. (October 2009). *The ECB's role in financial supervision* (UCD Centre for Economic Research Working Paper Series No. WP09/15). Dublin, Ireland.

Whelan, K. (2010). Policy paper: Policy lessons from Ireland's latest depression. *The Economic and Social Review, 41*(2), 225–254.

Whelan, K. (2013). *Ireland's economic crisis the good, the bad and the ugly*. Retrieved from http://www.karlwhelan.com/Papers/Whelan-IrelandPaper-June2013.pdf

Wiederschein, H. (2012). Hightech-Archäologie: Das 1000-Skelette-Projekt. *focus.de*. Retrieved from http://www.focus.de/wissen/mensch/archaeologie/tid-25675/leprakrank-kuestenbewohner-moench-hightech-archaeologie-entlockt-knochenfunden-verblueffende-erkenntnisse_aid_747111.html

Williams, P. (2013a, June 24). Inside Anglo: The secret recordings: Exclusive: Tapes reveal the lies and deception that led to the bank bailout. *independent.ie*. Retrieved from http://www.independent.ie/business/irish/inside-anglo-the-secret-recordings-29366837.html

Williams, P. (2013b, June 25). Abuse the bank guarantee, don't get caught – David Drumm: Anglo bank chief's extraordinary comments to staff after bailout. *independent.ie*. Retrieved from http://www.independent.ie/business/irish/anglo/abuse-the-bank-guarantee-dont-get-caught-david-drumm-29369275.html

Witchalls, P. J. (2012). Is national culture still relevant? Ist das Konzept von Nationalkultur noch zeitgemäß? *Interculture Journal: Online Zeitschrift für interkulturelle Studien, 11*(19), 11–19. Retrieved from http://www.interculture-journal.com/index.php/icj/article/viewFile/178/280.

Wong, B. B., & Candolin, U. (2015). Behavioral responses to changing environments. *Behavioral Ecology, 26*(3), 665–673. doi:10.1093/beheco/aru183

Wood, J. T. (2009). *Communication in our lives* (5th ed.). *Wadsworth series in speech communication*. Boston, MA: Wadsworth Cengage Learning.

Wood, J. T. (2015). *Communication in our lives* (7th ed.). Stamford, CT: Cengage Learning.

Woodham Smith, C. (1991). *The great hunger: Ireland 1845–1849*. London, United Kingdom: Penguin Books.

Worchel, S., & Austin, W. G. (Eds.). (1986). *Psychology of intergroup relations*. Chicago, IL: Nelson-Hall.

World Bank Group. (2017a). *World development indicators: GDP growth (annual %)*. Retrieved from http://databank.worldbank.org/data/reports.aspx?source=2&type=metadata&series=NY.GDP.MKTP.KD.ZG

World Bank Group. (2017b). *World development indicators: Unemployment, total (%of total labor force) (national estimate)*. Retrieved from http://databank.worldbank.org/data/reports.aspx?source=2&type=metadata&series=SL.UEM.TOTL.ZS

World Bank Group. (2017c). *World development indicators: Inflation, consumer prices (annual %)*. Retrieved from http://databank.worldbank.org/data/reports.aspx?source=2&type=metadata&series=FP.CPI.TOTL.ZG

World Bank Group. (2017d). *World development indicators: Real interest rate (%)*. Retrieved from http://databank.worldbank.org/data/reports.aspx?source=2&type=metadata&series=FR.INR.RINR

World Bank Group. (2017e). *World development indicators: GDP growth (annual %): Ireland, European Union*. 1973–1993. Retrieved from http://databank.worldbank.org/data/reports.aspx?source=2&country=IRL#

World Bank Group. (2017f). *World development indicators: Unemployment, total (%of total labor force) (national estimate): Ireland, Germany, France, United Kingdom, Italy*. 1983–1994. Retrieved from http://databank.worldbank.org/data/reports.aspx?source=2&country=IRL#

World Bank Group. (2017g). *World development indicators: Unemployment, total (%of total labor force) (national estimate): Ireland*. 1994–1994. Retrieved from http://databank.worldbank.org/data/reports.aspx?source=2&country=IRL#

World Bank Group. (2017h). *World development indicators: GDP growth (annual %): Ireland, European Union*. 1990–1999. Retrieved from http://databank.worldbank.org/data/reports.aspx?source=2&country=IRL#

World Bank Group. (2017i). *World development indicators: GDP growth (annual %): Ireland*. 1995–2000. Retrieved from http://databank.worldbank.org/data/reports.aspx?source=2&country=IRL#

World Bank Group. (2017j). *World development indicators: Unemployment, total (% of total labor force) (national estimate): Ireland*. 1995 and 2000. Retrieved from http://databank.worldbank.org/data/reports.aspx?source=2&country=IRL#

World Bank Group. (2017k). *World development indicators: GDP growth (annual %): Ireland, Republic of Korea, Singapore, Hong Kong, EU*. 1970–1999. Retrieved from http://databank.worldbank.org/data/reports.aspx?source=2&country=IRL#

World Bank Group. (2017l). *World development indicators: Decline of unemployment in the Celtic Tiger years*. 1994–2007. Retrieved from http://databank.worldbank.org/data/reports.aspx?source=2&country=IRL#

World Bank Group. (2017m). *World development indicators: GDP growth (annual %): Ireland*. 2007, 2008, 2009. Retrieved from http://databank.worldbank.org/data/reports.aspx?source=2&country=IRL#

Yaropolov, A. (2014). *Verrechnungspreise für immaterielle Wirtschaftsgüter*. Hamburg, Deutschland: Igel Verlag.

Yolen, J. (1986). *Favorite folktales from around the world*. New York, NY: Pantheon Books.

Young, G. L. (1974). Human ecology as an interdisciplinary concept: A critical inquiry. In A. Macfadyen (Ed.), *Advances in Ecological Research* (8th ed., pp. 2–88). London, United Kingdom: Elsevier.

Zamansky, J. (2013). The chickens come home to roost for Standard & Poor's. *forbes.com*. Retrieved from https://www.forbes.com/sites/jakezamansky/2013/02/05/the-chickens-come-home-to-roost-for-standard-poors-2/#7abd1b74375f

Zanna, M. P. (Ed.) (1993). *Advances in experimental social psychology: Vol. 26. Advances in experimental social psychology*. San Diego, CA: Academic Press.

Zappone & Anor -v- Revenue Commissioners & Ors Katherine Zappone and Ann Louise Gilligan, Plaintiffs v. The Revenue Commissioners, Ireland and The Attorney General, Defendants, and The Human Rights Commission, Notice Party. High Court Record No.: 2004 19616 P; Neutral Citation: [2006] IEHC 404, http://courts.ie/judgments.nsf/6681dee4565ecf2c80256e7e0052005b/a4fe4e30eef23925802572790040d30c?OpenDocument&Highlight=0,zappone#top (High Court December 14, 2006).

Zhang, R., & Ting-Toomey, S. (2014). Analyzing an intercultural conflict case study: Application of a social ecological perspective. In M. B. Hinner (Ed.), *Freiberger Beiträge zur interkulturellen und Wirtschaftskommunikation: Vol. 8. Chinese culture in a cross-cultural comparison* (1st ed., pp. 481–510). Frankfurt a. M.: Peter Lang GmbH.

www.ingramcontent.com/pod-product-compliance
Ingram Content Group UK Ltd.
Pitfield, Milton Keynes, MK11 3LW, UK
UKHW021921120926
8556IPUK00042BA/1092

9 783631 841488